D1520208

THE LITERATURE OF PHOTOGRAPHY

THE LITERATURE OF PHOTOGRAPHY

Advisory Editors:

PETER C. BUNNELL
PRINCETON UNIVERSITY

ROBERT A. SOBIESZEK
INTERNATIONAL MUSEUM OF PHOTOGRAPHY
AT GEORGE EASTMAN HOUSE

THE HISTORY OF
THE DISCOVERY
OF
PHOTOGRAPHY

BY
GEORGES POTONNIÉE

ARNO PRESS
A NEW YORK TIMES COMPANY
NEW YORK ★ 1973

Reprint Edition 1973 by Arno Press Inc.

Reprinted from a copy in
  The George Eastman House Library

The Literature of Photography
ISBN for complete set: 0-405-04889-0
See last pages of this volume for titles.

Manufactured in the United States of America

———◆———

Library of Congress Cataloging in Publication Data

Potonniée, Georges.
    The history of the discovery of photography.

    (The Literature of photography)
    Translation of Histoire de la découverte de la
photographie.
    Includes bibliographical references.
    1. Photography--History. I. Title. II. Series.
TR15.P6213 1973   770'.9   72-9222
ISBN 0-405-04929-3

THE HISTORY OF
THE DISCOVERY OF PHOTOGRAPHY

THE HISTORY OF
THE DISCOVERY
OF
PHOTOGRAPHY

BY

GEORGES POTONNIÉE

TRANSLATED BY

EDWARD EPSTEAN

NEW YORK

TENNANT AND WARD

1936

TRANSLATOR'S NOTE

In the Summer of 1932, out of affection and respect for Hofrat Dr. J. M. Eder, of Vienna, I promised him to make an English translation of the Fourth Edition (Halle, 1932) of his *Geschichte der Photographie*. I not only translated this work, but wrote the translation of its 1053 pages in longhand. The publication of the work was prevented by the demand of the German publishers for remuneration for the rights of translation.

Since that time I have translated and published that most important of the sources of information on the beginnings of photography: *La Vérité sur l'Invention de la Photographie, NICÉPHORE NIEPCE, sa Vie, ses Essais, ses Travaux,* by Victor Fouque, published at Paris in 1867. I now offer to the student of the history of photography an English translation of Georges Potonniée's *Histoire de la Découverte de la Photographie,* (Paris 1925).

The reader is asked to note three things. (1) M. Potonniée deals with photography up to the end of the daguerrean period —about 1851, the history of its development from that time to the present day being left for consideration in a second part of the work, not yet published. (2) The illustrations accompanying the text in the French edition are not reproduced in this volume, the originals, in many cases, being unobtainable here, and the prints in the published work not lending themselves to presentable reproduction. It is hoped that their omission in these pages will stimulate the desire to possess the original French work, to which the illustrations add a lively interest. (3) I have not accented the name Niepce in this translation, following M. Potonniée's Reference 1, Chapter XII, according to which the family Niepce today omit the accent.

I am indebted to my friends John A. Tennant, of New York, and L. P. Clerc, of Paris, for their kind and constructive criticism.

EDWARD EPSTEAN

New York, January, 1936

CONTENTS

CONTENTS

AUTHOR'S PREFACE

THE immense development of photography, its universal use, its importance as an auxiliary in all other sciences, based on the direct observation of nature, in short, of almost all the sciences; its very great importance as a medium of expression for the diffusion of thought by images, animated or still, and its profound influence exercised by these two methods on the development of civilization, has given to the world one of the greatest discoveries of all time.

It is continually widening its usefulness and its development shows no sign of slowing up. We may suppose that as long as civilized man inhabits this earth, he will make use of photography. We cannot, therefore, remain indifferent to its history, either in our time or in the future.

Until now the various histories of photography published in France have been very brief; in short, they have dealt only with a very limited part of the subject and have not treated the matter in detail. Thus, in order to obtain a complete survey of the whole subject, we are obliged to go to books written in English or German. This has many inconveniences. Since the works have not been translated, they are accessible only to few French readers. Moreover, foreign authors, being naturally better acquainted with the work of their own countrymen, deal with it more elaborately. Of course this is detrimental to our own inventors. And since many of the details of the discovery — which originated in France — could not possibly be known to them, except by unpublished documents accessible

only in our country, these writers and their works
are not free from error.

The history of photography is essentially French.
It was a Frenchman, Niepce, who invented photography and a Frenchman, Daguerre, who made it
public. And as, following the law of natural growth,
the prodigious discovery developed, it was in France
that its great improvements were achieved; the
photomechanical process, colour photography and
animated photography. Therefore it is fitting that
we should write a history of photography. There is
another reason which we must not omit to mention: in 1839, having purchased the secret of photography, France refused to draw from it any profit
whatever and liberally presented it to the world.
Is it not just to accord her the glory?

These are the reasons which decided me to undertake a work of which the first part is here offered
to the public.

1924   GEORGES POTONNIÉE

THE HISTORY OF
THE DISCOVERY OF PHOTOGRAPHY

CHAPTER I

Definition of Photography

PHOTOGRAPHY is the art which renders permanent, by other means than that of manual design, the images perceived in the camera obscura. It was invented by the Frenchman, Nicéphore Niepce, in 1822.

Photography is one of the graphic arts: a novel method of designing. But under this title, photography has changed the habitual processes of ancient time; because as far back as we can ascertain human beings have used manual design. Certain paintings, certain Egyptian designs — those of Beni-Hassan, for example — were made more than five thousand years ago, and the perfection of their technique compels us to conclude that they had reached the results of an incomparable period which showed a further advance over those achieved by tentative or experimental methods. The designs in colours found at Fontdegaume, in the grotto of Altamira, go still further back to the Magdalenian period; fifteen thousand years old perhaps, and already presenting characters of complete design. They show indications delineating outlines, the colour which identifies and the modeling which presents light and shade effects. And what wonderful presentations of animals one can see in Paris at the Institute of Human Paleontology or at the Museum of Saint-Germain; so perfect that they equal the best modern designs and of such quality that, it would seem, the artists of those remote ages had nothing to learn.

And, antedating these designs, others were found still more ancient, but less clever, and others again older than these, and still others, always more ancient, always becoming more awkward, until there were found attempts so elementary that one concluded that this was the beginning: the very first trials at manual design. Now these rudimentary images were found buried in the lower quaternary period which savants have reconstructed down to thirty thousand and even fifty thousand years. We can learn nothing concerning these figures — so vague — except the fact that these handmade designs are extremely ancient. For a period of some ten thousands of years they have expressed the rudimentary thought of our ancestors. And at an era buried in obscurity, these designs, evolved little by little towards mere symbols and were finally expressed in writing.

"For writing is only design, becoming more and more simplified. Everywhere men started to express their thoughts by means of design. The more complicated, the more abstract, these thoughts became, so much more did the symbol replace the material representation. Later the symbol gave place to the sign or abridged figure." (1)

Thus, the object, at first designed as a whole, was later represented by a small part of the design only; later this symbol itself—after how many thousands of experiments?—represented by the monosyllabic word designating the object, and finally also by similar sounds, the idiograph becoming a letter.

The proofs of these facts abound in Egyptian monuments where the idiographs are always interspersed with phonetic signs, and this method of writing extended unchanged for a period of more than four thousand years.

Without any intention to belittle the art of drawing, we must recognize that the change to writing marked a great advance. Humanity has certainly produced painters of genius; but no one would assert that their work has expressed human thought as completely, or with such diversity or with such facility as our writers.

Meanwhile, pure design and the art of writing—evolved from the design traversed historic times, antiquity and the middle ages; but only in modern times, in the fifteenth century, which brought forth so many new ideas, both design and writing faced a crisis. Writing became printing. The artists of that time were tormented by their fears of the future. They began to question the accuracy of their vision and sought the aid of mechanical means to improve their representation of nature. This new science was given a name: it was perspective. The teachings of antiquity on this matter, which may be found in Vitruvius, were lost sight of during the middle ages and Montucla (2) is correct in saying that perspective drawing was reborn at the end of the fifteenth century. I shall not here cite the numerous works in which during the course of the following centuries the laws of perspective were set forth. These lists would be beyond the scope of my subject and are always accessible in the histories of mathematics. (3) It must be noted, however, that among the many devices for the automatic attainment of correct perspective, the camera obscura was employed in drawing early in the sixteenth century. Long after this, however, the restless spirit of the artists kept them from taking full advantage of the use of the apparatus which at most they employed as an accessory to manual design, keeping their

4

methods unchanged.

It will be seen in the course of this work how the genius of an inventor sensed what until this time had been only a confused and formless dream, and applying to his work the chemistry of light, so foreign to it, eventually succeeded in rendering permanent, by his new method, the image received in the camera obscura.

Thus a gradual evolution of drawing produced photography, and, after many centuries, created a new form of writing. For it is superfluous to repeat that photography in the form of cinematography is nothing but simple writing, clear, intelligible, even to the illiterate, not only in his own country but in all countries, a really universal language which the writers of the world are slowly substituting for, or as supplementing, the printed word. And so great is the power of its expression that in the whole world legislatures are compelled to regulate its use.

What then is this photography, hardly a century old and still in its infancy: what is its value today? True its translation in black and white of the colours of nature is defective and does not last. It copies nature, but with difficulty. It will give the illusion of space, but only with the aid of special apparatus. It registers movement, but without relief and without colours, and it was only yesterday that photographic pictures, in halftone, were transmitted to distant parts. But these separate elements tried to unite and we may glimpse the imminent solution of these diverse problems or, still better, of the unique problem, photographic images which will be a complete representation of nature. The next few years will bring continued improvement. This illusion of life, this living picture, created by photography, will instantly transport us to a far distance where it will become real and in television, unsolved yesterday and today possible and at the door. Thus we can foresee a scene in some remote corner of the world, instantly transported, on the screen, to the opposite corner of the world; not a fantastic idea, but reality achieved.

REFERENCES: CHAPTER I

1. Gustave Lebon, *Les premières civilisations.*
2. J.F.Montucla, *Histoire des Mathématiques*, Paris, year VII.
3. An extensive list will be found in the 1690 edition of *Cursus Mathematicus* by Milliet Dechales.

CHAPTER II

Porta, Alleged Inventor of the Camera Obscura

INVENTIONS arise from the application of accumulated knowledge.
They are not born of themselves and ideas are not more the product
of spontaneous generation than are human beings. The invention of
photography would not have been possible had it not been preceded by
that of the camera obscura.

For a long time the invention of the camera obscura was and is still
attributed to the physicist, Jean-Baptiste Porta.

Giovanni Battista della Porta was born in Naples at an unknown
date. His biographers give the years 1550, 1545, 1540, 1538, which is of
little importance. Educated together with his brother Vincent by their
uncle, they received a thorough training and later enjoyed the greatest
respect of the scientists of their time. They lived, unmarried, in the
same house. They seem to have worked together, and if certain authors
are to be believed, Vincent Porta was the real inventor and Jean Baptiste Porta merely the recorder of their scientific associated work. Jean-
Baptiste Porta travelled a great deal in Italy, France and Spain, visiting
the libraries and studying with scientists and professors. He thus
acquired a vast store of information of which one gets an idea from his
works. He was a member of the *Academia degli Otiosi* and of the *Lincei;*
he founded a scientific society which met at his house under the name
of *i Secreti* and its members had to be distinguished by some useful
discovery in the natural sciences.

But in those ignorant and barbaric times, chemistry, physics and
medicine were confused with magic, and the society of the Secreti was
dissolved by the Pope. The members of the society defended themselves
against the accusation that they indulged in illicit science. Jean-Baptiste Porta also believed in astrology and meddled with the rendering
of oracles. Some of his predictions having been realized, his reputation
spread and the crowd besieged his home to secure horoscopes. Thus,
this was undoubtedly one of the principal reasons for the dissolution of
the Secreti. After their troubles with the ecclesiastical tribunal, Porta,
it is said, abandoned the study of science and devoted himself to literature. He wrote twenty-four or twenty-five theatrical plays which,
however, do not give us a very high idea of his talent. He died in Naples

6

on February 4, 1615, leaving the reputation of a great scholar, a pious man, agreeable, spirited and of pleasant manners.

Porta's works give a complete picture of the science of his time, a veritable encyclopedia. This was really the object of his life; to write an encyclopedia. He had announced it and he had prepared its prospectus. He included in it all that was known of astrology, physics, alchemy, etc., and a good many things gathered in a book, little read. I believe he did more. Many experiments described in his books had been known for a long time; transmitted by word of mouth, like the secrets of the laboratory, from master to pupil, from scholar to scholar, from magician to magician. Porta made them public. This explains the success which his work achieved and his lasting reputation. I have given elsewhere a list of his works. (1) I shall speak here only of his most famous book *Natural Magic*, the only one of interest to photographers. (2)

In the preface of the 1588 edition the author states that he had written this book when he was fifteen years old. Modern writers who claim that Porta was born in 1538 deduce from this that the first edition of *Natural Magic* dates from 1553. Abbé Leclerc, in his library of *Richelet* (3) gives the date as 1555; but he adds that he had not seen this book and that Porta's statement seems incredible to him. His argument, drawn from Porta's own works, seems reasonable. However this may be, the earliest edition of *Natural Magic* which we possess — at Paris, at least — is dated 1558. This date has been questioned, but one cannot doubt it, because the work can be found at the Bibliothèque Sainte-Genevieve in Paris under the letter R.283 and under the title: *Magiae Naturalis sive de Miraculis Rerum Naturalium, libri IIII, Jo.Baptista Porta, Neapolitano, authore. Neapoli apud Matthiam Cancer MDLVIII.* Michaud, in his universal biography, states that this work consists of only three volumes. This is a mistake because there is a fourth volume, and it is just in this fourth volume that the description of the camera obscura is found which I quote here: (4)

"The manner in which one can perceive in the dark the things which on the outside are illuminated by the sun, and with their colours.

"If one would see this, it is necessary to closely shut the windows and door down to the smallest possible aperture, lest even a little daylight entering the interior should cause the demonstration to fail. The light should be admitted only through a single conical hole bored through the wall, the base of the cone being turned to the sun and the pointed end towards the interior. The wall opposite should be kept white, or covered with a sheet or paper. One will then perceive everything that is lighted by the sun, only the people passing on the street will have their feet in the air and what is on the right will be on the left side. Everything will be reversed. The images will be as much larger as the paper will be farther away from the opening; but the nearer the paper is placed, the smaller they will become. I will now reveal a matter which I have always hidden and believed it best to conceal: if one would see all these things in their colours on the paper, one uses a mirror. Not a mirror which disperses the rays, but one which collects them. Move it farther away or place it nearer until you find the proper distance where the image is in the center of the mirror and the observer, looking attentively, can recognize the faces, the gestures and movements of the passersby . . . . This will make it possible for anyone ignorant of the art of painting to draw with a pencil or pen the image of any object whatsoever." (5)

Such is the first description of the camera obscura given by Porta. Some years later Porta published an enlarged edition of his *Magic* which comprised twenty volumes instead of four. Nicéron (6) and Böhmer (7) state that this edition in twenty volumes dates from 1569; the oldest edition which the Bibliothèque Nationale in Paris has is dated 1588. (8) This edition is greatly enlarged and is a combination of medicine, perfumery, physics, natural history, optics, cooking, alchemy, etc. The author, at times somewhat naive, sometimes a charlatan and at other times the scholar, sets out to teach but more often perplexes his reader. In this work Porta again describes the camera obscura as he had done thirty years earlier, but he adds these new details: "Now I will make known a matter which I have always hidden and thought best until now to keep silent. If one places a crystal lens (9) in the opening, soon all things will appear more distinct. One will see the faces of the passersby, the colours, the clothing, the gestures and, in short, everything as if they were quite close . . . . Would you like to see this apparition set upright? This is very difficult, often attempted, but nobody has succeeded. In short, as a matter of fact, one has placed plane mirrors in a slanting position with reference to the opening. These mirrors reflected the image on the screen. Everything appeared turned in its proper direction although obscure and not very distinct. But one can succeed in this also: in the opening there is placed an eye-piece, composed of convex lenses, and the image is sent on to a concave mirror . . . . It receives the reversed images and sends them out correctly. If a piece of white paper is placed above the opening, pictures of the objects outside will be seen on it so clear and so sharp, that one never tires of enjoying and admiring them. We must warn, however, that this experiment must not be made without due care (he means that it will be useless T.N.) because it is necessary that the curvature of the lenses of the eye-piece and that of the concave mirror shall have a definite relation."

Natural Magic, as I have said above, is so extended that it seems to be a resumé, a compendium of all Porta's works. There he has accumulated the fables and searched for everything that might possibly seem strange and new, as he seems to have done in all his other books. But in spite of all his extravagances, he has published hardly the twentieth part of the author's experiences and of his translations from Italian, French, German, English, etc. One consults this sort of handy encyclopedia without finding anything which would disclose the sources which the author may have perused. This explains that already in Porta's time the invention of the camera obscura was attributed to him. Kepler in 1604 (10), states that Porta informed him of the camera obscura. This assertion was later repeated by all the writers of the seventeenth and eighteenth centuries. This is also found in the *Encyclopédie* (11) and in Abbé Nollet's works. (12)

1. *Bulletin de la Société Française de Photographie*, 1923, p.52.
2. Aside from the *De refractione Optices*, where a prediction of stereoscopy is found, his other works do not deal with optics. See *Bulletin de la Société Française de Photographie*, 1922, p.206.
3. Lyons edition, 1728.
4. Liber quartus, Caput II, p.143; a typographical error paged this as 135. Libri must have consulted this example, because he gives as reference p.135 in the notes, which accompany his report on Melloni to the Academy of Sciences of Naples.
5. Ut quisque picturae ignarus rei alicujus effigiem stylo describere possit.
6. *Mémoires pour servir à l'histoire des hommes illustres dans la République des Lettres* (Memoirs of Letters relating to the history of famous men of the Republic) by the late R.-P. Nicéron, Barnabite, Paris 1745. Porta's biography, which is inserted in this work is by Jean-Bernard Michault, Scientist of Dijon (1707-1770).
7. Böhmer Georg. Rudolph, *Bibliotheca scriptorum historiae naturalis*. Lipsiae 1785-1789.
8. Jo. Bapt. Portae, Neapolitani, *Magiae Naturalis libri XX, ab ipso authore expurgati et superäucti, in quibus scientiarum naturalium divitiae et delitia demonstrantur, Neapoli DDLXXXVIII.* (J.B.P., Neapolitan, *Natural Magic*, vol. XX, expurgated and enlarged by the author in which the wealth and defects of the natural sciences are demonstrated.) An edition of 1589 contains a portrait of the author bearing the inscription: *"anno aetatis quinquagesimo"* (in his fiftieth year).
9. *Si crystallinam lentem foramini appones* (If a crystal lens is placed in the opening). This word designated then, rock crystal; it is said that crystal glass was first invented in England in the eighteenth century.
10. Johann Kepler. *Ad Vitellionem Paralipomena*, Francfort, 1604.
11. *Encyclopédie ou Dictionnaire raisonné des Sciences, des Arts et des Métiers* (Encyclopedia or classified dictionary of Science, Art and Trade) edited by a Society of men of letters, Paris, 1753, vol.3, article: "chambre obscure ou chambre close" (camera obscura or enclosed room).
12. Abbé Nollet, *Leçons de Physique expérimentale*, Paris, 1743.

CHAPTER III

The Camera Obscura Before Porta

MEANWHILE towards the end of the eighteenth century, after the Italian campaign, the Commissaries of the Republic had brought to France the manuscripts of Leonardo da Vinci, which were studied and translated by Venturi. (1)

This famous scholar discovered that Vinci had described the camera obscura before Porta in a passage which he cited: "*When the images of objects which are illuminated penetrate through a small hole into a very dark room, these images are received on the inside of the room on a white paper, situated some distance from the opening. You will see on the paper all these objects in their proper form and colour. They will be reduced in size, they will present themselves in a reversed position, owing to the intersection of the rays. If these images come from a place which is illuminated by the sun, they will seem as if painted on the paper, which must be very thin and viewed from the back. The hole should be made in a very thin iron plate.*" (2) Leonardo da Vinci was born in 1452 and died in 1519, one hundred years before Porta; therefore Porta finds himself greatly anticipated.

The life of Leonardo da Vinci is too well known to attempt relating it here. It is well known that he became famous as a painter, sculptor, and no less renowned as an engineer, optician, architect and a man of letters. Louis XII on his expedition to Italy, having entered Milan in 1499, desired to honour this extraordinary man and granted him a pension. Invited by King François I, in 1515, to establish himself in France, Vinci, then sixty-three years old, went to Fontainebleau and later resided at Amboise, where he died on May 2, 1519.

Vinci produced very little work; he worked slowly, turning and returning to his subject, and taking it up again continually. He had a habit of carefully jotting down his observations, his thoughts and his deductions, every day, in short notes, in the order in which they happened, for the purpose of using them later. It is in these fragments, ignored by his contemporaries, that moderns have found so many astonishing things. They were bequeathed by Leonardo da Vinci to one of his pupils who had followed him to France, François Melzo, together with his drawings, apparatus and books. All this made quite a considerable lot which Melzo took back with him to Italy. But Melzo's heirs gave little care to them. The precious writings were abandoned in their country house at Vavero where they were looted. The Melzi gave some to others without any consideration of their value, and were astonished when they learned that any value attached to these waste papers. Later Pompée Aretin recovered a certain number of them, which he gathered into a collection of 392 pages which became known as the *Codex Atlanticus;* others, recovered by Arconati, were donated in 1637 to the Ambrosian Library at Milan and so, little by little, there was assembled in this Library the greater part of Vinci's manuscripts. At the end of the eighteenth century the Ambrosian Library contained fourteen volumes of Vinci's manuscripts, and we know two or three others were known to be in the hands of private individuals. This Ambrosian collection, reduced to thirteen volumes, was taken to Paris in 1796. Twelve volumes were deposited at the Institut and the largest one, the *Atlanticus*, went to the Bibliothèque Nationale, from which in 1815 it was removed again by the Austrian Commissary and returned to Milan.

Until Venturi's time it was difficult to unravel this mass of sentences, compiled without system and in a cypher written backward (minor writing, not easily read). From all this were culled different fragments relating to painting, which Raphael du Fresne published in Paris, in 1651, under the title: *Traité de peinture de Léonard de Vinci.*

Venturi classified the manuscripts and designated them by the first letters of the alphabet. The description given above is found in Manuscript D, folio 8; the *Codex Atlanticus* also contains this passage relating to the camera obscura: "*If the façade of a building, or a place, or landscape is lighted by the sun, and a very small hole is drilled in the wall of a room in a building facing this, which is not lighted by the sun, then all the objects illuminated will send their images through this aperture and these will appear, upside down.*" We do not know in which year the two quoted fragments were written. It is true that the manuscripts give the various dates, but without order and the leaves have many times been repaired. (3) It is probable, however, that they were written not later than the last years of the fifteenth century and, in any case, Porta did not appear on the scene until a long time later.

Venturi's brochure nevertheless in no manner modifies the generally accepted opinion and when, on August 19, 1839, Arago made public before the Académie des Sciences the daguerreotype process, he presented the history of the camera obscura in the following terms: (4) "A Neapolitan physicist, J.-B. Porta, recognized about two centuries ago that if one bored a very small hole in the window shutter of a closed room or, better still, in a thin metal plate fastened to the shutter, all the lighted exterior objects, of which the rays can penetrate the hole, will be painted on the wall of the room facing it. Porta discovered shortly after that it was not necessary for the hole to be small, that it could be of any size whatever, if the hole is covered with one of the highly polished glasses which, owing to their shape, are called lenses ....

"Porta constructed portable camera obscura. Each of these had a tube of varying length, equipped with a lens. The whitish screen of paper or cardboard upon which the pictures were to be projected was placed in the focal plane. The Neapolitan physicist intended his small apparatus for persons who had no knowledge of drawing."

Supported by the authority of Arago's great name, these inaccuracies were looked upon as equal to a dogma and the writers of our days continue to copy them over and over again in their histories of photography. Meanwhile Libri, a colleague of Arago since 1840, in his history of mathematics (5) recalled Venturi's text and the description of the camera obscura by Leonardo da Vinci. He even quotes a second example. (6) A work by Caesar Caesariano, published at Como in 1521 (7), contains in effect a passage describing an optical experiment made by a Bene- dictine Monk, Papnutio, but without giving either place or date. In effect this reads: In the shutter of a completely closed room Papnutio placed a conical box, which was 0.13m at the large end and at the small end 0.05m. A minute opening in this small end permitted the images on the outside to pass, projecting them on a piece of white paper. All the earth and all the sky are shown, says the author, in their colours and design. This description resembles so closely that given by Porta in 1558, that it is reasonable to suppose that Porta copied this from Caesariano's work, with which he was undoubtedly acquainted. Venturi had already pointed out (8) that the composition of Greek fire given by Leonardo da Vinci was repeated word for word by Porta. (9) He con- cluded from this that the two authors had drawn their information from the same source, which is unknown to us.

After Libri, other references have been found regarding the camera obscura. (10) In January 1544, the Dutch mathematician Gemma Frisius (1508-1555) observed a solar eclipse by means of a camera obscura and thus obtained the proportion and figure of it (11): "*There exists*" he says (for observing the eclipse) "*another process much more certain and the easiest of all, which has been pointed out by Erasmus Reinhold in his commentaries on a Theory of Peuerbach. Into a room in which all the windows are closed, a ray of the sun is permitted to enter through a narrow, round opening and is projected on a screen . . . . We have also observed an eclipse of the sun at Louvain in 1544.*" The *Théoriques* of Peuerbach or Purbachius (1423-1461) were printed at Venice in 1488, twenty-seven years after the death of their author. But this work was reprinted a great number of times with commentaries by different scholars. The text of Gemma quoting the commentaries of Erasmus Reinhold (12) seems to make an allusion to an edition of Peuerbach which appeared at Wittenberg in 1542. This incunabula, badly printed, bears no frontispiece but only this kind of a title in the body of the work: *Theoricae novae Planetarum Georgii Purbachii foeliciter incipiunt.* The dedication indicates that the marginal notations are by Erasmus Reinhold of Saalfeld and it is dated April, 1542. The volume is not paged and I have not been able to find any notation in which Reinhold recommends the use of a camera obscura. Eder, in his History of Photography (13), confirms that Reinhold made an observation of the eclipse with the camera obscura in 1540 but gives no reference.

Jerome Cardan, in 1550, also described the camera obscura (14): "*If you care to see what goes on in the street when the sun is bright, place in your window a glass disc and the window having been closed* (shuttered T.N.) *you will see images projected through the aperture onto the opposite wall; but the colours are dull. Place then a piece of very white paper at the place where the images are projected . . . .*" It is generally agreed that by this glass disc (orbis e vitro) a bi-convex lens is meant; however, Waterhouse thinks that it means a mirror.

Daniel Barbaro (15) in 1568 at Venice described a camera obscura equipped with a diaphragm and lens, but recommends that a convex lens be preferred, giving the opinion that it would be easy by this method to shade and colour the image as it appeared on the paper.

Benedetti (16) in 1585 at Turin also mentioned the camera obscura equipped with a lens, and the Sicilian Maurolycus (17) in 1575 investigated the path of the rays in the camera obscura without ever giving us the name or description of this optical apparatus.

A synopsis of the list which I have given of these scholars will show that the camera obscura has been described by:

Leonardo da Vinci	before 1519
Papnutio	before 1521
Reinhold	in 1540 or 1542

THE CAMERA OBSCURA BEFORE PORTA

Gemma Frisius	in 1544
Cardan	in 1550 (equipped with a lens)
Porta	in 1558
Barbaro	in 1568 (equipped with a lens and diaphragm)
Benedetti	in 1585 (equipped with a lens)

Porta in 1588 and at the earliest in 1569 (equipped with a lens)

J.B. Porta ranks only sixth in this list in the use of the camera obscura, and only third or perhaps fourth who had made use of a lens.

I find it unnecessary to add that Porta had never constructed portable cameras. It is easily seen from all these descriptions that, in its beginnings, the camera obscura was a real room, part of a house arranged for this purpose and into which the spectators entered. This form of the camera obscura remained unchanged for a long time. After the sixteenth century it was furnished with a reflecting mirror and a diaphragm, no longer novelties any more than lenses. For a long time the action of mirrors had been investigated and often described, just as it was known that a sharper definition of the image could be obtained by narrowing the aperture. As far as lens glasses are concerned, they also were ancient. It is certain that lenses were known to antiquity. The property to amplify a picture of objects is clearly described in the work on optics by the Arabian writer, Alhazen (eleventh century). Bacon is the first who spoke of glasses for correcting the defects of vision. He said "Hoc instrumentus est utile senibus et habentibus oculos debiles." (This instrument is useful to old people and people whose eyes are tired). However, the invention of eyeglasses is not attributed to him, but to the Florentin, Salvino degl'Armati, who died in 1317, or to the Pisan, Della Spina, who died in 1313.

Neither Vinci nor Caesariano claimed the credit for having discovered the camera obscura. It seems, however, that they cited it as a phenomenon known to scholars of their time and that it had not been used a great deal. It is true, for instance, that we do not hear of an observer viewing in the camera obscura the spectacle of the goings-on in the street or in the country before Leonardo da Vinci; but the investigations are far from being complete, and it will be seen in the next chapter that a limited use of the camera and the camera itself were known in the thirteenth century.

The painter Alberti, who lived in the fifteenth century (1398-1484) has also been regarded as the inventor of the camera obscura. However, the description of his apparatus, which we read in Vasari (18), had no

other object in view than that of optical projection, or perhaps panoramas, which were invented towards the end of the eighteenth century.

Vinci and Caesariano speak of the camera obscura as opticians and
in the manner in which scholars speak of operations in the laboratory.
Reinhold and Gemma thought of it only for astronomical observations;
Cardan (1501-1576), great miracle worker, and who, together with
Arnaud de Villeneuve (1238-1314), without the master, made at least
Porta's model. Porta had only to imitate it. Cardan made with it a
diverting spectacle, and sometimes a terrifying marvel for the simple-
minded. Porta affirms (19) that often he had presented before great
persons, to his friends, and to inquisitive fools, spectacles which astonish
us somewhat by their extent. Outside of his house, on a conveniently
chosen site, a forest, in a solitary neighborhood, rigged up like a theatre,
actors in costume hunted and killed exotic, little-known animals, often
naively represented. Or again, soldiers of contending armies simulated
with naked swords the science of war and murder; and again, apparitions passed in phantasmagoric disturbances. Thus, while on the outside, the horns and the trumpets made a racket, the audience, not being
able to see how this was produced, and, shut in the room, viewed these
things passing by on the screen of white canvas, but had their doubts
whether what they saw were not diabolical sorceries.

But we must always remember the use of the camera obscura for
manual designing; because this idea expressed by Barbaro and Porta of
reproducing images in tracing their outlines and adding to them the
lights and shades and colours of nature, continued without change until
Niepce; all this without anyone's having the slightest idea—with only
one exception as we will see—that a new art of representation might
result from it.

THE CAMERA OBSCURA BEFORE PORTA
REFERENCES: CHAPTER III

1. Venturi, *Essai sur les ouvrages physico-mathématiques de Léonard de Vinci*. (Notes on the physico-mathematical works of Leonardo da Vinci) Paris, year V, (1797). Venturi (1746-1822) professor at Modena, later at the University of Pavia, then Italian chargé d'affaires at Bern, was at Paris in 1797, attached to the Count of San Romano, who looked after the interests of the d'Este family after the Directoire.
2. Venturi reproduces the diagram of the phenomenon of the intersection of rays drawn by Vinci.
3. The manuscript C, for example, on p.16 carries this remark: "On April 23, 1490, I began this book." Manuscript F contains the following: "Begun at Milan, September 12, 1508." See *Les manuscrits de Léonard de Vinci* (manuscripts of Leonardo da Vinci) published facsimile with text and translation by Ravaisson-Mollien, Paris, 1881-1889.
4. *Comptes rendus hebdomadaires des séances de l'Académie des Sciences*, 1839, 2nd semester, p.250.
5. *Histoire des Sciences Mathématiques en Italie depuis la Renaissance des Lettres jusqu'a la fin du XVIIe siécle* by Guillaume Libri, Paris 1838-1840. Libri-Carucci (1803-1869) born in Florence, took refuge in France owing to political events in Italy, after 1830. Naturalized in 1833, he became a member of the Académie des Sciences, inspector general of the University and of Libraries of France. He embezzled several valuable books, among them two volumes of manuscript leaves of Leonardo da Vinci, A and B, which he went to England to sell. He was sentenced by default in 1859.
6. *Rapport sur le Daguerréotype lu à l'Académie des Sciences de Naples* (Report on the daguerreotype read before the Academy of Sciences of Naples, by Macedoine Melloni, translated by MM*** and Al.Donné, reviewed by Libri, member of the Institut, Paris, 1840, p.16, note.
7. *Vitruvio de Architectura Libri Decem traducti de latino in vulgare* (Vitruvio on Architecture, ten books translated from the Latin into common language by Caesare Caesariano, Como, 1521, Book I, leaf 23, verso.
8. Venturi, work cited, p.31.
9. *Magia Naturalis*, Book XII, Chapt.II.
10. Waterhouse, *Notes on the Early History of the Camera Obscura*, London, 1901.
11. *Gemmae Frisii, medici et mathematici De Radio Astronomico et Geometrico Liber*, Antwerp, 1545, leaf 31.
12. Erasmus Reinhold (1511-1553) published the famous *Tables Prunétiques* after the system of Copernicus, and also published the *Théoriques* of Peuerbach. Montucla, in his history of mathematics, denotes him as a man of genius.
13. Eder, *Geschichte der Photographie*, Halle, 1905.
14. Hyeronimi Cardani, Medici Mediolanensis, *De Subtilitate*, Libri XXI, Nuremberg, MDL, p.307.
15. *La pratica della Perspettiva di Danielo Barbaro*, Venice, 1568, Cap.V.
16. Io.Baptista Benedicti, *Diversarum speculationum mathematicarum et physicarum liber*, Turin, 1585.
17. *Theoremata de Lumine et Umbra ad perspectivam radiorum incidentium*, Venice, 1575.
18. Vasari, *Vite de più eccellenti pittori, scultori e architetti*.
19. *Magiae Naturalis Libri XX*, book 17, chapter 6.

CHAPTER IV

Roger Bacon and the Camera Obscura

SOME believed to have seen a description of the camera obscura in the writings of the monk Roger Bacon (1214-1294) in the thirteenth century. However, the passages cited are so improbable that this opinion is generally rejected. But the text produced by Pierre Duhem (1) hitherto disregarded by the historians of photography, permits no doubt that the camera obscura was known in that century.

Roger Bacon, in Book II, Chapter VIII, of the treatise: *De multiplicatione specierum* (1267), inserted at the end of the *Opus Majus* in the edition by Jebb (2), while examining the laws of the propagation of light, speaks of a ray of light passing through any form of aperture and projecting itself in the form of a round spot, especially if the aperture is narrow. The larger the opening, the more distant and larger must be the projection, taking on the round shape or according to the form of the opening. He adds a diagram.

This shows the rays of the sun passing through an aperture (foramen) and projecting their image, after crossing, on the wall (paries). Notwithstanding the troublesome word "wall" which seems to indicate a room, this passage has always been rejected as a description of a camera obscura. Some think that this is the exposition of a theory and does not refer to an existing apparatus. Others object that these phenomena of vision can be observed outside the camera obscura. Everyone has seen the orb of the sun falling into a shadowy path through the foliage and, there, the observation can be made in the open at twilight. Bacon later develops theories in order to explain the phenomenon, which are outside of our subject.

A manuscript written before 1277 (3) by a certain Witelo or Witeck relating to the same optical problem contains and develops this proposition: "Omne lumen per foramina angularia incidens rotundatur." "All light passing through angular apertures is projected in a circular form." Nothing is known of the author except his German or Polish origin. His text, which is still more vague than that of Bacon, cannot reasonably be taken to describe a camera obscura, but it seems to demonstrate that the observation of the passage of a ray of light through a more or less narrow opening and its resulting projection (crossing of rays forming a circle) was investigated again in Europe in the thirteenth century. Its origin was old. The theory is found in the works of Aristotle (384-322 B.C.) and is confusedly pointed out in the *Optics* of Alhazen (eleventh century), whose work was inspired by Aristotle, and who again furnished all the material used by Bacon and Witelo. But this is not the camera obscura.

The third quotation is derived from a manuscript which is preserved both at the Bibliothèque Nationale, Paris, and at the Bibliothèque municipale of Bordeaux (4) and which is a treatise on astronomy, with no indication of the date of its publication or of its author. Pierre Duhem in publishing it in extenso shows, by piecing together different parts of the text, that this author had before him the works of Bacon and of Witelo. When their theories conflicted, the anonymous author adopted those of Bacon and repudiated the German thesis. It is evidently a contemporary polemic of the two controversial works.

"Radii incidentie" says that anonymous author "cadenti per foramen planum angulare, cujus tamen latera non multum se excedant, in pariete opposita rotundatur . . . Sed, dicit aliquis, rotunditatem incidentie esse a rectitudine radiationis a corpore solari sphaerico descendentis . . . ; quod probari videtur, quoniam tempore eclipsium solarium, hujus modi incidentia radiorum solarium novacularis et omnino disposita ad modum illum quo disponitur pars solis quae a lunari corpore non obrumbratur." "The incidence of a ray falling through an angular hole lying in a plane, whose sides, however, do not much exceed each other, appear round on the wall opposite . . . But, says someone, the roundness of the incidence is from the straightness of the radiation descending from the spherical solar body . . . ; which seems to be proved, since, at the time of solar eclipses, this sort of incidence of the solar rays is knife-like and wholly of the same shape as that part of the sun which is not overshadowed by the lunar body."

And so the solar eclipses were observed by means of an arrangement having a narrow aperture, through which the rays passed, and a screen which received the projection of the luminary under observation; Bacon's diagram thus corresponded to reality. As a matter of fact, a similar arrangement is described in another anonymous manuscript (5), of the end of the thirteenth century, which may be attributed to Bacon, although without any evident proof but also without any absolute objection. "If, moreover, on the day on which the sun is eclipsed, you watch the whole eclipse without injuring the eyes, i.e. when the eclipse of the sun begins and however great it may be and as long as it lasts, observe the falling of a solar ray through the middle of some round hole, and look carefully at the distinct circle which the ray makes in the place upon which it falls. When you see the roundness of this circle becoming defective in any part, you may know that at the same time the brightness is failing in the body of the sun in the part opposite to that part. For when in the distinct circle the roundness begins to fail, then the sun is beginning to be eclipsed from the west; and likewise, as the roundness of the distinct circle increases, the eclipse of the sun decreases proportionately in quantity. For whatever number of degrees of the diameter of the sun are eclipsed, just so many degrees disappear of the distinct circle which the ray of the sun forms in the place where it falls after it has gone through the middle of the round hole. And this is the end of that."

This text is of great interest to photographers, therefore I reproduce the Latin text, notwithstanding its length. The reader, at any rate, can always pass over these lines: "Si autem die qua sol eclipsabitur, totumque eclipsim conspicere absque oculorum lesione, hoc est quando incipit et quanta sit, et quamdiu durat solis eclipsis, observa casum solaris radii per medium alicujus rotundi foraminis, et circulum clarum quem perficit radius in loco super quem cadit, diligenter aspice. Cujus circuli rotunditatem cum in aliqua parte videris deficere, scias quod in eodem tempore deficit claritas in corpore solis ex parte opposita illi parti. Nam, cum in circulo claro incipit rotunditas deficere, tunc incipit sol eclipsari ex parte occidentis; et similiter, dum crescit rotunditas circuli clari, decrescit eclipsis et proportionaliter secundum quantitatem. Quot enim digiti diametri solis eclipsantur, tot pereunt digiti circuli clari quem figurat radius solis in loco casus sui postquam transierit per medium foraminis rotundi. Et sic est finis hujus."

Here again we do not know whether this observation was made in diffused light or in complete darkness, whether this deals with an arrangement installed in an open place or in a dark room. Jean Peckham (1228-1291), Archbishop of Canterbury, a contemporary and believed to be a pupil of Bacon, a Franciscan and scholar of physics like himself, states in his *Perspectiva* (6): "Et hujus rei conjecturam ex solis eclipsibus sumunt. Quando enim, tempore eclipsis solis, *in loco tenebroso per quodcumque foramen radii solis excipiuntur*, est videre basim pyramidis illuminationis corniculatim ea ratione obumbrescere, qua solem luna tegit." "And the accomplishment of this they take from eclipses of the sun. For when, at the time of an eclipse of the sun, *the rays of the sun are received in a dark place through any hole*, it is possible to see the horned base of the pyramid of light fall into the shade in the same manner as the moon covers the sun." This illustrates the last point and proves that the observation was made in a dark place.

There is only left to me to point out a text which will eliminate all doubt. It is due to Guillaume de Saint-Cloud, an astronomer of the thirteenth century. A note by Littré, inserted in Volume XXV of the Literary History of France (7) informs us about Guillaume de Saint-Cloud, known solely because a manuscript at the Bibliothèque Nationale (8) contains two short works by him, a calendar for the years 1096 to 1496 and an almanac written in 1290. The manuscript discloses the fact that the calendar was made by order of Queen Marie of Brabant, second wife of Philippe III, the Bold (1245-1285); she was born in 1260, became queen in 1274 and died in 1321. He was assuredly a famous scholar, for the queens, both widows, were not in the habit of entrusting their scientific commands to unknown men. We find at the end of the almanac this passage, which Littré translated with abbreviations (9): "In the year of our Lord 1285, on the 5th day of June, it happened that those who too intensely observed the sun (during the eclipse) their vision was impaired when they turned their eyes back into the darkened room. This condition of being dazzled lasted with some two days, with others three and with some others several days, according to the length of time they had stared at the sun and according to the degree in which their eyes were sensitive . . . In order to eliminate this and to be able to observe without danger the time of the beginning, of the end, and the extent of the eclipse, *they made in the roof of a closed house, or in the window, an opening turned towards that part of the sky where the eclipse of the sun would appear, and the size of the hole was about the same as that made in a barrel for the purpose of decanting wine.* The light of the sun entered through this opening, before which, at a distance of twenty or thirty feet, something flat, for instance a sheet, was placed. A ray of light will be seen delineating itself on the sheet in a round shape, even if the aperture is angular. The spot illuminated will be larger than the opening and so much greater as the sheet is moved away from it, but then it will be more feeble than if the sheet is placed closer." "*Fiat in domo clausa foramen in tecto domus vel (in) fenestra versus parte illa coeli qua debet eclipsi solis apparere et sit quantitas foraminis sicut ejus foramen dolii ex quo extrahitur vinum.*"

Guillaume, continuing his demonstration, states that the center of the sun passes through the center of the hole, but that the upper marginal rays are projected on the lower part of the sheet and inverted; that on the sheet the projected image will diminish as soon as the eclipse begins, but from the opposite side of the diminution of the sun; that the image will begin to enlarge from the other side as soon as the eclipse has passed into its second phase, and that, for the same cause, objects are seen reversed as in a concave mirror. This is made plain in the accompanying diagram. He states, "Suppose A B to be the sun, C the center of the hole, A D a solar ray, arriving from the eastern side of the sun, B E a ray from the western side. It is manifest that when ray A diminishes in the sun, it will also diminish at D in the projected image on the sheet after passing through the hole, since it is ray A which falls at D, and if the ray diminishes at B, it will also be diminished on the sheet at E for the same reason." This figure which, together with the demonstration, are identical with those given by Bacon.

There is no longer any doubt; this description so complete can only be that of the camera obscura. Reinhold, in 1540, pointed out as new a method which had been employed for two hundred and fifty years. Duhem established by means of a very close analysis that all these writings are the works of Bacon or of Bacon's disciples. This led him to the absolute conclusion that the camera obscura was invented by the Franciscan monk in the thirteenth century. After this for him there was no doubt; Bacon is the inventor of the camera obscura. To me the matter seems less certain.

The commentator remarked that in the anonymous manuscript 15,171, attributed to Bacon and in that of Guillaume de Saint-Cloud, the descriptions of observed eclipses in the camera obscura appear there as outside of the scope of the work and without any close relation to the rest of the text; it is evident that they treat of a novelty, something that will make a sensation and that the authors were anxious to make it public. But on the other hand, Jean Peckham and the first anonymous writer mentioned seem to contradict Bacon's explanations; the projected image is round because the sun is round and this is proved at the time of solar eclipses where the projection is hollowed. Thus, those who opposed Bacon's theories—who were not his pupils—also were familiar with and observed the eclipses by the same arrangement as Bacon.

In short, everything that is known has been cited here and the reader is free to draw his own conclusions. But this is what seems probable. A solar ray filtering through some narrow aperture into a darkened room and there showing as a luminous round spot is a phenomenon known for many centuries. The first use made of this seems to have been the examination of solar eclipses without danger to the eye. Who was the first to do this? Roger Bacon might be named without hurting the truth but without certainty. Some time later it was learned that through this hole contrived in the wall or window, the image of all exterior objects delineated themselves in the room, and one could observe also the passers-by and the public square. Who was the first to see this? We have no clear description of it prior to that of Leonardo da Vinci. A passage in Roger Bacon which I have quoted in speaking about projections (Chapter XLIII) where concave mirrors are described reflecting exterior objects, is too vague to reach any conclusion. Between Bacon and Vinci more than two hundred years elapsed. Two centuries of silence as to the camera obscura. This seems incredible and can only mean that we have no knowledge of other writers who speak of the subject. If we could trace them, the history of the camera obscura would unroll the successive steps of its progress from antiquity to our day and one would recognize without always knowing the authors, it would be seen how the arrangements became more and more complicated by the increasingly ingenious applications. Thus, it is vain to single out any one as inventor of the camera obscura because there is no such individual. If this honour must be bestowed upon any one of the scholars who have most contributed to it, whether it be Vinci, Bacon or Guillaume de Saint-Cloud, of whom we know so little, it must be bestowed on Porta. However, what a difference from the camera of Bacon to that of Vinci! And then again, how much greater the difference between that of Leonardo and of those who followed him! And today we call an apparatus camera which, by no stretch of the imagination can be said to resemble the century-old arrangements which I have exhumed. One reason why there are so many contradictory opinions lies in the use of the sole name, camera obscura, to describe so many entirely dissimilar things.

1. *Le système du monde* (System of the World) by Pierre Duhem, Paris 1913-1917, 5 volumes were published, vol.III, p.499 and following, vol.IV, p.10. These passages were pointed out by Lagrange in *Photo-Revue*, August 15, 1923.
2. *Fratris Rogeri Bacon ordinis minorum Opus Majus ad Clementem quartum Pontificem Romanus* . . . nunc primum edidit S.Jebb . . . . London MDCCXXXIII, p.358: *Incipit Tractatus Magistri Rogeri Bacon, De multiplicatione specierum, pars secunda,* caput VIII, p.409. *Opus Majus,* was dedicated by Bacon to Pope Clement in 1267.
3. *Alhazeni Arabis libri septem nunc primum editi* . . . . *Item, Vitellionis Thuringopolini libri X. Omnes instaurati . . . a Frederico Risnero,* Basle, MDLXXII.
4. Bibliothèque Nationale, latin sources No.16089. Municipal library at Bordeaux No.419.
5. Bibliothèque Nationale, latin sources No.15171. Pierre Duhem: *Le Système du Monde,* vol.III, p.501.
6. *Joannis Archiepiscopi Cantuariensis Perspectivae communis libri tres.* Jam postremo correcti ac figuris illustrati. Coloniae Agrippinae, anno MDLXXX.
7. *Histoire littéraire de la France, ouvrage commencé par les religieux bénédictins de la congrégation de Saint-Maur et continué par des membres de l'Institut* (Académie des Inscriptions et Belles-Lettres), vol.XXV, Paris, 1869.
8. Mss.7281, latin sources, folios 141 to 154.— Mss.15171, latin sources, folios 88 to 101.
9. Mss.7281, folios 143 verso and 144 recto.

CHAPTER V

The Camera Obscura of the Seventeenth Century

THE primitive arrangement of the camera obscura, because of its lack of mobility, naturally limited the use that could be made of it. Moreover, in the early years of the seventeenth century, already the transportable camera was beginning to be discussed. The astronomer Kepler (1571-1630) possessed a camera obscura about 1611, which is described in a letter from Sir Henry Wootton to Lord Bacon (1561-1626), part of which is given here (1): "*I passed the night at Lintz (Linz T.N.) in Austria .... I found Kepler there, a man famous in the sciences .... He informed me he had a little portable tent which he could set up anywhere in the open country, wherever it pleased him, which turned like a windmill so that one would see, in succession all points of the horizon; totally closed and dark with the exception of a small hole about an inch and a half in diameter. In this hole there is a long perspective tube with a convex glass at the end which enters the opening (2); at the other end is a concave glass, which reaches into the interior of the tent, about half way, and by which the visible radiations from all the exterior objects are introduced and fall on a sheet of paper upon which they are received. It is quite simple after this to trace with a pencil or pen all outlines of the design and to reproduce them true to nature. This completed, the tent is turned with care to take a new view of the landscape, and thus one can design everything around the horizon.*"

Kepler's tent is known only from what we read in this letter which itself is comparatively unknown. We have no illustration of it, however the description of it resembles almost line for line another apparatus described and illustrated thirty-five years later by Athanasius Kircher, in his *Ars Magna*. (3)

Kircher, who had seen this machine used in Germany, describes it as having the form of a large sized cube which encloses a smaller one and both are hermetically closed. The outside box, constructed from light material, was opaque and had a hole equipped with a lens which occupied the center of the sides, while the interior box was made only of thin and transparent paper. In the board a trapdoor permitted the observer to slide into the apparatus. He then saw the images sent through the lens appearing on the paper walls which enclosed him. The outfit, supported by two horizontal struts, was so light in weight that two men could transport it wherever it was desired. From this illustration the Jesuits of Paris about 1671, constructed a similar machine in the form of a portable chair and informed Kircher that they were delighted with it although the construction of it was costly. (4)

These, then, are the first examples of mobile cameras; they had to be sufficiently large so that the operator could enter them.

At Ingolstadt, in 1612, the Jesuit Scheiner, in order to observe the sun spots, employed an apparatus of which he gives an illustration in his *Rosa Ursina*. (5) This is a long, very long tube equipped with lenses, at one end, terminating at the other end in a kind of framework. The bottom of the frame carries a piece of white paper upon which the image is received. In order to permit the examination in semi-darkness, the machine was covered—a prototype of the tele-objective—with fabrics, papers or laths. The complete apparatus was placed in a room and the tube with its lens pointed at the sun through the open window. Scheiner enumerates six other methods of observing sun spots, and states that the seventh one, here described, by means of the helioscope, in which method the lens records the solar image on the paper, gives the most brilliant, easiest and surest result.

This arrangement seems to have been adopted by other astronomers. Gassendi (6) describes a similar arrangement by the aid of which, in 1631, he observed the passage of Mercury across the sun, and which he was accustomed to use for the observation of sun spots and eclipses. This famous passage of Mercury crossing the sun, which took place on November 7, 1671, was observed by many astronomers. Those who employed the camera obscura saw nothing, says Montucla. (7) But Gassendi is quoted among those who succeeded in the observation. His arrangement was nothing else but the camera obscura and, as a matter of fact, it was a transition from the primitive camera obscura to the portable boxes, the use of which soon became general.

It seems that the construction of small cameras, i.e. those which were really portable, did not begin until the middle of the seventeenth century. Eder (8) finds the first mention of this in *Oculus Artificialis* by Zahn, published in 1665. Others existed, however, before this date, as is shown by the following passage in Hérigone (9): "*Various methods of obtaining the perspective of an object which one wishes to see before his eyes . . . . The others figure that one can obtain an object in perspective in its colours by means of its replica which records itself on a piece of white*

*paper stretched taut at the bottom of a chalice-shaped cup and on the oppo-
site side of the tube through which the images entered, a convex lens; the
right portions of the perspective will, however, represent the left portions of
the object."*

Hérigone does not give us an illustration of his apparatus; but his text
is so clear that one can easily visualize it. This must be regarded as one
of the first portable cameras constructed. In any case I have not been
able to find an earlier example. Neither Jean Dubreuil (10) nor Father
Nicéron (11), who wrote at that time, mentions the camera obscura.

I believe that the use of this camera was taken up again in France
about the middle of the seventeenth century. In a later edition of the
Perspective curieuse by Nicéron, dated 1646 (12), therefore later than
1638, there is not a single word in which the author quotes the camera
obscura as known in Rome by the lecture given by Scheiner on *Rosa
Ursina;* while the third edition of 1652 (13) contains a full description of
the camera obscura and of its use. The author states: "After a room has
been shut on all sides so that no perceptible light can enter, a hole is
made in one of the walls or in the shutter, in front of which hole a paper
or blank sheet is placed at a certain distance, perpendicular to the horizon, which serves as the canvas upon which the exterior images are
received. This reception is so perfect that the eye is completely deceived
by this natural image so that, if science and reason did not correct the
deception, one would believe that the eye sees the actual objects, especially if one inserts in this hole, about the size of a twenty sol piece, a
convex lens of long focus; because these exterior objects project not only
their real size, the figures and colours, but also their movements, which
is always lacking in the painter's work . . . .

Nicéron says that a similar perspective (show T.N.) could be seen at
the Samaritaine, on the Pont-Neuf. We know that in this neighborhood
a lot of outlandish spectacles attracted the idlers; the camera obscura
was one of the attractions. But what use was made of it? "Sometimes
the eyes of those who were in the room were so deceived that, having
lost their purse, they saw it in the hands of those who counted and
divided the money in some wood or garden plot, and they believed that
this spectacle was done by magic . . . . And charlatans have deluded
some naive and ignorant people by persuading them that what they saw
was a manifestation of the occult science of astrology or of magic, and
they had no difficulty in astonishing them and this afforded an opportunity to abuse the simpletons and draw whatever profit they could

from this." The subjects of the "Roi Soleil", having lost their key or purse, or faced with a perilous decision or anxious to find out what the future had in store for them, hied themselves to the camera obscura as the people of our day run to the crystal gazer. Again, just as today, the artistic atmosphere returns them to their homes, improved in knowledge, satisfied and relieved of their purses.

The dialogue was always the same. "For" continues Nicéron, "if some-one behind the screen (white paper) impersonated the *Spirit*, so-called, and speaks in the manner of those who pull the strings of marionettes, the simpletons believed that the speech proceeded from the personages represented, once the marionettes opened their mouths. And as soon as the window was opened, everything vanished as on the witches sabbath. It was there, they explained to the people, that the figures vanished."

The camera obscura was used not only by charlatans but artists also used it. They were constructed if they were meant to be moved, "*like a military tent or like a tent used in the country*" (Kepler's camera); or again, "*as the sedan chairs on which people were carried through the streets*" (Kircher's camera). "It is sufficient to remark" still quoting Nicéron "that if a painter in a transportable camera *makes four drawings and joins them together where he can put the matter to a test*, he will have the kind of perspective which he seeks" (Hérigone's camera). "A painter must have *a sort of portfolio or lantern* pierced in such a manner by a hole that . . . he will see below everything projected by the light-rays through this hole on a very white piece of paper. Now, looking through another opening made on the side of the portfolio, he will trace all on the same place on the paper in order to carefully reproduce an immobile painting from the mobile picture which latter, however, will vanish as soon as the first hole is covered or when he changes his position."

Thus in the middle of the seventeenth century several models of transportable cameras and hand cameras were known in France. As a matter of fact, these various apparatus were still very unhandy.

Oculus Artificialis by the Premonstratensian Zahn (14) published in Wurzburg in 1665, twenty-three years after Hérigone's book, contains several illustrations of cameras easily transportable and, as the author states, were made to demonstrate in any place whatever the curious and ever-changing aspects of nature. The earliest model is a box AB about 25 cm. long and equally high, of which the length, calculated for the focus of the lenses, is 65-70 cm. The back A is formed by a wooden shutter which can be lowered or raised by sliding in grooves, and inside the shutter a cardboard pierced with a circular opening, through which one looks inside the camera. Some distance from this partition, about 6 or 7 cm. another partition is placed parallel in the interior of the camera, and its opening covered by a piece of thin white paper impregnated with oil so that one can see through it the image which will be projected on it; in the front of the box, tubes H I K telescope one into the other, shortened or lengthened, as may be necessary proportionately to the focal length and carrying one or two bi-convex lenses; a cork closes them.

But the men of the seventeenth century, like all contemporaries of Porta, wanted to see the images as they really were; they disliked to observe people who walked with their feet in the air, or landscapes showing the sky forming the base of the picture. And so cameras were constructed with the images showing the figures set upright. Nicéron (15) states that the pictures were set upright by means of lenses or mirrors. Zahn (16) presents illustrations of reversing mirrors and points out three methods of placing them. The first before the lens. The arrangement is so awkward that he seems to speak as of a mere experimental model. This heavy box, higher than it was wide, a hole pierced in the base at B, reflects the visible object in mirror H, at an angle 45° to the interior. In the interior, also, a little above and placed in a double bottom e f, the lens receives the image from the mirror and sends it on to the paper screen a. The upper partition is pierced by a round opening through which the screen can be examined; a hinged lid covers all.

The second arrangement places the mirror back of the lens and behind the screen (or paper). A box A B C D, already better constructed, carried in front a lens H placed in collapsible tubes, then oiled paper a b inside the box receives the image at the focus of the lens and reflects it onto the mirror c d, inclined towards the front where the observer views it. The third arrangement, by far the best, and the use of which has persisted through the years, places the mirror between the objective and the screen.

In an edition, dated 1686, wherein Zahn (17) published the second and third installments of his *Oculus Artificialis*, we find illustrations and methods of construction of cameras more complicated than those just mentioned, and in which sets of movable mirrors show the images one after another naturally or reversed. This is the first time where the author speaks of a glass prepared to receive the image (vitrum parastaticum), and he advises it as preferable to oiled paper. This glass was made opaque on one side only by means of a light coating of an adhesive matter, like white lead. It is possible that it may have been roughened.(18) However, oiled paper remained in use for a long time, inasmuch as Abbé Nollet, in 1765, still describes a camera obscura equipped with an oiled paper screen. Zahn also speaks of the apparatus used by charlatans. Such are the magic vases. At the left-hand lower side can be seen at A in the extreme base of the vase an opening artfully disguised as an ornamental motif. It is there where the lens was placed. The image was received on a mirror f inclined at an angle of 45° which reflected it upwards to C D. At C D a ground-glass, perfectly fitted, formed the lower end. Water or coloured liquid filled the upper part of the glass and the observer perceived the images moving about in the water. The author here shows us two dogs which appear to be swimming in the vase. But these experiments were not always of so innocent a character. Imagine such an apparatus backed up against a wall and arranged with an opening which permits it to receive pictures from the outside; the quack's show and the audience of the spectacle were in semi-darkness, moved by the setup of the scene and expectantly awaiting the beginning of the show. Imagine on the outside a mechanized scene, with figures animated by real persons and you will have the explanation of many illusions, the chimeras which history has handed down to us as a souvenir, and an idea of the numbers of people to whom the future was shown in a glass of water.

Cameras were usually equipped with a single bi-convex lens; however, combinations of several lenses were far from being unknown. In the sixteenth century concave and convex lenses were employed and after the invention of the telescope or astronomical eyepieces by the maker of spectacles Zacharias Janse (19) of Middelbourg, in 1590, combinations of different lens glasses came into frequent use.

On one of the pages of *Rosa Ursina* by Scheiner (20) (1575-1650), there is shown a camera obscura equipped with a series of lenses consisting of bi-convex or plano-concave lenses in different arrangements, chiefly with the object of presenting the image sometimes in a natural position, sometimes reversed. *La Vision parfaite* of Father Cherubin (21) (1677), shows that bi-convex, plano-convex, plano-concave, bi-concave, and also meniscus lenses were used.

These authors point out how they were made and the proper qualities that they must possess for their right use. Zahn states that it is preferable to employ three lenses in place of two for the lens combination in the camera obscura, in order to obtain more brilliant images.

30

THE CAMERA OBSCURA OF THE SEVENTEENTH CENTURY

It should be noted also, that in the seventeenth century, the word "camera" indicated solely the old camera of Vinci and Porta. Portable cameras are called, as has been noted above, *vaisseau en forme d'entonnoir*, *portefeuille*, *sorte de lanterne*, etc. Zahn, in order to distinguish them from the camera obscura called the cameras described in 1665 *cistulae parastaticae*, and those of 1686 *machinae parastaticae*. As a matter of fact, these were not cameras but boxes or optical apparatus. However, the name of the camera obscura persisted even for the small portable boxes.

1. This translation is taken from *Cosmos*, January 1858.
2. That is, towards the exterior. The tube was introduced from inside the tent.
3. Athanasii Kircheri, Fuldensis Buchonii e Soc. Iesu Presbyteri . . . *Ars Magna lucis et umbrae in decem libros digesta*. Romae 1646, liber X, Magia, Part II, p.806.
4. Athanasii Kircheri . . . editio altera priori multo auctior, Amsterdam 1671, p.714.
5. *Rosa Ursina* . . . by Christophoro Scheiner . . . , Bracciano 1630, p.150.
6. *Institutio Astronomica* . . . by Petro Gassendo . . . , Paris 1647, pp.186 and 199.
7. *Histoire des Mathématiques*, vol.II, p.321.
8. *Geschichte der Photographie*, Halle, 1905, p.33.
9. *Supplementum Cursus Mathematici* . . . by Pierre Hérigone, Paris, MDCXLII. On the perspective, Chap.6, p.113.
10. *La perspective pratique* . . . by a Parisian Jesuit, Paris, MDCXLII.
11. *La perspective curieuse* by P.F.Jean-François Nicéron, Parisian of the order of Minims, Paris, 1638.
12. R.P.Joannis-Francisci Niceronis . . . *Thaumaturgus Opticus* . . . opus curiosum et utile Pictoribus, Architectis, Statuariis, Sculptoribus, Caelatoribus et quibucumque aliis, quorum opera in delineandi studio posita est. Lutetiae Parisiorum . . . MDCXLVI.
13. *La perspective curieuse* by the Rev.P.Nicéron . . . with the optic and catoptric of R.P.Mersenne, of the same order, brought to light after the death of the author, Paris, MDCLII.
14. *Oculus Artificialis teledioptricus sive Telescopium* . . . Author R.P.F.Joanne Zahn . . . Wurzburg, 1665, pp.176 and 181.
15. *Perspective curieuse*, edition of 1652, p.21.
16. *Oculus artificialis*, p.180.
17. R.P.F.Joannis Zahn, Carolopolitani Sacri Candidi Canonici Ordinis Prae monstratensis in superiore Cella Dei professi pro explicando et demonstrando *Oculo Artificiali Teledioptrico*, etc. Wurzburg, MDCLXXXVI, fundamentum III, p.221.
18. Glass was known ever since antiquity; the invention of glass for window panes only dates from the thirteenth century. For a long time it was an object of luxury, even after Colbert in the seventeenth century had sent for workmen (glaziers) from Venice in order to spread the glass industry in France. At the end of the eighteenth century oiled paper was often still used for windows. Antiquity equally knew the art of engraving on glass with sand. The middle ages had forgotten these processes which were reinvented in the fifteenth century. But it was not until the eighteenth century that the discovery was made of etching glass with hydrofluoric acid. In 1686 unpolished glass became a rarity.
19. *De Vero Telescopii Inventore cum brevi omnium conspiciliorum historia* . . . . (On the history of telescopic glass with a short history of all relating to it). Author; Petro Borello, Hagae Comitum MDCLV.
20. *Rosa Ursina*, book II, p.107.
21. *La Vision parfaite ou le concours des deux axes de la vision en un seul point de l'objet.* (Perfect sight or the coincidence of two axes of vision at one point of the object) by Father Cherubin, Capucin, Paris, MDCLXXVII.

CHAPTER VI

The Camera Obscura of the Eighteenth Century

IN the course of the eighteenth century numerous models of the camera were taken up by the public, but without essential modification from those of the camera obscura described above. They were made larger or smaller, more or less elegant, more or less handy, for transport and use; but the optical apparatus remained the same.(1) L'Encyclopédie (2), in 1753, describes three models of the camera obscura and refers to the Cours d'Optique (Optical Course) of Professor Wolf, published in Halle in 1707.(3) But Wolf contented himself with copying the descriptions of Zahn's *Oculus Artificialis*. However, at the time when l'Encyclopédie was published, about 1750, these heavy boxes had become antiquated. Abbé Nollet (1700-1770) at almost the same time asserts that he had used demountable cameras.(4) "The camera obscura which was also in the form of a box, whether demountable or not, is not so portable as one would have desired; moreover, one is reduced to obtaining only very small images, because if a long focus lens is used, the box must be proportionately longer. It is now about twenty-five years (5) since I have thought of a camera which is very light, takes up very little room and of which the objective has a focus of thirty inches (0.81m) and even more. This is a pyramid composed of four strips of wood, A B C D meeting at the top in a collar of the same material E F, and at the bottom joined by a baseboard at the four corners of the chassis G H I K. These boards are hinged, and each side of the chassis folds towards the center, so that when the four hooks are opened to give free play at the hinges G H I K, they fold and open and close like the ribs of an umbrella and, on each side, are the crossbars which form the chassis. The top piece E F is pierced in order to receive a cardboard tube L equipped with a lens focused towards the base of the pyramid. The part L which turns like the rest, is equipped with another collar M N which turns upwards when desired, carrying on its circumference two small copper tubes N, n, split lengthwise, so that they can fly back. In these tubes, gliding up and down, are two small metal uprights which carry a cap o, at the bottom of which a plane mirror is adjusted . . . . It is possible, without moving the pyramid, to turn the mirror towards any point of the horizon, and incline it as much as required in order to find the objects which one desires to see . . . . The whole is covered with a heavy green cloth, again enclosed inside of black taffeta, on all three sides of the machine and part of the fourth. At the lower part of the two uprights a thick black curtain is attached, for the purpose of covering the head and shoulders . . . . In use this machine is placed in a badly lighted room, somewhat elevated, on a very solid table covered with a large sheet of white paper. One selects the kind of weather when the objects are well illuminated; one seats himself with the back turned towards them and puts one's head inside the curtain . . . ."

Nothing remains, evidently, but to make the drawing on the paper covered board. Do you want to take the camera away?: "The machine is folded, the hangings and curtain are rolled on the standards and the whole put into a long and narrow cloth bag which is easily transportable."

This camera was still in use at the beginning of the nineteenth century together with another demountable model constructed by Castellan which was made up of movable shutters which were ready for use when assembled. When demounted and the partitions placed on top of each other, this camera was extremely light and convenient for travel. La Société Française de Photographie possesses a camera obscura belonging to Daguerre and which he was accustomed to use for drawing.

This is made from two pieces of wood which slide smoothly one into the other. The front piece carries a bi-convex lens and is advanced or drawn back to obtain the proper focus; the rear part contains a mirror inclined at 45°, which reflects the reversed image onto a ground-glass let in the top of the box. A hinged cover is raised, permitting one to view the image sheltered from the glare of the light. This looks strangely like the first boxes described, the cameras of Nicéron and those of Zahn. The arrangement had not been changed since the seventeenth century.

The optical equipment remained defective. However, in 1747, Euler proposed to correct, by employing certain substances, the aberration which results from the decomposition of light in spherical lenses, thus discovering achromatism. In the years which followed, Aiscongt and Dollond constructed achromatic eye-glasses in England. In France, D'Alembert and especially Clairaut studied these optical problems; but it seems that there was no improvement in lenses used in the camera obscura before Wollaston in 1812.

The bi-convex lens projected on the screen an image parallel to its curvature, in the form of a concave sphere. Attempts were made to employ concave screens for the reception of the image, but without

34

success. On a plane screen, only one part of the image was sharp: either the center was sharp and the margins blurred, or if the screen was moved backwards, the margins became distinct and the center confused. Wollaston remedied this defect to a certain degree by the use of a meniscus lens in which the two curvatures were as 1 : 2. The concave surface faced the exterior, the convex, the interior of the camera. A fixed diaphragm with an opening whose diameter was equal to half that of the lens increased the sharpness.

In 1819, Charles Chevalier (7) replaced lens and mirror by a prism with curved faces and, in 1823, he equipped the camera obscura with the "meniscus" prism. All the cameras used in the first years of the nineteenth century were of this type, with the exception of the antique camera of Vinci, still sometimes employed.

The use made of these camera obscura underwent no further change. Porta and Barbaro stated in the sixteenth century: "This is such an entertaining spectacle that those who see it never tire of it" and: "Those who do not know how to draw could in this way draw anything." *Le Dictionnaire technologique* (8) in 1828, two hundred and sixty years later, merely states: "The camera obscura not only affords a recreation in presenting animated pictures of a different kind and very amusing, wherever there is a window out of which a good view can be obtained; but it can also be used for rapidly sketching views and landscapes or perspective outlines of extreme accuracy which, without this apparatus, would require a long time . . . . All one needs to do is to trace the projected picture with a pencil." Between these two extreme periods we find no other mention of the subject. Scheiner in 1612, Hérigone in 1642, Kircher in 1645, Nicéron in 1652, Zahn in 1665, Cellio in 1686 (9), Wolf in 1707, Smith, in his *Optics* in 1738, saw no other use for the camera obscura than the astonished amusement of the spectator and the copying of images by manual design. I quote from *l'Encyclopédie* (10): "The camera obscura furnishes a very amusing spectacle because it presents perfect images resembling the object; because it imitates all the colours and even the movements which no other representation can produce. By means of this instrument those who are uninstructed in drawing are nevertheless able to draw with the utmost precision and exactitude." This is the opinion of Abbé Nollet, the opinion of all up to Cayeux (11) who in 1809 also invented a camera obscura for the purpose of facilitating drawing by hand; until Soleil, who constructed in 1812 his *pronopiographe*, a camera obscura for showing *"living pictures of outdoor* *objects"; until the belated inventor Newton, who in 1844 obtained a camera obscura for copying designs, and put the artist inside the camera just as Barbaro and Porta had done.

Thus, the chief, if not exclusive, aim of those who until this time had employed or constructed the camera obscura was the reproduction by copying of the outlines of the image as seen on the ground-glass. And so during the long space of time for three centuries we find no attempt, nor even a clearly expressed desire, to fix the image of the camera obscura by any process other than that of manual design.

CAMERA OBSCURA OF THE EIGHTEENTH CENTURY
REFERENCES: CHAPTER VI

1. Abbé Nollet, *Leçons de physique expérimentale*, Paris, 1743.
2. *Encyclopédie ou Dictionnaire raisonné des Sciences, des Arts et des Métiers* (see Footnote 11, Chapter II. T.N.)
3. Wolf (1679-1754) professor at Halle in Prussia, began his lectures on mathematics in 1707. He published *Corpus Philosophiae* in which is contained a part on mathematics. 24 volumes, Leipzig, 1728 to 1746.
4. *Leçons de physique expérimentale*, 5th edition, 1759, vol.5, p.532.
5. Abbé Nollet's camera was approved by the Académie des Sciences in 1733.
6. Charles Chevalier, *Notice sur l'usage des chambres obscures et des chambres claires*. (Note on the use of the camera obscura and camera lucida). Paris, 1829.
7. Arthur Chevalier, *Etude sur la vie et les travaux scientifiques de Charles Chevalier*. (Study of the life and scientific works of Charles Chevalier), p.8.
8. *Dictionnaire technologique ou Nouveau dictionnaire universal des Arts et Métiers et de l'Economie nationale et industrielle*. (Technological dictionary or new universal dictionary of arts and trades and national and industrial economy). Paris, 1828.
9. *Comptes rendus hebdomadaires des séances de l'Académie des Sciences*. (Weekly reports of the sessions of the Academie des Sciences) 1839, 2nd semester, p.289.
10. Vol.III, p.62, 1753 edition.
11. *Archives des Inventions et Découvertes*, vol.I.

CHAPTER VII

Mechanical Processes for the Reproduction of Designs

IN the meantime many instruments and processes other than the camera obscura had been proposed for designing with the greatest possible accuracy. In all of these it was merely a question of following the outlines of the image as seen in the apparatus and maintaining by means of manual design the correct proportions of this image, either enlarged or reduced in their proper relation.

Alberti (1398-1484) suggested, as early as the fifteenth century, drawing by means of certain frames or eyepieces: Pietro del Francesca, at the same time laid down the rules for perspective by an identical method.(1) Several painters of the sixteenth century used a pane of glass or a piece of gauze stretched on a frame for drawing in perspective. In 1505 Viator invented a plane table and rule for viewing squares in perspective. Thirty years later Albert Dürer (1471-1528) (2) constructed two drawing tables where we find for the first time a fixed point serving as a sighting instrument.

In 1559 Daniel Barbaro suggested a method almost similar. In 1583 Barozzius, in his *Perspective*, described an instrument which he had invented and in addition all those which had been conceived before him. About 1800 the pantograph, was invented by the German geometrist Scheiner for enlarging or reducing designs. At the same time Cigoli invented the squaring apparatus, which bears his name, for designing in perspective correctly on the horizontal plane.

Samuel de Marolais, in 1615, de Vauzeland, in 1635, in particular Father Nicéron, in 1638, described processes very similar to the foregoing. Jean Dubreuil, in his *Perspective Pratique* (1642) presents illustrations of different apparatus for designing, among which is a perspective lattice work of which the inventor is unknown. This last process, it was said, was used by a famous painter in portraiture. Still more instruments and other processes are mentioned by Hérigone in 1642 and by Bosse in 1648. De Monconys (1664) reports that he had seen in England a machine constructed by Thompson by means of which all sorts of portraits and etchings are copied on parchment as clear as glass. We find in the *Mémoires de l'Académie des Sciences* (4) several processes used in the last quarter of the sixteenth century for designing on glass and fabrics stretched on a frame. Father Cherubin, in 1677, (5) invented an apparatus "for designing from a distance by means of a dioptric eye-piece". Cherubin's design gives an idea of the different kinds of apparatus enumerated above.

In the eighteenth century instruments and processes became more numerous. There are those of Father Lamy in 1701, Hales in 1710, Abbé Hautefeuille in 1722, Nollet in 1733, Leblond in 1738, Langlois in 1743, Bion in 1752, Louvrier in 1753, Buchotte in 1754, Leroy in 1756, Sikes and Storer in 1778, Eckart in 1779, Charles in 1786 (who invented the megascope), Bonjour in 1786, an anonymous inventor in 1787 and many others up to Wollaston who conceived the camera lucida in 1806. This list might be continued until photography was made public; it seems that with the nineteenth century, the number of inventors continued to increase.

James Peacock in 1794, Bunel in 1800, Isaac Hawkins in 1803, Nicholson in 1805, Schmalcalder in 1806, Lemoine in 1808, George Adams in 1809, Laffore in 1817, Verzy in 1819, Senefelder in the same year, Aueracher in 1820, Napier in 1820, Boucher, Chevalier, Smith in 1821, Clinchamp in 1822, Brunelle de Varenne in 1824, Alasson, Edgeworth, Baldance, Ronalds, Puissant in 1825, Lalanne, Barbaroux in 1828, Guérard, Févret de Saint-Mesmin in 1829, Gavard in 1830, Symian in 1832, Coclough, Madame Burgess in 1833, Milne-Edwards, Lefèbre and Percheron, Sauvage, Zust, Varley in 1836, Viennot in 1837 and many others who are mentioned in the *Archives des Inventions et Découvertes*, all having suggested new methods, or constructed new apparatus, intended to reproduce, enlarge or reduce drawings.

And even this long list is incomplete. It does not include the *Physionotrace* of Chrestien, about 1785, probably the prototype of the *Physionotype* of Sauvage, also intended to obtain portraits, which dates from 1834. There is no trace of the process of reproducing pictures by the English painter Joseph Booth, applied for and patented by a special act of Parliament describing his process of 1792. This history of Booth, also that of Wedgwood and his friends of the "Lunar Society", greatly interested the photographers of the year 1863. (6) Nothing came of this but heated discussions.

The list also omits the instrument of the engineer Boucher conceived in 1808, which is recorded in the *Mémoires de l'Académie royale des Sciences* (1825, vol. VIII), and the history of Gonord, miniature painter and engraver who invented in 1805 a *procédé par aspiration* (aspiration proc-

39

ess) by which he obtained on the same engraved plates impressions of different sizes, and which was advanced as a forerunner of photography. (7) Gonord always refused to make his secret known; it is believed that he employed gelatine. He certainly used analogous methods, such as were used at the end of the eighteenth century by Pictet at Geneva and Hassenfratz at Paris; of the same nature as those of Stone Coqueret and Legros d'Anizy in 1809, and those of Robertson in 1818. As early as 1701, Father Lamy described a method of reproducing drawings on concave and convex bodies both in intaglio and relief by means of a mesh.

In conclusion, I desire to retain, of the long and incomplete list of more or less mechanical processes of design, *only* that, despite the great number of inventors and their labours through so many years, no one conceived a different kind of designing other than drawing by hand, as practised by men since immemorial time.

The idea of photography did not enter their minds!

PROCESSES FOR THE REPRODUCTION OF DESIGNS
REFERENCES: CHAPTER VII

1. Rouget de Lisle. *Notice chronologique sur les diverses méthodes abrégées de reproduire ou de multiplier dessins.* (Chronological note on the different abridged methods for reproducing or multiplying designs.)
2. Alberti Dureri. *Institutionum geometricarum libri quatuor, versi olim germanica in linguam latinam et nunc iterato editi,* Arnheim, 1605, pp.183 and 185.
3. The date 1535 under fig. 18, page 49 of the French edition, is reproduced from the oldest edition accessible in France. It is possible that there is an older one made during the life of Durer, who died in 1528.
4. Vol.IX, p.650.
5. *La Vision parfaite.* (The Perfect Vision), Paris, 1677.
6. See: *Photographic News,* November 13, 1863; *Photographic Journal,* January 15, 1864, *British Journal of Photography,* January 15, 1864.
7. *La Lumière,* May, 1851; June 9, 1855; *Bulletin de la Société d'Encouragement pour l'Industrie Nationale,* 1807 and 1814; *Le Lycée,* 1819.

CHAPTER VIII

Tiphaigne de La Roche

THE first idea of photography seems to have been discerned by some in a work written by the Norman, Tiphaigne de La Roche, about the middle of the eighteenth century. A passage in this book, long forgotten, which it is believed relates to photography, was discovered in 1846 and incompletely published in the *Mosaique de l'Ouest*, later in the *Vieux-Neuf* by Fournier. It is there that a historian saw it first and after that it was copied by everyone. (1)

Charles-François Tiphaigne de La Roche was born at Montebourg (2), Department de la Manche, in 1729 and died there in 1774. Little is known of his life.(3) He was a doctor of medicine of the Faculty at Caen, where he lived. He later became a member of the local Académie des Sciences, Arts et Belles-Lettres and published in the *Bulletin* of this Society, in 1758, a scientific memoir. In Paris, where he also lived, he achieved a modest reputation as a writer. Grimm and Fréron, it is said, quoted his novels. In the style of the time (4), they dealt with imaginary voyages full of fantastic detail by which the author sought to amuse the reader, or to mask certain startling ideas. His first work of this kind was published in 1753 under the title *"Amilec ou la graine d'hommes qui sert à peupler les planètes"* (Amilec, or the seed of people to populate the planets).

But the book of interest to us, the book that has become so precious to photographers, and of which I shall reproduce a passage is entitled *Giphantie*, anagram of Tiphaigne, and dates from 1761. (5) In his preface the author declares "that regarding the earth as his fatherland and all men as his brothers, he felt it his duty to travel all over his fatherland and to visit his brothers". But after "having traveled all over the earth and visited all the nations, he did not find himself recovered from his weariness". And the disabused Tiphaigne having read again the memoirs written by him "on the different people, on their prejudices, their morals, politics, laws, religions and history" threw the whole thing into the fire. Alas, only a chapter was preserved which is precisely this *Giphantie*. The book commences: "I was at the frontier of Guinea, at the edge of the desert which borders it on the north, etc." The traveler then advanced into the desert "provided with some tablets to appease thirst and hunger, one winter's day (for these were the dog-days), the wind blowing from the southwest, the sky was cloudy and the air mild". But this benign southwest wind played our traveler a nasty trick. It blew, it blew a hurricane, it bowled him over, it rolled him around in a sandstorm, it buffeted him, lifted him up and transported poor Tiphaigne, much shaken and half conscious, until the hero finally awakened at a rock in an unknown country. Seeing a wonderful garden, he walked towards it, seeking for some inhabitant, when he met a Spirit who addressed him. "I am" said the Spirit "the Prefect of this island which is called Giphantie; it is inhabited by the elementary spirits, etc., etc." And the ghostly prefect who had preserved Tiphaigne from worse shocks during his hazardous transport by the hurricane, proposed to honour philosophy by showing our traveler the wonders of Giphantie. The prefect, going first, Tiphaigne followed him, and marvels are offered to the reader. They are extensive; let us hope that our forefathers were amused by them.

At the foot of a flight of stairs there is a road running under ground. "We enter; my guide having conducted me through several dark passages, leads me out again into the light. He brought me into a fair-sized hall, almost bare, where I was struck with astonishment by the spectacle confronting me. I saw through a window the sea, which did not seem more than two or three furlongs distant. The sky, full of clouds, transmitted only a pale light threatening a storm. The sea, agitated by the high rolling waves and the shore whitened by the spindrift of the surf, glittered as it broke on the shore. By what miracle, I cried, the sky so serene a moment ago suddenly became darkened? And by what other miracle do I find the ocean in the middle of Africa? While saying this, I hastily went forward in order to convince myself of the reality of these seemingly unbelievable things, but when I tried to put my hand out of the window, I encountered an obstacle like a wall. Astonished by this shock following so many other incredible happenings, I fell back five or six paces. "It was your haste which caused your error," said the Prefect to me, "this window, this vast horizon, these heavy clouds, the stormy sea, all this is nothing but a painting. One surprise followed another. Impressed more than ever, I drew closer; my eyes were still more fascinated and even touching the painting with my hand I could hardly convince myself that it was a painting which could produce so complete an illusion.

"The elementary spirits" continued the Prefect, "are not as clever painters or as skillful physicists; you will judge this by observing how they operate. You know that the rays of the light, reflected from different bodies, create an image and reproduce these bodies on all polished surfaces, on the retina of the eye, for instance, on water, and on glass. The elementary spirits have sought to fix these passing images; they have compounded a very subtle substance, very viscous, which will rapidly dry and become hard, by which a painting can be made in a trice. They coat a piece of material with this substance and turn it towards the objects which they wish to paint. The first effect of the material is the same as that of a mirror, one sees all the objects near or distant of which the light can bring the image. But what the glass is unable to do, the fabric owing to its being coated with the viscous substance keeps the image. (6) The mirror reproduces the objects faithfully but does not preserve them. Our canvas renders them not less faithfully and preserves everything. The impression of these images on the canvas which receives them is instantaneous. After the impression is taken in the open air, it is then taken into a dark place. An hour later, the coating is dry and you have an image so much more precious than anyone can produce, and so perfect that time cannot destroy it. We have taken from their source the purest of light matter, while the colours which the painters draw from different materials never fail to change in the course of time. Precision of design, fidelity of expression, and strokes of varying strength, the gradation of shades, the rules of perspective, we leave all this to nature, which by this sure method never contradicts itself and traces on our canvas visible images and create doubt in our minds as to whether what we call realities are not another kind of phantom deceiving our eyes, our hearing, our touch and all our senses at the same time.

"The elementary spirit enters therefore into all physical details; first into the nature of the glutinous matter which intercepts and preserves the rays; second it enters into the difficulties of its preparation and use; and third it enters into the action of light and of the dry material; three problems which I submit to the physicists of our days and which I leave to their wisdom."

Some historians look upon this mass of fantasies as a divination of genius, and the description as anticipating photography. I must refuse to see in it so much as this. First of all, these historians neither knew nor transcribed more than a part of the above-quoted text. As a matter of fact, we find in the works on photography, copied one from the other, only the portion which ends with these words: "You know that the rays of light reflected from different bodies create an image, etc." All before this has escaped them. Therefore, one recognizes that the painting by Tiphaigne is animated; the ocean is not motionless, "it is agitated by the high waves . . . it dashes its waves on the shore." This alone would explain Tiphaigne's error and the violent blow he felt on his face. But in 1846, so long before the motion picture, a similar complication embarrassed the commentators and they passed it in silence. Would that it did not embarrass us!

The reading of the novel shows that its author never had the slightest scientific pretentions. He wrote a satire on the morals of his time and the animated picture is only an allegory as he takes care to inform us later. Even without this warning, we perceive, fixed on canvas, as is customary in painting—not a copy but the reality of nature—movement, relief, colour—What childlike simplicity!—We understand that so unreal a conception could not correspond with the possibility, and that Tiphaigne has not dreamed of anything which might some day become reality.

The real inventor of photography, most modest and learned, certainly had neither the ambition nor the desire to attain such results. And that is why I repeat: "The images" explains Tiphaigne "record themselves on the retina of the eye, on water and on glass." The author stops right there; aside from the fact that he mentions mirrors, he never dreamed of the camera obscura. It was only chance which made his dreams so curious. Tiphaigne only expressed a naive and popular dream. This desire to preserve the image reflected from life in a glass persisted until much later, in 1839, when the daguerreotype appeared, the public was persuaded that Daguerre had succeeded in fixing the fugitive image of the mirror. This error prevailed for many years, the facts notwithstanding. (7)

No, Giphantie did not forecast photography! Moreover, instead of having aided whatever led to its discovery, it is photography which discovered the simple novel and rescued it from eternal oblivion.

1. Mayer and Pierson. *La Photographie*, Paris, 1862 — Ed.Fournier, *Le Vieux-Neuf, histoire ancienne des inventions et découvertes modernes*, Paris 1859 — *La Mosaïque de l'Ouest*, 1846-1847.
2. Montebourg, county seat of the Canton de la Manche, arondissement of Valongnes, seven km. distant from the city of the same name (T.N.).
3. *Bulletin de la Société des Beaux-Arts de Caen*. vol.IX, fasc.2, July 1892.
4. Swift wrote *Gulliver's Travels* in 1728; Voltaire the *Micromégas* in 1752.
5. Mayer and Pierson state that *Giphantie* was published at Cherbourg in 1760. Decauville-Lachenée says it was published at Babylone (i.e. Paris) in 1760. Fournier repeats this. Barbier states: Giphantie, at the Hague (Paris) 1760. The example at the Bibliothéque Nationale is entitled: Giphantie, à la Haye, House of Daniel Monnier, MDCCLXI, without the author's name. A pencil note on the frontispiece reads: Ch. Fr. Tiphaigne de La Roche (after Barbier). It is a small volume of 196 pages in two parts.
6. This description seemed so probable to Fournier that he did not hesitate to write: "This is what has been done for daguerreotypy: Tiphaigne, thus, attempted seriously some experiments with the use of the camera obscura, an instrument long well-known." (*Le Vieux-Neuf*, vol.I, p.21). Incidentally, we must note that Tiphaigne does not say a word about the camera obscura. De la Blanchère, (*Répertoire encyclopédique de photographie*, Paris 1863, vol.I, p.472) copying Fournier, amplifies it and states: "Photography started in the seventeenth century, in 1670; Tiphaigne de La Roche discovered the method of fixing luminous rays." And so are legends born; they grow older and make history.
7. E.Lacan, *De la Photographie*, Moniteur, January 12, 1855.

CHAPTER IX

Chemists and Photochemistry

I F we agree with the majority of the historians that the chemistry of
light created photography, that this is an inevitable consequence,
deduction from photochemistry, it follows logically that the chemists —
and their ancestors, the alchemists — are the creators of photographers
and participated in the invention of photography. This obliges con-
scientious authors to give place in their works to those who investigated
the action of light, its chemistry and its physics, which are closely allied
with it. This singularly broadens the whole matter because, as we know,
light goes back to the beginning of time.

And thus Bacon, Djafar (1) and Aristotle became photographers in
spite of themselves and the historians without fear have added to them
the fabulous Hermes Trismegistos. Let us be grateful, therefore, to these
zealous historians who refer the discovery of photography to some time
after the creation of the world.

When, on the other hand, we take the opinion of the inventors themselves, if we hold closely to the clear-cut declaration of Niepce, following
that of Davy, that chemistry was a means and not the cause, these
drawn out tales become useless. It will suffice, in order to arrive at a
correct idea of the matter, to acquaint oneself with the resources and
effective means which Niepce could have found in the science of his
time.

Far be it from me to think that the writers who have gotten up these
lists of precursors and who searched so far into the past could have
pursued equivocal ends and that, in giving the inventor of photography
so many collaborators, they intended to diminish his glory in order to
accord to each of them a part of that which is legitimately due only to
Niepce, but their learning led them to strange conclusions. For example:
open the history of a scholar of high repute, Dr. Eder (2), and you read
there that in the year 1727 the German physician Schulze discovered
that a mixture of chalk, nitric acid and silver turns black in the light.
This Schulze, after having poured this mixture into a bottle, cut with
a knife words and sentences like paper stencils which he fixed on the
glass with wax. The whole being exposed to the light, the words and
sentences soon designed themselves in black on the mixture. The stencil

47

having been removed, Schulze showed this mysterious writing on the silver mud to his astonished friends. When he stirred the flagon, everything disappeared. Here are Schulze's own words, as quoted by Eder: (3)

"Vitrum pro maxima sui parte opacis corporibus obtegerem, relicta exigua portione quae liberum luci accessum permitteret. Sic non rara nomina vel integras sententias chartae inscripsi et atramento notatas partes scalpello acuto caute exscidi, et sic sententias sedimento cretaceo tam accurate et distincte inscriberent ut multis curiosis, experimenti autem nesciis, ad nescio quod artificium rem hanc referendi occasionem subinde dederim." (I cover the greatest part of the glass with opaque matter leaving a small portion which would allow free access to the light. In this manner I have inscribed some words or even whole sentences on paper and have carefully cut out with a sharp knife the parts written with ink, and in this manner they inscribed sentences on a chalky sediment so accurately and distinctly that I have now and then caused many of the curious, who were, however, unacquainted with the experiment, to attribute this to some artifice. T.N.).

This shows that Schulze had no other ambition than to let the spectators suppose that he had there the result of some sort of witch-craft. Dr. Eder drew from this the formidable deduction: "Therefore Schulze, a German, must be proclaimed the inventor of photography." Dr. Eder writes: "Moreover, I am the first to have so designated him." (4) I believe him willingly and he might well have added: "and the last".

It is, therefore, necessary to protest against these errors and to show, as I have done in the case of the sketchers, that the chemists have in no manner nor at any time anticipated photography. Let us leave aside the Greeks and Arabs, who, not being Germans, could not possibly be suspected of having invented anything whatsoever. I know very well that in the case of paintings which are deteriorated by air and light, one need only quote the passage from Vitruvius (5) in which he recommends that picture galleries be placed facing the north; but I certainly think that Vitruvius had no thought of photography. No more I expect had those observers in the far past thought of attributing the colouration of vegetables, the bleaching of linen or of wax to the influence of daylight; neither was photography in the thoughts of the alchemists who used the power of the sun for the transmutation of base lead into gold or for remedies more mysterious than efficacious.

We thus arrive easily at the eighteenth century and at this Schulze who invented photography without suspecting it. Silver nitrate which he used had long been known, for its discovery is attributed to Geber, or Djafar (6), born in Mesopotamia at the end of the eighth century. Albert in the thirteenth century pointed out that it blackens the skin, and in 1658 Glauber states that it can be used to blacken wood, furs and feathers. Schulze made no other use of silver nitrate and this property of blackening in the light than that described above. Almost at the same time (1737) the Academician Hellot (7) suggested a system of writing with silver nitrate. The characters traced remained invisible as long as the paper was kept in the dark and, in order to make it appear, it was necessary only to expose the letter to the rays of the sun.

The experiments of Schulze and of Hellot were often taken up again and described, in particular by Hooper in 1775, Halle in 1784, Duchesne (8) in 1801 and by many others. About 1770, Lewis in England, Walerius in Sweden, state that silver nitrate can be used for dyeing the hair, for making designs on ivory, marble, etc. (9) It follows from the explanations of these authors that the blackening of silver salts was at this time common knowledge. (10) There is nothing to show that any of them speaks of a process which would permit the reproduction of natural objects.

The beginning of the chemistry of light is usually ascribed to the work of Scheele (1742-1786). This is not without reason, because if he was not the first to discover the influence of light on different matters, he was certainly the first to systematize his researches with the object of an organized and complete study of photo-chemistry. His theories are forgotten and in any event present nothing of interest applicable to our subject. They are explained, together with his other investigations in his book, written in Latin and published in 1777. It was translated into French in 1781 under the title: *De l'air et du feu* (Concerning Air and Fire). We read there that sunlight reddens nitric acid and that it blackens silver chloride, but that it is without effect on silver chloride which has been immersed in nitric acid. Paper impregnated with silver chloride blackens unequally under the different colours of the spectrum and much more rapidly under the influence of the violet rays. He also points out that the reaction of ammonia is not the same on silver chloride blackened by light as on that which has not been exposed to light.

Twenty years before Scheele, the Italian Beccari demonstrated that the blackening of silver chloride is caused by light. A century before Beccari, Bayle obtained this blackening and believed that it was caused

49

by air. The earliest mention of silver chloride known to us is contained in a treatise on metals by Fabricius dated 1566. Arago, in 1839 (11), relates this fact and attributes to Fabricius the discovery that silver chloride blackens in the light, or at least his note is written in such a manner as to give that impression. This had the result that the writers who copied from Arago, practically all, repeated his error. Eder (12) asserts that he was the first who called attention to this misconception. However, Becquerel (13) long before Eder states positively that Fabricius never spoke of the blackening of silver chloride.

In the seventeenth century the sudden discovery of phosphorescent stones gave rise to a veritable infatuation among the chemists who at that time were nothing but alchemists. They devoted themselves intensively to research on these new phosphorescent bodies and their eagerness greatly assisted the birth of modern chemistry. (14) Scheele's experiments in the following century, without causing any such great commotion, had the similar happy influence on the study of light. After Scheele, many scholars endeavoured to determine the nature of light, and to discover the causes of the phenomena which had recently been observed. It is useless to enumerate in detail the explanations which were proposed by so many ingenious minds and to parade the investigators, heated in the defense of their contentious theories or battling for phlogiston or for anti-phlogiston by opposing memoirs. But it is very necessary to point out that the investigation of the action of light was widespread at the end of the eighteenth and in the early years of the nineteenth century.

We have seen above how the sensitivity of silver nitrate and silver chloride to light was discovered. These researches continued. Bergmann (1779), Senebier in particular (1782), Vassali (1792), Mrs. Fulham (1794), Buchholz (1800) obtained the blackening of various gold and silver salts. Vauquelin (1798 to 1809) obtained the blackening of silver chromate and silver citrate. Mercury salts which changed colour in the sun were investigated by Bergmann (1779), Fourcroy (1791), Trommsdorf (1796), Abildgaard (1800), Leroux (1801), Harrup, etc. Phosphorous, by Böckmann (15), Berthollet, Vogel; nitric acid by Scheele, iron salts by Klaproth, Kastelin, etc. The bleaching properties of light were especially indicated by Dufay (1737), Bonzius (1757), Opoix (1777), Berthollet (1791). We must certainly mention the experiments of Hagemann on guaiaca gum and above all those of Senebier.

Senebier (16) (1742-1809), librarian of the city of Geneva, made many observations on the colouring and bleaching of resins, wood and flowers. He experimented with guaiacum, mastic drops, sandarac, anime (17), gamboge, gum arabic, incense, ammoniacal gum, that of tacamahac, of scammony, of pine. (18) Wollaston, in 1804, investigated again the roots of guaiacum.

I do not cite all the writers who dealt with these substances. Among all these patient, learned and informed investigators, no one can be found who makes any mention of a process of design for the reproduction of nature. They sought for the application of their labours to industrial uses, but they certainly never thought of photography. (19)

Wedgwood and Davy had before 1802 copied designs (tracings T.N.) by means of silver nitrate but had failed to fix them. Seventeen years later, in 1819, Herschel pointed out the action of hyposulphite of soda on silver salts without perceiving the application of this idea to the designs of Wedgwood and Davy. It needed the thunderbolt of 1839, the publication of Daguerre's process, the claims of Talbot, all the clamour made about the new-born photography, to open Herschel's eyes and urge him to call Talbot's attention to the fixing salt which we still use today.

However, their minds were still far from grasping the idea of photography, because it had quite escaped the keen intelligence of Herschel who, however, had only to unite the two elements which he knew, but failed to connect with the problem.

1. See Footnote 6.
2. Eder, *Geschichte der Photographie*, Halle, 1905.
3. Eder, work cited, p.51. The text of Schulze is taken from *Acta physico-medico, Academiae Caesarae Leopoldino Carolinae*, 1727, L.528.
4. "Demnach muss Schulze, ein Deutcher, als der Erfinder der Photographie bezeichnet werden, als welcher er allerdings zuerst vom Verfasser dieses Werkes erklärt worden ist." (Accordingly Schulze, a German, must be described as the inventor of photography which, to be sure, he was proclaimed, first of all, by the author of this book.) Eder, work cited, Chapt.VII, p.51. See *Bulletin de la Société Française de Photographie*, November 1921.
5. *De Architectura libri decem*.
6. Geber or Yeber, Arabian alchemist lived about the end of the eighth century or at the beginning of the ninth. His full name was, Abou Moussah Djafar Al Sofi.-Djafar (Ben Mohammed Abou Maschar) Arabian astronomer also known as Albumazar, born at Balkh (Kjoracan) about 776, died in 885 A.D. (Larousse).
7. *Mémoires de l'Académie des Sciences* 1737, pp.101-228.
8. *Dictionnaire de l'Industrie*.
9. Eder, work cited, p.63, which gives in detail the works of all chemists.
10. In a translation of Porta: *La Magie naturelle ou les Secrets ou Miracles de la nature*. (Natural magic or the secrets or miracles of nature), Rouen, 1631, book II Chapt.XV: On feminine attire and delicacy. The manner of dyeing the hair: "Take a silver solution and burned bronze, mix the whole with four times as much strong lye, bring it to a boil and wash the hair. Dry it; wash it again with hot water and the operation is complete."
11. *Comptes rendus*, 1839, 2nd semester, p.250.
12. Eder, work cited, p.18.
13. Ed.Becquerel: *La Lumière*, Paris, 1868, 2nd part, p.45. The same information is given by Fabre in his *Traité Encyclopédique de photographie*, Paris, 1889.
14. Ed.Becquerel, *La Lumière*, 1st part, Paris, 1867.
15. *Annales de chimie*, 1813, vol.85.
16. Senebier, *Mémoires physico-chimiques sur l'influence de la lumière solaire*. (Physico-chemical notes on the influence of sunlight) Geneva, 1782.
17. Resin of the locust tree.
18. Senebier, work cited, vol.III, p.165.
19. This refers to the same details which Eder gives on the work of these chemists. (Eder, work cited, Chapters, I, VI, VII, IX, X, XI, XII, XIII.) But this impression grows stronger when one reads the original documents on the article on chemistry of this period.

CHAPTER X

Charles and His Silhouettes

A MONG the scientists who did not dream of photography, we must except the physicist Charles who, it is said, employed silver salts and made portraits by the action of light.

Charles (1), born at Beaugency in 1746, had the most varied talents: musician, painter, writer and moreover financier. It was not until his later years that he devoted himself to the study of the physical sciences, with great success. His fine collection of apparatus, gathered at great expense, was very much admired. King Louis XVI commanded it to be placed in the Louvre and Charles gave lectures there for thirty years, attracting the most brilliant audiences. (2) He was noted especially for the boldness of his experiments. He suggested that balloons should be inflated with hydrogen, and on August 2, 1783 he made an ascension at the Champ de Mars which remained famous. As a reward he received a large money prize and was elected member of the Académie des Sciences in 1785. He died in 1823.

His photographic works became known from a sentence in the report which Arago made to the Chamber of Deputies on July 3, 1839 concerning the proposed purchase of the daguerreotype process. After relating, rather inexactly, the history of the camera obscura and of silver chloride, Arago says (3): "We must return to the early years of the nineteenth century in order to find the first traces of the photographic art. At that time our countryman, Charles, used in his lectures a coated paper in order to produce silhouettes by the action of light. Charles died without describing the preparation which he used; and in order not to fall into inextricable confusion, the historian of science must rely only on authentic printed documents. In all justice, we must reconstruct the first outlines of the new art from a memoir of Wedgwood, the celebrated manufacturer, famous in the industrial world, for his improvement of pottery (4), and for the invention of the pyrometer, used for measuring the highest temperatures." Arago said at first (5) (February 4, 1839): "We must ascertain if M.Charles of the Académie des Sciences, who made silhouettes in his public lectures, preceded or followed M. Wedgwood." Later, returning to this subject, he now affirms: "Charles preceded Wedgwood."

Arago, who seems to speak as an eyewitness, does not point out either the year or the place where Charles made his experiments nor the arrangement of the apparatus, nor even if he had an apparatus, nor the results. However, this statement, so vague, is all we have relating to the photographic experiments of Charles. Baron Fourier (6), his biographer, does not mention a word of it. No one, who had heard the lectures at the Louvre, confirms Arago's statement, although many well-known men who attended them were still alive in 1839. Among the numerous writings which Charles edited, in the analysis of his work presented to the Académie, nothing refers to these experiments, there is no allusion to it. Charles and his contemporaries remained silent. Only those historians who did not know Charles were loquacious.

Gaudin (7) in 1844 added to Arago's statement: "This property (the blackening by light) was first recognized in silver chloride. According to the investigations of M. Arago this phenomenon was published for the first time in a work by Fabricius printed in 1566, later employed towards the end of the eighteenth century by Charles, famous physicist at the Conservatoire des Arts et Métiers de Paris. He used it for the purpose of producing silhouettes on paper coated with silver chloride."

While it is true that the erroneous information about Fabricius originated with Arago, that about Charles is entirely due to Gaudin. This author, some years later (8), was not quite so sure of his facts; but gave the use of silver chloride then as only probable. Conduche (9), in 1855, in a history which he announced as ready for publication, promised to reproduce concerning the silhouettes of Charles "notes extracted from contemporaneous documents and of unquestioned authority". I have searched in vain for this work and I believe that it was never published. Francis Wey (10) adds a new detail: "Charles *after Wedgwood* made fruitless attempts."

This contradicts Arago who said: "Charles *preceded* Wedgwood." Where did Francis Wey get his information?

Belloc (11) asserts that Charles used silver nitrate. De la Blanchère (12) in 1863, informs us about Charles' nationality: "Charles, an *English physicist*, Wedgwood and Humphrey Davy made many experiments without result." But from this date on, all the circumstances surrounding Charles' experiments begin to be known. The journal *Le Rayon Bleu* (13) discovers in 1869 a mass of new detail: "Professor Charles, in his leisure during the early years of aeronautics, gave public lectures attended by great crowds. One day he showed to his assistants a peculiar image obtained by means of the action of luminous rays on certain salts. In order to demonstrate this, he projected an image on a screen in a darkened room, on which he had previously placed a sheet of paper, immersed in a solution of silver chloride. The luminous parts of the image were rendered in black on the paper, and remained visible for several minutes. The paper was passed from hand to hand, but little by little, under the action of the surrounding light, the parts which in the darkened room were not subjected to the action of the luminous rays also changed and blackened. The image was thus effaced little by little. On another occasion Professor Charles made a silhouette of one of the spectators. He placed him in full light facing the opening of the camera which was equipped with his converging lens. The shadow of the sitter projected itself on a screen, covered as before with a piece of paper impregnated with silver chloride. The silhouette showed white but, once taken out of the darkened room it blackened rapidly just as the background. Wedgwood operated in the same manner with the exception that he used nitrate of silver instead of silver chloride."

This writer was remarkably informed! At least Blanquart-Evrard (14) thinks so, because later, in 1870, he reproduced almost verbatim this passage: "About 1780 Professor Charles, a physicist and chemist of that time, at his public lectures in Paris, made, under the guise of recreation, portraits in silhouette of his pupils, projecting their shadow upon a piece of paper coated with a solution of silver chloride. He, therefore, applied to the obtaining of images in the focus of the camera obscura the property which this chloride possesses to become blackened by the luminous rays."

The improbability of the operations described, the low sensitivity of silver chloride, does not stop these authors for a moment. Gaston Tissandier (15) completes the story by showing the apparatus used by Charles: "About 1780 Professor Charles was, after the sublime discovery of the Brothers Montgolfier, alone responsible for the creation of the hydrogen gas-filled airship following the hot-air balloon. He was the first to make use of the camera obscura in attempts to produce rudimentary photographs. In his lectures on physics, where a great number of eager hearers gathered, he did not fail to produce before his audience an extraordinary experiment, marvelous even in his period; by means of strong sunlight he projected the silhouette of one of his pupils on a piece of white paper. This paper was· previously impregnated with silver chloride. Under the influence of the light it quickly blackened in the

parts which were illuminated; it remained white in those parts on which
the shadow was projected in such a manner that a faithful silhouette of
the person showed itself in white on a black background. We have reproduced the curious experiments of Charles as found in the rather vague
and incomplete tales of the times in which the famous physicist lived.
(16) We can see in our present engraving processes how the experiment
begins; the silhouette of the person shows itself in black; several minutes
later the part of the paper represented in white becomes black . . . .
Charles also reproduced roughly, it is true, engravings which he placed
on sensitized paper; but the historical documents, very incomplete in
this respect, do not permit us to describe exactly the methods employed
by the illustrious inventor of the hydrogen gas balloon. Wedgwood, able
English physicist, made an analogous experiment to that of Professor
Charles on a sheet of paper immersed in silver nitrate; he received the
image of the camera obscura on the sensitized paper, obtaining, however, only a rough outline which could only be preserved in the dark."

We note that Tissandier so completely informed on Charles and so
badly misinformed on Wedgwood, had not read Davy's memoir. (17)
From what source did all these authors draw their information? Their
successors did not seek out the sources but simply copied them. Baron
Ernouf (18) in 1877 republished this history, and, moreover, tells us that
Niepce had made use of Charles' works. Gossin (19), whose work is
otherwise seriously written, also believes that he must reproduce the
same story. The truth of the matter is undoubtedly presented by
Davanne when he says that Charles had studied the sensitivity of certain salts to light, but even this is only a supposition. (20) Nevertheless,
the story is confirmed by a serious document.

The report on Blanquart-Evrard's processes, read before the Académie des Beaux-Arts at the session of June 19, 1847, contains these
words (21): "Wedgwood and Davy in England, Charles in France,
obtained on paper prepared with silver chloride reproductions of gravures, designs and even of some partially transparent natural objects
such as leaves of trees, petals of flowers, etc. But their papers were not
sufficiently sensitive to light for the obtaining of images in the camera
obscura." The presence of Biot on the commission, responsible for this
report, gives it a great deal of value as far as Charles is concerned,
because Biot had analyzed Charles' works.

Thus the writers who have known least of Charles' experiments have
talked about him most extensively. They have concealed the origin of

their information and it is not rash to say that their stories are fables. Further, would it not be wise to adhere closely to Arago's statement: that the historian must rely only on authentic documents to avoid falling into the most inextricable confusion? And the conclusion which must be drawn from this impartial examination is that no more importance attaches to the silhouettes of Charles than was given them by the author himself. And again, how did Arago construe this word "silhouettes"? We know no more about this than we know about the rest.

HISTORY OF THE DISCOVERY OF PHOTOGRAPHY
REFERENCES: CHAPTER X

1. Baron Fourier, *Eloge historique de M.Charles*. (Historical eulogy on M. Charles), Paris, Didot, undated. This eulogy, pronounced before the Académie des Sciences, June 16, 1828, will also be found in *Mémoires de l'Académie Royale des Sciences*, 1829, vol.VIII, pp.75-87.
2. For Charles' lectures, see *Mémoires récréatifs, scientifiques et anecdotiques* by E.G.Robertson, Paris, 1831, 1-75-78.
3. *Comptes rendus*, 1839, 2nd semester, p.250. The entire text of this report will be found in the pamphlet: *Historique et description des procédés du daguerréotype et du diorama*, by Daguerre, Paris, 1839.
4. Arago here confuses Josiah Wedgwood, the father, with Tom Wedgwood, the son.
5. *Comptes rendus*, 1839, 1st semester, p.170.
6. J.-B.-J.Fourier, 1768-1830, was a member of the Académie des Sciences in 1817, of the Académie française in 1827. He pronounced the historical eulogies on Delambre, on Charles, on W.Herschel and on Bréguet.
7. Gaudin, *Traité pratique de photographie*, Paris, 1844.
8. Gaudin, *Résumé général du daguerréotype. La Lumière*, July 17, 1852.
9. *La Lumière*, March 15, 1856.
10. Francis Wey, *Notice sur J.N.Niepce, La Lumière*, July 6, 1851.
11. Belloc, *Les quatre branches de la Photographie*, Paris, 1855.
12. H. de la Blanchère, *Répertoire encyclopédique de photographie*, Paris, 1863, vol.I, 293.
13. *Le Rayon Bleu*, Journal de Photographie, January 15, 1869.
14. Blanquart-Evrard, *La photographie*, Lille, 1870.
15. Gaston Tissandier, *Les Merveilles de la photographie*, Paris, 1874.
16. Tissandier does not say where this rather obscure and incomplete reference to Charles' period can be found. I did not think it necessary to reproduce the fantastic illustration which accompanies the text in Tissandier's book.
17. See chapter following.
18. Baron Ernouf: *Les inventeurs du gas et de la photographie*, Paris, 1877.
19. H.Gossin: *La Photographie*, Paris, 1887.
20. Davanne: *La Photographie*, Paris, 1879.
21. Report on the processes and products of photography by Blanquart-Evrard read by Picot, for the mixed Commission composed of Hersent, president, Biot and Regnault of the Académie des Sciences, Aug. Dumont, Petitot, Debret, Le Bar, Baron Desnoyers, Gatteaux and Picot. Extract from the minutes of the session of the Académie Royale des Beaux-Arts held on Saturday, June 19, 1847.

CHAPTER XI

The First Conception of Photography

WE must give credit to Thomas Wedgwood who, about the end of the eighteenth century, it seems, conceived the idea of the photographic design: an incomplete idea, expressed without hope of realization, and which would never have become known without the actual invention of photography.

Thomas Wedgwood (1), third son of Josiah Wedgwood, the famous English potter, born in 1771, died in 1805, devoted himself during the short time of his life to various scientific researches. About 1791 he and some of his friends, whose names history has preserved: Wedgwood, James Watt, Boulton, Priestley, the poet Darwin, the botanist Withering, the chemist Keir, Edgeworth, etc., often met in the evenings for a discussion of science and literature and they called themselves the Lunar Society. It is believed that Wedgwood's experiments in photography originated from these meetings. A letter from James Watt, of 1791, speaks of *silver pictures*. Another from Leslie leads us to suppose that this work continued in 1800. Wedgwood never mentioned them and since we find no trace of them in his correspondence nor in his references to his experiments in physics, it is evident that he never attached the slightest importance to them.

After Wedgwood, owing to illness, left England in 1802, a young man whose name later became very famous, Humphry Davy (2), the collaborator of Wedgwood, published their works in a bulletin not widely read at that time, the *Journals of the Royal Institution of Great Britain*. The memoir was ignored. Much later, after Davy's death, his brother undertook to collect and publish the works of the famous physicist in an edition which appeared in 1839-40. The memoir of 1802 was included and since at that time Talbot's process attracted a great deal of attention in England, following the announcement of the discovery of the daguerreotype, Dr. Davy added this note: "Recently this method of designing has again been employed by Mr. Talbot." Thus the experiments of Wedgwood and Davy became known. (3)

Here is a verbatim transcription of the memoir of 1802; notwithstanding its length, it is too important to abbreviate it.

"An Account of a method of copying Paintings upon Glass, and
of making Profiles, by the agency of Light upon Nitrate of
Silver. Invented by T. Wedgwood, Esq. With
Observations by H. Davy.

"White paper, or white leather, moistened with solution of nitrate of
silver, undergoes no change when kept in a dark place; but on being
exposed to the daylight, it speedily changes colour, and after passing
through different shades of grey and brown, becomes at length nearly
black.

"The alterations of colour take place more speedily in proportion as
the light is more intense. In the direct beams of the sun, two or three
minutes are sufficient to produce the full effect. In the shade, several
hours are required, and light transmitted through different coloured
glasses acts upon it with different degrees of intensity. Thus it is found
that red rays, or the common sunbeams passed through red glass, have
very little action upon it: Yellow and green are more efficacious, but
blue and violet light produce the most decided and powerful effects.
(Note by Davy. The facts above mentioned are analogous to those
observed long ago by Scheele, and confirmed by Senebier. Scheele found
that in the prismatic spectrum, the effect produced by the red rays upon
silver muriate was very faint, and scarcely to be perceived; whilst it was
speedily blackened by the violet rays. Senebier states that the time
required to darken silver muriate by the red rays is twenty minutes, by
the orange twelve, by the yellow five minutes and thirty seconds, by
the green thirty-seven seconds, by the blue twenty-nine seconds, and
by the violet only fifteen seconds. Senebier, *de la Lumiere*, III, 199.)

"The consideration of these facts enables us readily to understand
the method by which the outlines and shades of paintings on glass may
be copied, or profiles of figures procured, by the agency of light. When a
white surface, covered with solution of nitrate of silver, is placed behind
a painting on glass exposed to the solar light, the rays transmitted
through the differently-painted surfaces produce distinct tints of brown
or black, sensibly differing in intensity according to the shades of the
picture, and where the light is unaltered, the colour of the nitrate
becomes deepest.

"When the shadow of any figure is thrown upon the prepared surface, the part concealed by it remains white, and the other parts speedily become dark.

"For copying paintings on glass, the solution should be applied on leather; and in this case it is more readily acted upon than when paper is used.

"After the colour has been fixed upon the leather or paper, it cannot be removed by the application of water, or water and soap, and it is in a high degree permanent.

"The copy of a painting, or the profile, immediately after being taken, must be kept in some obscure place. It may indeed be examined in the shade, but in this case the exposure should be only for a few minutes; by the light of candles and lamps, as commonly employed, it is not sensibly affected.

"No attempts that have been made to prevent the uncoloured part of the copy or profile from being acted upon by light have as yet been successful. They have been covered with a thin coating of fine varnish, but this has not destroyed their susceptibility of becoming coloured; and even after repeated washings, sufficient of the active part of the saline matter will still adhere to the white parts of the leather or paper, to cause them to become dark when exposed to the rays of the sun.

"Besides the applications of this method of copying that has just been mentioned, there are many others. And it will be useful for making delineations of all such objects as are possessed of a texture partly opaque and partly transparent. The woody fibres of leaves, and the wings of insects, may be pretty accurately represented by means of it, and in this case, it is only necessary to cause the direct solar light to pass through them, and to receive the shadows upon prepared leather.

"When the solar rays are passed through a print and thrown upon prepared paper, the unshaded parts are slowly copied; but the lights transmitted by the shaded parts are seldom so definite as to form a distinct resemblance of them by producing different intensities of colour.

"The images formed by means of a camera obscura have been found too faint to produce, in any moderate time, an effect upon the nitrate of silver. To copy these images was the first object of Mr. Wedgwood in his researches on the subject, and for this purpose he first used the nitrate of silver, which was mentioned to him by a friend, as a substance very sensible to the influence of light; but all his numerous experiments as to their primary end proved unsuccessful.

"In following these processes, I have found that the images of small objects, produced by means of the solar microscope, may be copied without difficulty on prepared paper. This will probably be a useful application of the method; that it may be employed successfully, however, it is necessary that the paper be placed at but a small distance from the lens.

"With regard to the preparation of the solution, I have found the best proportions those of one part of nitrate to about ten parts of water. In this case, the quantity of the salt applied to the leather or paper will be sufficient to enable it to become tinged, without affecting its composition, or injuring its texture.

"In comparing the effects produced by light upon muriate of silver with those produced upon the nitrate, it seemed evident that the muriate was the most susceptible, and both were more readily acted upon when moist than when dry, a fact long ago known. Even in the twilight, the colour of moist muriate of silver spread upon paper slowly changed from white to faint violet; though under similar circumstances no immediate alteration was produced upon the nitrate.

"The nitrate, however, from its solubility in water, possesses an advantage over the muriate: though leather or paper may, without much difficulty, be impregnated with the last substance, either by diffusing it through water, and applying it in this form, or by immersing paper moistened with the solution of the nitrate in very diluted muriatic acid.

"To those persons not acquainted with the properties of the salts containing oxide of silver, it may be useful to state that they produce a stain of some permanence, even when momentarily applied to the skin, and in employing them for moistening paper or leather, it is necessary to use a pencil of hair, or a brush.

"From the impossibility of removing, by washing, the colouring matter of the salts from the parts of the surface of the copy which have not been exposed to light, it is probable that, both in the case of the nitrate and the muriate of silver, a portion of the metallic acid abandons its acid to enter into union with the animal or vegetable substance, so as to form with it an insoluble compound. And, supposing that this happens, it is not improbable but that substances may be found capable of destroying this compound, either by simple or complicated affinities. Some experiments on this subject have been imagined, and an account of the results of them may possibly appear in a future number of the Journals. Nothing but a method of preventing the unshaded parts of the delineation from being coloured by exposure to the day is wanting, to render the process as useful as it is elegant."

This is the only information we have on these experiments. If one can imagine what kind of images could be produced by Wedgwood's process, copying by contact and merely the outlines of objects, rendering the blacks in white and reversed, and without any gradation of tones and, incapable, according to the author's own admission, of presenting a distinct resemblance, one cannot wonder that Wedgwood kept silent on such poor attempts. Anyone who has examined a negative image knows how remote it is from presenting a correct idea even approximating the subject. Of what use were these copies if one could examine them, only briefly, in daylight? Wedgwood's silence is better understood than Davy's assertion: "Nothing but a method of preventing the unshaded parts of the delineation from being coloured by exposure to the day is wanting, to render the process as useful as it is elegant." Quite so, neither elegant, nor easy, certainly not having the slightest practical use.

It is not in this that Wedgwood's merit lies, but rather in the conception of the new and bold idea, up to that time never expressed, of fixing the images of the camera obscura. For Davy states this precisely: "*To copy these images of the camera obscura, such was the first object of Mr. Wedgwood in his researches on this subject. For this purpose he used nitrate of silver which was mentioned to him by a friend as a substance very sensible to the influence of light.*" The inventor, having conceived the idea of photographic design, pursued it by research in chemistry for a practical method of attaining his purpose. Davy by no means possessed the same keen perception and his memoirs show that he interested himself less in the reproduction of images of the camera obscura and much more in the study of the effects caused by the action of light on silver salts, as all chemists before him.

The same method of procedure will be observed in Niepce, who, in the invention of photography, also conceived first the project of rendering permanent the images of the camera obscura, and not seeking until later the means of accomplishing this in the scientific works of his times. It is well to emphasize these facts, which historians always present in reverse order. They suppose that chemical researches on light created photography and write history from that viewpoint. This is diametrically opposed to the facts.

If Wedgwood and Niepce, who were the first and almost at the same time, had the absolutely new idea of a method of drawing other than by hand, we must agree with Litchfield (5) that Wedgwood and Davy had no exact and definite idea of it. They were discouraged by this matter which, as a matter of fact, never yet existed: a design produced by the spontaneous action of natural forces. For, no matter how far they might have delved into the science of past times, they could find only images traced by the hand of man, guided by the human eye. The important consequences following so unexpected a result, did not occur to the mind of either of them. Davy improved very little on Wedgwood's attempts and obtained small images with the solar microscope, i.e. without contact; but they soon abandoned their work which they believed could not be realized. Photography, which Wedgwood foresaw for an instant, gave them nothing but a confused vision, a chimera soon forgotten in the fog and haze of dreams.

This is why Niepce succeeded, having clearly seen that which escaped Wedgwood. It was after having determined the principle of this difficult problem, having foreseen the consequences and calculated the chances of success, that he undertook to discover and did discover photography. The following pages will show that Niepce's experiments started with lithography, that is to say, the design, and that his ideas followed the same road as Wedgwood, but his progress deviated after Niepce had arrived almost at the object of his purpose, bold as it seemed to him. A manuscript which I have found in the correspondence of the inventor deposited in the Museum at Châlon, which has never before been published, will supply the proof, I believe, of what I advance. This describes with an extreme nicety the task which he proposed to himself and the means employed in order to attain it, also what was considered for its complete success. I quote this paper verbatim:

INTRODUCTION

"I designate by the name heliography the discovery which is the object of this work. It is due to the observation of a light phenomenon until now almost unperceived. It is the fruit of several years of research for the solution of a question, equally interesting and curious, which is obtained by finding in the emanations of the luminous fluid an agent capable of imprinting in an accurate and durable manner the images transmitted by the optical processes; to imprint them, I do not say with the splendour and variations of their colours, but with all the gradations of tone from black to white. In short, I think that if it is not impossible

to discover with the aid of chemical combinations a phosphorescent substance which would have the particular property of retaining the coloured rays of the prism, it would be very difficult to procure by this
process a print which will not quickly undergo a change.

"Nevertheless, I propose to hazard below some ideas by means of
which this work may be achieved: but, far from laying claim to the
brilliant result which these ideas seem to predict, it satisfies me to have
been able to obtain what I had in view and to attain the purpose which
I had proposed; I do not flatter myself at all that I have entirely succeeded, nor have been as fortunate as I might have desired. There are
two reasons which prevented me. First, I occupied myself with the
principle of seeking among the substances of the three kingdoms those
which would best meet my object. I lost much time engaging in a mass
of experiments on each of them. Then I had to surmount difficulties of
all sorts, difficulties of manipulation which could only be overcome by
constant practice, thus causing many failures and often producing
strange anomalies in results; especially difficulties in manipulation which
occur more or less directly in the production of the principal effect;
magical effects, the imperceptible causes of which escape the watch-
fulness of even the most attentive observer.

"If I venture, nevertheless, to recommend to the indulgence of the
public the premature fruits of my researches, it is only because they
indicate at least a piquant objective by the attraction of its novelty,
and in the hope that I will not invoke in vain the useful support of many
persons more capable than I to assure its success. May I add also that
I have been greatly assisted by the encouragement of some distinguished
artists of the Capital and many members of the Royal Society of
London.

"Since the work which I undertake must be merely a simple statement of facts which observation and experience have enabled me to
gather, the order which I must follow in the arrangement of the matter
and the limits prescribed are naturally predetermined. Thus I shall
speak at first of the chemical properties of light in its state of composition; in order to bring into proper relation those which are closest to my
subject, I have characterized them according to the noticeable changes
which they effect in substances and I shall distinguish them by the
names: *colouring property, decolourizing property* and the *solidifying
property* of light. I pass then to the experimental examination of these
three kinds of properties of which the last has furnished me, by its

remarkable results, the solution of the problem which I had proposed and which will engage all my attention hereafter. I end this paragraph by reporting in a detailed manner that which pertains to the practical processes, namely the manipulation.

"Included in the following paragraph with other phenomena of light, I turn to some considerations of those which are manifested when light is dispersed by a prism and displays its richest colours. I shall make known the various hypotheses which they have aroused, the conflict which exists between them with regard to the nature of the active principle attributed to each of the prismatic rays, and how the conflict permits thus the free scope of opinions. This will permit me to announce my own hypotheses and I will support them by comparative experiments which I have made with diffused light and in the interior of the camera obscura.

"The third and last paragraph will comprise under the title *Applications of Heliography:* 1st, the manner of applying it to gravure on copper; 2nd, on silver plates for drawing; and 3rd, two processes of applying it to glass; the first one, where the print of the image is viewed by transparency, reproduces the illusions of the Diorama, and the other process, viewed by reflection, seems to modify certain local colours. The observation of this effect and the inferences which I have drawn from it made me believe in the possibility of linking it, without much effort, to Newton's theory of the phenomenon of coloured rings. Finally, my idea in this respect is only mere conjecture and I present it with all the reserve required by so delicate a matter, and with the diffidence prompted by the realization of my position."

As is readily seen, this is a preface which the inventor proposed to place at the head of a work which was never written; it contains a brief but complete exposition of his studies and works. The original paper, in Niepce's handwriting, is not dated; but it is easily proved that it was drafted in 1829. It was entrusted in 1866, with the rest of the correspondence, by the son of the inventor, to Victor Fouque, the historian of Niepce, who made no use of it in his book: *La Vérité sur l'invention de la photographie*, simply mentioning it therein, on page 247. Long afterwards, what remained of this correspondence—93 pieces out of 103— was presented to the Museum at Chalon-sur-Saône by the grandson of Nicéphore, Eugène Niepce, at the time of the dedication of the statue of the inventor at Chalon on June 21, 1885. A note placed at the end of the manuscript indicates that a copy of it was given on September 4, 1839 to M.de Hamel. I do not known whether the latter ever used it. Thus, this particular evidence, this program of the invention of photography remained unknown until this day.

1. *Tom Wedgwood*, by R.B.Litchfield, London, 1903.
2. Born at Penzance, Cornwall, in 1778, member of the Royal Society of London in 1803, baronet in 1818, president of the Royal Society in 1820: died at Geneva in 1829.
3. Litchfield, work cited XIII, *The Photographic Work*.
4. This bulletin did not appear regularly. It was only a small publication, printed once or twice a month, in order to inform subscribers to the Royal Institution of the proceedings. The number that contains Davy's Memoir is dated June 1802.
5. Litchfield, *Tom Wedgwood*, chapter XIII.

CHAPTER XII

Nicéphore Niepce (1)

THUS, before Niepce, who invented photography, it is only Wedgwood who can be found to have thought of it. It is now time to state who Niepce was. (2)

Joseph-Nicéphore Niepce belonged to a rich and educated family of the old Burgundy bourgeoisie. Long before the sixteenth century the Niepces, by their riches, by their property, by their position, mixed with the nobility of the province. The great-grandfather of Nicéphore, Antoine Niepce, lived at the castle of Saint-Loup de Varenne, a small place of less than three hundred fifty inhabitants at that time, situated eight kilometers (five miles) south of Chalon, where he died about 1720, leaving eleven children. The youngest, Bernard, born in 1691 (3), squire, King's Counsellor, Comptroller of garrisons, Collector of taxes for Bourgogne and Bresse, acquired in 1740 a house in Chalon in the street of the Révérends-Pères de l'Oratoire. He lived there only a short time and died in 1760 on his property at Gras, in the township of Saint-Loup de Varenne. This Bernard had three children, a daughter and two sons, one of whom, Claude, was the father of Nicéphore and the other, Bernard, the grandfather of Niepce de Saint-Victor. (4)

These were the ancestors of Nicéphore. His mother, Claude-Anne Barrault, was the daughter of a well-known lawyer, and received, as also her sisters, a dowry of 100,000 crowns, a very fine dowry for that period. In his luxurious house at Chalon, Barrault, a cultured amateur and patron of art, had collected a number of paintings which were highly regarded in the neighborhood. This cultured man was also interested in science and Nicéphore mentions in his correspondence (5) a solar microscope which belonged to his grandfather Barrault. The solar microscope was then a show piece in the laboratories of physicists. (6)

Nicéphore's father, Claude Niepce, Lawyer, King's Counsellor, and also Receiver of taxes of the town of Chalon, died before 1794 in this house in the rue de l'Oratoire which had been acquired by his family in 1740. Nicéphore was born in this house March 7, 1765. He had one sister, Victoire, and two brothers, Claude and Bernard. But his favorite comrade, his lifetime friend, his playfellow and fellow-student was his elder brother, Claude.

Fine studious children (7), they were carefully instructed by a clerical tutor and followed in general the lines of instruction given by their neighbors, Pères de la Congregation de l'Oratoire, whose reputation in the teaching of the sciences had long been established. The two students in their free time showed even then a passion for mechanics which became their life work. With no other tools than their knives, they made small wooden machines which Nicéphore's son found forty years later, and which he cleverly readjusted so that they once more functioned. Young Nicéphore was destined, as was customary in rich families for younger sons, to enter the service of the church. He was religiously inclined and so remained during his whole life. Having finished his studies and being too young to be ordained priest, he was sent as a professor to the school which the Oratorians conducted at Angers.

Then came the Revolution. The Oratorians were suppressed in April 1792; but the members of the Order probably dispersed before this date. Nicéphore gave up his ecclesiastical career and became a soldier. He was appointed on May 10th of the same year as sub-lieutenant of Infantry.

It is remarkable how a peaceful cleric could change himself so easily into a military man. We must remember that these were troublous times. The emigration caused many vacancies in the regiments because most officers were recruited from the nobility. The National Assembly decreed on September 28, 1791 that all French citizens between the ages of 16 and 25 in good health, who could procure a certificate of civism, were eligible for a sub-lieutenancy after having passed a public examination held at the Military Divisional Headquarters. The colonels then proposed these young men for appointment by the King, which admitted them to their regiments. Six weeks later the Legislative Assembly simplified this more by a new decree ordering that half of the vacancies were to be reserved for sub-officers and the other half for the sons of citizens active in the National Guard.

The exclusive choice of nobles for the officers' ranks had been regarded as a crying abuse during the monarchy and provoked bitter recriminations by the citizens. It is not surprising, when this easy access to all the officers' ranks was given to the sons of citizens, that they threw themselves greedily into the army. The exaltation which marked the beginning of the Revolution was added to by this outburst of patriotism. Other causes determined Nicéphore. His family was connected with the ecclesiastic and royalist nobility; they held places in the department of finance. This alone was enough to arouse suspicion and even persecution.

NICÉPHORE NIEPCE

Although the father of Niepce, together with all the notables of Chalon, took the oath of loyalty some time after August 10, 1792, he had to leave the town and went to Dijon where he died a short time after. (8) Other members of the family became the victims of violence. The Niepce fortune suffered greatly. The suppression of the places and offices they held, the confiscation of the estates of the Duc de Rohan, of which Niepce's father managed a part, the forced sale of their real estate, payable in scrip, dispersed the greatest part of their possessions. Nicéphore, like many others who did not dare to return to Chalon until long after in 1801, sought refuge from suspicion in his regiment and also as a proof of his loyalty. And so he entered the 42nd Regiment of Infantry, formerly called Angoumois.

During January and February 1793 he took part in the expedition to Sardinia, where the 42nd, 52nd and 26th Regiments of the Line together with the grenadiers of the National Corsican Guard were engaged. It was not a success. Towards the end of February Vice-Admiral Truguet (9), commanding the expedition, assembled his troops at Toulon, complaining bitterly that the soldiers had not seconded the work of the marines and shot at each other. Niepce, however, was appointed lieutenant in the 83rd Demi-Brigade on May 6, 1793 and sent to the army in Italy. He took part in two bloody battles against the Austrians and Piedmontese on June 8th and 12th under the command of General Brunet near the village of Breil on the highway running from Nice to Coni. The battle of June 8th resulted in almost a defeat and that of the 12th was completely so, for which Brunet paid with his life.

Niepce's military career terminated quickly. Moreover, the military service suited neither his character nor his abilities. He was attached to the staff and, because of his liberal education, was assigned to the Adjutant-General Frottier, on the 18th ventôse in the year II, corresponding to March 2, 1794. Almost at once he contracted typhus which was decimating the army. After his convalescence his condition, shattered health and impaired sight, obliged him to ask for his discharge. He went to live at Nice in the house of a lady by the name of Roméro, whose daughter Agnès was for some time past the widow of a lawyer by the name of Mignon. The two ladies looked after him with much devotion; the daughter was tall, intellectual and cultured and, although she was five years older than Nicéphore (10) and had two children, Niepce fell in love with her and married her at Nice on the 17th thermidor, year II (August 4, 1794). The following November he was appointed a member

71

of the Administration of the Nice district, which had been annexed to France on January 31, 1793. He did not keep this post long, but resigned and settled at Saint-Roch, a village near Nice, living contentedly on the revenue from his properties. The newly married couple had a son born to them on April 5, 1795, who was given the name Isidore.

Niepce's activities in this place indicated in no way his avocation. He was a born inventor and we have shown that already as a school-boy he constructed ingenious playthings together with his brother Claude. This association of thought and effort of the two brothers continued during their whole lifetime and it is, therefore, difficult to separate in after years their individual share in their inventions, which were not successful. It is perhaps just to recall here that Claude also had a part in the invention of photography.

Claude, like Nicéphore, fled from Chalon and from the revolutionary outbreaks, but his adventurous spirit led him to become a sailor. At the end of 1791 he entered the naval service on board the store ship *Dromadaire* and for two years sailed the sea. After a second embarkation at Boulogne which lasted only a few months, he also left the service and joined his married brother at Saint-Roch towards the end of 1794. The Revolution of thermidor undoubtedly influenced the decision of both Niepces.

Here we find them leading together a most peaceful life in their house at Saint-Roch under the beautiful sky of this climate. Notwithstanding the losses suffered owing to the Revolution, the combined income of the two brothers amounted to about 15,000 livres. Considering the value of money at that time, this spelled affluence. Their literary tastes, their culture and their aestheticism were sufficient to assure them a happy leisure. Mme. Niepce and Nicéphore, having resided more than fifteen months at Nice in a world of army officers, were the intimates of all those who constituted good society in the town. Claude too was cultured and had enjoyed an excellent education. Thus we find them satisfied to devote their time to their social obligations, the care of their property and intellectual diversion. For Nicéphore was on occasion a clever poet, and, as was the fashion of the time, steeped in Latin, and a follower of Abbé Delille. If the lowly position of an inventor can be reconciled with admission to Society, the family Niepce certainly occupied it.

It is just this difficult career which these two middle class men had followed and in which their fortune had been swallowed up, which made for their success and their beautiful poise. It is true that instinct does not always prevail over education and that one cannot resist one's destiny. It seems that the restless spirit of Claude always gave the impetus to the desire of the two brothers. It is Claude who was the first to imagine the construction of a machine "destined to move boats without sails or oars". (11) The first attempts, followed by incomplete experiments, took place at Saint-Roch. The Niepces, believing that their stay at Chalon no longer presented any danger for them, finally returned, in 1801, to their native town and lived again in the same house in the rue de l'Oratoire where their mother had continued to reside.

They continued their work there and in 1807 patented their engine which they rather ingeniously named *pyreolophore*. "It was based on the direct action of a flame on air and the violent rarefaction of this fluid produced by sudden heating of lycopodium powder"; later they used petroleum. It will be seen that this is simply an internal combustion engine. This motor, in 1807, eighty years before the automobile! Undoubtedly it was too soon and before its time as, although this engine had made a boat move on the pool of Battrey at Saint-Loup, afterwards on the River Saône and finally at Bercy on the Seine, and although it was favorably reported to the Académie des Sciences (12) by Berthollet and Carnot, it was never fully exploited, thus inflicting cruel disappointment and finally ruin on the two brothers.

In that same year, 1807, the government having offered a prize for the plan of an hydraulic engine to replace that of Marly, Claude and Nicéphore submitted a project to Carnot for his approval. In his reply (13) Carnot shows a high regard for their work. "Messieurs, it seems that the result proves the necessity for substituting a combustion engine for Marly's machine. I am very sorry that you have been unable to engage in this earlier, especially in using the principles of the pyreolophore motor. You will always be acclaimed for the invention of this engine, for which mechanics hope and aspire . . . ." He assured them of his high esteem and affection.

Owing to their straitened circumstances, created by the continental blockade, the researches of Claude and Nicéphore turned again to the cultivation of woad at their place at Saint-Loup de Varenne in the district of Gras; they experimented with the extraction of coloured starch from woad for the purpose of replacing indigo, later endeavoring to obtain sugar from beets and pumpkins, and cultivating different textile plants. (14) Their experiments, continued until 1816, earned for them flattering letters from the imperial government.

HISTORY OF THE DISCOVERY OF PHOTOGRAPHY

Thus we see the cultured mind of Niepce approaching the principal scientific experiments of his time before realizing the discovery of photography. It is, therefore, not true, as has been written, that it was chance that guided him to a recognition of the facts. The inventor gave long and patient thought to it and persevering calculations, unique sources of his happy discoveries.

NICÉPHORE NIEPCE
REFERENCES: CHAPTER XII

1. Niepce with an accent is the form given in all original documents. Little by little it was written Niepce (without accent) and even the family adopted this mode of writing the name.
2. All the details known of Nicéphore Niepce's life are contained in the work: *La Vérité sur l'Invention de la Photographie*, by Victor Fouque, Paris and Chalon, 1867. They were published briefly by the son of the inventor, Isidore Niepce in his pamphlet: *Historique de la découverte improprement appelée daguerréotype* (History of the discovery improperly called daguerreotype), Paris, 1841. Fouque, who was the registrar of the city of Chalon-sur-Saône, had used in part for his work the 101 letters written by Niepce or addressed to him and which Isidore managed to recover after a good deal of search. Only 93 of them were placed in the Museum at Chalon by the son of Isidore Niepce, on the occasion of the dedication of the statue of the inventor in the public place at Chalon on the 21st of June, 1885. The Conservatoire des Arts et Métiers at Paris possesses copies of 62 letters.
3. Fouque, on p.19 of his work gives the date as 1671. I based my date on a manuscript of Isidore Niepce, preserved in the family.
4. The part which Niepce de Saint-Victor plays in the history of photography will be seen later.
5. Letter from Nicéphore to Claude, May 5, 1816.
6. Abbé Nollet states that in 1743 the solar microscope came to Paris from London. It had been invented a short time previous by Lieberkuyn (1711-1756) of the Royal Academy of Sciences at Berlin.
7. For the sake of clarity I give an extract of the genealogy of the Niepce family:

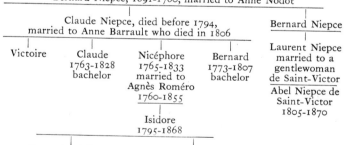

Jean Niepce, living in 1595, married to Damoiselle Jeanne Jaillet

Antoine Niepce, died in 1720, married to Christine Perrot
they had 11 children

Bernard Niepce, 1691-1760, married to Anne Nodot

Claude Niepce, died before 1794, married to Anne Barrault who died in 1806 | Bernard Niepce

Victoire | Claude 1763-1828 bachelor | Nicéphore 1765-1833 married to Agnès Roméro 1760-1855 | Bernard 1773-1807 bachelor | Laurent Niepce married to a gentlewoman de Saint-Victor — Abel Niepce de Saint-Victor 1805-1870

Isidore 1795-1868

François Alphonse died in 1874 | Eugène died in 1893

8. This resulted from Nicéphore's marriage contract, see Fouque p.25.
9. *Moniteur*, January 27, March 10 and 15, 1793.
10. The marriage contract mentions the age of Niepce as 29½ years and that of his wife as 30 years. This cannot be true. Agnès Roméro did not state her age correctly. Her grave in the cemetery of Saint-Loup-de-Varenne gives her true age: died July 26, 1855 at the age of ninety-five. She was born in 1760.
11. This was not a new idea nor did the Niepces believe it to be new. Nicéphore writes in a letter dated June 27, 1816: "Monsieur de Chardonnet explained to me how Monsieur de Jouffroy had obtained a patent (for an engine operat-

ing boats) thirty years ago and had submitted a plan and notes to the Académie des Sciences. During the Revolution, the pieces had been taken apart
and delivered to Fulton who had used a good part of them." The Marquis
de Jouffroy (1751-1832) propelled a boat by the aid of a hot air engine on
the Doubs in 1776. On July 15, 1783 in the presence of thousands of spectators, a large boat equipped with paddle wheels and which Jouffroy baptised
"Pyroscaphe" went up the Saône at Lyons rapidly. This demonstration
created a great deal of attention. Claude Niepce was then twenty years old,
Nicéphore eighteen. It is well known that successful attempts were made at
Paris by Jouffroy in 1816 but the company which was established to exploit
his patents and those of his rival Périer both failed.

12. This report will be found in *Mémoires de l'Académie des Sciences*, 1807.
13. Fouque, p.36.
14. "Other inventions and numerous experiments on the manufacture of beet
    sugar from native shrubs, or plants which might yield a blue colour, on the
    cultivation of woad and the extraction of its coloured starch to take the place
    of indigo, as well as experiments with several species of plants, useful for
    textile purposes, fill the years from 1807 to 1813." (Unpublished manuscript
    of Isidore Niepce).

CHAPTER XIII

From Lithography to Photography

IT was after 1813, on the introduction of lithography, that Niepce turned to photography. Lithography (1), as we know, had a difficult beginning. The first establishment founded by the inventor in Munich, in 1796, was not a success. In 1800 Pleyel, a musical publisher, brought Niedermayer, a friend of Senefelder, to Paris, but both soon abandoned the venture. André d'Offenbach, an associate of Senefelder, who opened in 1802 the first lithographic printing establishment in Paris, succeeded no better. The new Société d'Encouragement pour l'Industrie Nationale (2) awarded him a medal, which was of no help because André was compelled to sell his process in 1806 to Choron, Baltard and others. The first satisfactory proofs seem to date from 1808 and are the work of Lomet. Guyot des Marais, Duplat, Marcel de Serres printed lithographs in the following years. Nevertheless, in 1814 there existed no lithographic printing establishment in Paris. The fortunes of the new art fared better in Germany; the first lithographers of Munich, Stuttgart and particularly those at Vienna prospered. Perhaps the reason why so little was known in France about the process, or why the results were so unsatisfactory, lies in the fact that the inventor kept the secrets of his process as much as possible to himself and divulged the details as little as possible, even to his associates, friends and workmen. The first printed information on lithography dates from 1810. It is *Le Secret d'imprimer sur pierre* published by the Stuttgart printing works. Senefelder did not publish his work until 1819 (*Lehrbuch der Lithographie*, 1818, T.N.). (3) About 1812, Count Lasteyrie-Dusaillant, the son-in-law of Lafayette, having learned practical lithography at Munich, attempted to spread the process in France and succeeded. Lithography became a fashionable hobby even with those who could not draw. (4) The lack of commercial progress for some time may well be attributed to the disasters of 1813 and 1814.

The intellectual class took up lithography in 1813, Niepce among the others. This discovery, which he considered marvelous, made a profound impression on him. But, guided by his peculiar logic, which he had applied in the cultivation of woad, the extraction of native sugar, etc., he at first turned to the industrial side of the process to search the country for stones suitable for lithography. These are extremely rare, owing to the requirement of a particular quality. A fortune awaited anyone who could find lithographic stones of quality and in abundance. Nicéphore, however, found none and his researches, paid for by the Société d'Encouragement (5) although continued until 1817, had to be abandoned.

Lithography is the drawing on a stone of particular quality with an ink made from soap and a greasy substance. By giving it a weak acid bath and then impregnating it with gum water, the design is strengthened and the stone is given a new quality. This results in the ink taking only on the design, which is greasy and rejects the moisture when an inked printers' roller passes over it. From this, printed impressions can be obtained in large editions. While this is the principle of the process and will suffice here as a general explanation, the practice of the art is much more complicated. Nicéphore made lithographs in 1813 but did not know how to draw. Fortunately his son Isidore, then about 18 years old, had an amateur's talent for design and sculpture. It was he who made the drawings on stone from which his father printed. The year after, 1814, Isidore enlisted in the guards under Louis XVIII and Nicéphore found himself without his artist. (6)

The inventor now reproduced engravings and, since the chemical side of the process interested him more than the artistic, he searched for different protecting varnishes which would better resist the action of the acid. Later, in order to save himself the trouble of drawing by hand, he made the light act through the engraving on the varnish. He realized, of course, that his drawings were defective and therefore attempted to copy the engravings automatically. Soon his ideas expanded and, following a marvelous progression, he considered that, if he could but perfect some new method of designing this image on the stone, the very image of nature could thus be fixed without great difficulty, resulting in a great improvement over the present feeble copies from engravings. This is the genesis of his discovery and the progression of his ideas. (7) In all Nicéphore's mental work Claude had a part. The idea of photography was theirs in common. Their correspondence leaves no doubt on this subject. They have stated it many times and insist upon it. It was Nicéphore alone who pursued the experiments.

It was perhaps in 1814, certainly in 1815, that this idea, so weighty in its consequences, germinated in the minds of the two brothers. They were then 52 and 50 years old respectively. The first photographic attempts of Nicéphore are obscure. Isidore, absent from home, had no chance to report them, and the only record we have of the progress achieved by the inventor is known to us only because Claude and Nicéphore, separated, found it necessary to write to each other.

Nicéphore, his wife, their son and Claude lived together in the family home on the rue de l'Oratoire at Chalon until 1806 when their mother died, surrounded by her family. In the spring the family left for their beautiful Gras estate at Saint-Loup-de-Varenne where they passed the summer. Although each of the brothers owned property in their own right, their fortunes were administered in common and Nicéphore voluntarily took charge of the details of the management. Here, liberated from their social duties, they leisurely pursued their researches in textiles, sugar and woad, without paying much attention to their practical application. But, above all, they tried to perfect their engine, the *pyreolophore*, the work of their lives. At Gras they had a perfectly equipped workshop with a helper. A boat, constructed there and equipped with a pyreolophore, was navigated on the pond at Battrey which covers about five or six hectars (thirteen acres), hidden in the woods of Saint-Loup. Later they launched a more important boat on the Saône, and in 1815 they thought the time had come when the invention should be more widely exploited.

These and similar experiments were costly; despite the apparent success, something always was missing, requiring changes, more trials and new additions. Real definite success always eluded them. Their situation became precarious; they were constantly put to expense and this machine, like a cancer, little by little, ate up their fortune. Fortunately they figured that the exploitation of so fine a discovery would more than indemnify them, but whom could they interest at Chalon? Shipping flourished there, and the water traffic was important, but, notwithstanding this, it was only a provincial town. Niepce's attempts to start a shipbuilding company for the exploitation of the machine with borrowed capital failed one after another. In March 1816 Claude left for Paris with the idea of interesting the Marquis de Jouffroy in their enterprise. Planning to leave Chalon for a few months only, he never returned. The conferences with de Jouffroy never took place, because, alas, in the trials the pryeolophore failed to move a large craft at Bercy on the Seine. Propositions and experiments did not help and Claude, who lacked the wise moderation of Nicéphore, made up his mind that Paris was not the place for him but that in London he would be listened to, and he left for

79

England in August 1817. He continued his efforts and his costly improvements there and his failure affected his brain, which was already weakened. He died insane at Kew, near London, in February 1828.

After his brother's departure, Nicéphore struggled alone at Saint-Loup, living there almost constantly financially embarrassed. However, he always met the renewed demands of Claude, doing his best, not troubled or excited like Claude, but quietly confident of the destiny of the pyreolophore, until he went to England, found his brother dying and realized the emptiness of their dreams.

FROM LITHOGRAPHY TO PHOTOGRAPHY
REFERENCES: CHAPTER XIII

1. Lithography was invented in 1796 by Senefelder who published *Art de la lithographie* at Paris in 1819.

2. Towards the end of the summer of 1801 scientists and industrialists sought to create a society in France modeled after that existing in England since 1754. They met at the house of Benjamin Delessert in the rue Coq-Héron where they founded on the 12 Vendémiaire, year X (October 5, 1801) the "*Société d'Encouragement pour l'Industrie Nationale*". The first meeting of the Society took place on October 4, 1801. The constitution of the Society was adopted on November 18, 1801. The Bulletin was started on September 1802. Count Lasteyrie-Dusaillant is mentioned among the charter members.

3. Eder, *Geschichte der Photographie*, 1932, F.N. p.249, gives the publication date as 1818. This difference in date may be explained by the fact that Eder gives the date of the German edition while Potonniée that of the French.

4. For about ten years after its introduction, it will be remembered, lithography was the hobby of amateurs. Criticisms of imperfect proofs which appeared in profusion were discussed seriously. Apparatus sold by the hundreds and even in castles lithographic presses were installed to which the amateurs consigned their outlines made from the surrounding landscape. These lithographic works even obtained the honour of being put into song. A forgotten ditty went all over France; it commenced thus: "Long live lithography! It is all the rage, etc." Francis Wey, *La Lumière*, July 6, 1851.

5. *Bulletin de la Société d'Encouragement pour l'Industrie Nationale*, 1817, vol. XVI, pp.189, 209.

6. "From 1814 to 1821 I was unable to follow the heliographic work of my father because having entered the Corps of the Royal Guards, Wagram Company, on June 16, 1814, I did not return to Gras until after the disbandment of the Company which took place at Béthune on March 21, 1815, when we were combined with the Havré Company on November 1st of the same year." Unpublished manuscript by Isidore Niepce.

7. Fouque p.49 and throughout the manuscript notes of Isidore Niepce, which confirm these facts.

CHAPTER XIV

First Work of Niepce in Photography

IN the letters exchanged by the two brothers, that is at least the letters which have been preserved, we find the details of the beginning of photography. In a letter to Claude of May 5, 1816, Nicéphore writes: "I have placed the apparatus in my workroom by the open window facing the bird house. I have made the experiment *in accordance with the procedure known to you*, my dear friend, and I saw on the white paper all of the bird house which one can see from the window, also a faint image of the casement which was less illuminated than the outside objects. It is easy to distinguish the effect of the light in the picture of the bird house and up to the window frame . . . . Your prophecy has come true. The background of the picture is black and the objects white, or rather lighter than the background." (1)

Since Claude, when he left Chalon in March 1816, knew of this process, and had realized that the image obtained would be a negative, it must be inferred that the first attempts were made by the two brothers together, before 1815, which point has not been stressed heretofore. From Nicéphore's letter to Claude of May 19, 1816 (2): "I enclose in my letter two gravures (3) made according to the process known to you . . . . In order that you may better judge the effect, it will be necessary for you to view it a bit in a weak light; place the gravure on an opaque background and hold it against the light. This kind of gravure changes, I believe, in the course of time, although it is protected from contact with the light by the reaction of nitric acid which is not neutralized. I fear lest it may be damaged in transportation. This is only an experiment; but if I could improve the effect a little more (which I hope to do) and especially if I could reverse the order of light and shade, I believe that the illusion would be complete. These two gravures were made in my workroom and the view only includes that part of the yard which is seen from the window. I have read that Abbé Nollet (4), who was able to make representations of a large number of distant objects, had to use lenses of a greater focus and had to place another glass in the tube which carried the lens. If you want to preserve these two *"rétines"* (pictures), which are hardly worth while, you need only to leave them in the wrapping paper and put them between the leaves of a book. I intend

82

pursuing three objects: 1st, to give greater sharpness to the reproduction of the object; 2nd, to transpose the colour (make a positive. T.N.) (5); and 3rd, to fix them (make permanent T.N.) permanently, which will not be the easiest."

Nicéphore to Claude, May 28, 1816 (6): "I am sending you four new prints (épreuves) two large and two small, which are sharper and more correct. I have obtained them by means of a very simple process which consists in narrowing the diameter of the lens with a perforated cardboard disc. The interior of the box receiving less light, the picture thereby becomes more lively; the outlines and the shadows as well as the lights are more clearly distinguished. You can better judge as to this by the roof of the bird house, by the lines of the wall, by the crossbars; the panes themselves seem transparent in certain places, and the picture reproduces exactly the impression of the coloured images. If everything is not distinct, it is due to the fact that the image of the object represented is too small and the object seems as if it were viewed from a distance. After this it is necessary, as I have told you, to have double lenses in order to take in properly distant objects and to unite the largest number of them on the rétine; but that is another matter. The bird house appears reversed, the barn, or at least the roof of the barn, is at the left instead of the right. The white mass, which shows only dimly at the right of the bird house, above the passage and shows on the paper only by reflection, is the pear tree, which stands a good deal further away, and the black spot above the tree top is an opening between the branches. The shadow on the right shows the roof of the kiln, which seems lower than it is in reality because the boxes (camera) are placed about five feet (1.62 m.) above the floor. Finally, my dear friend, the small white lines, which appear above the roof of the barn, are some branches of trees of the orchard, are a part of the picture and are represented in the rétine. The effect would be more striking, as I have told you, or better as I do not need to tell you, if light and shade were reversed; and I shall occupy myself with this before I attempt to fix the natural colours, which latter will not be an easy task."

Letter of June 2, 1816 (7): "I sent him (Isidore Niepce) in my letter of the 28th a small proof similar to those which I sent to you in my last and have impressed on him not to show it to any of his friends."

Letter of April 20, 1817 (8): "I thought I had informed you, dear friend, that I have given up the use of silver muriate and you know the reasons which led me to this decision."

The foregoing extracts then deal with the sending of seven photographs of which the subject is always the same and which are described minutely by the author, namely: the courtyard of the property at Gras, the bird house, the barn and the garden. They had been obtained with the aid of silver muriate or silver chloride which Niepce rendered sufficiently sensitive in order that they might attain an impression in the camera obscura (9); they were very poorly fixed with nitric acid (10); they were negatives. Perhaps these images were not as fragile as one might be led to think. In 1866, fifty years after their production, Fouque (11) affirms that he still had one of these proofs, "unfortunately almost effaced", and he assumes the authority to place the year 1816 as the date of the invention of photography. I can not share that opinion. (12) Negative images, not completely fixed, cannot be called photographs. This will please the detractors of Niepce. We see here the immense difference which already separates Niepce from Wedgwood. Davy in his memoir considers that a negative of an object made by contact constitutes a process as elegant as useful. Niepce, attaining negative images from nature, almost permanent, since they lasted half a century, considered the problem so little solved that he did not hesitate to abandon this primitive process in order that he might pass on to a new line of thought.

FIRST WORK OF NIEPCE IN PHOTOGRAPHY
REFERENCES: CHAPTER XIV

1. Niepce's correspondence at the Museum at Chalon is numbered in rotation. This letter is number 4. It is quoted in Fouque p.63.
2. This is number 7 at Chalon, Fouque p.67.
3. i.e. two photographs, as indicated by the text following in the letter.
4. Abbé J.Antoine Nollet, physicist, member of the Académie des Sciences (1700-1770) occupied himself particularly with electricity. His principal work is *Leçons de physique experimentale*, 6 vol., 1743. (T.N.).
5. Notice the lights and shades.
6. Letter No.9 at Chalon, Fouque p.69.
7. Letter No.10 at Chalon. This sentence has never been published.
8. Letter No.47 at Chalon, Fouque, p.87.
9. Ritter, in 1801, used paper coated with chloride of silver, still moist, in the camera obscura. The ultra-violet rays and those visible rays, most actinic, coloured the paper.
10. Scheele in 1771 pointed out that silver chloride, dissolved in nitric acid, is not coloured by light.
11. Fouque, p.247.
12. *Bulletin de Société Française de Photographie*, 1921, p.312.

CHAPTER XV

Apparatus and Experiments with Different Substances

THE inventor had to overcome many other difficulties. No one up to that time had produced a negative image from nature. He was unable to avail himself of the experience of others. Moreover, the camera obscura, which were used, were built for another purpose. He had not only to create the process, but first of all the material. Five cameras are in the Museum at Chalon-sur-Saône which Niepce built or modified for his use. The optical apparatus, consisting of assembled single lenses, gave an image sufficient for those who wanted to use them for copying with a pencil or merely for their amusement. The sensitized paper however revealed the defects—spherical, chromatic aberrations, distortion, astigmatism and blurring—and they became evident and Niepce was unable to remedy them. We have seen that he tried to attain sharpness by using a fixed diaphragm. He improved on this, showing his genius by constructing an iris diaphragm, a wonderful invention, forgotten with him and reinvented a long time after. This diaphragm is still in the Museum at Chalon. In the midst of these difficulties, leaving aside the daily perplexities and the serious annoyance with the pyreolophore, Niepce continued his researches.

I again cite the correspondence. Nicéphore to Claude, May 5, 1816: (1) "You have noted from my last letter that I have broken the lens of my camera. When in town last Monday I found only one lens at Scotti's of a greater focus than the first and I have had to lengthen the tube in order to obtain the correct focus . . . . My lens having been broken, I could not use my camera. I put an "artificial eye" in Isidore's jewel case, a small box 18 lignes square (36 to 40 mm.). Fortunately I still had the lenses of the solar microscope which, as you know, were left to us by our Grandfather Barrault. I found that one of these small lenses is of the correct length; and the image of the objects is received very sharply and clearly on a field of 13 lignes in diameter (29 mm.)".

June 16, 1816 (2): "Your support is sufficient to encourage me in an enterprise, the idea of which belongs to both of us. (3) In the circumstances, success will more than satisfy me. Although I am not afraid of the difficulties which beset me, thank God, I have no illusions about the imperfections of my first attempts, nor the improvements which I desire

86

EXPERIMENTS WITH DIFFERENT SUBSTANCES

to make. For several days I have worked, not so much in making new proofs by the same process, which seemed to me useless, but I have applied myself to the task of fixing the image in a satisfactory manner and to place the lights and shadows in their natural order. I have made several attempts along these lines, which I intend to repeat because I see a possibility of success. The idea which you kindly suggest, my dear friend, for attaining this twofold object is very ingenious and has also occurred to me, because it involves a number of combinations which I can make. But until now my experience has indicated only one substance which the light decolourizes easily and it does not offer as satisfactory result as a substance which has the property of absorbing light. I have read that a solution of muriate of iron (iron chloride T.N.) in alcohol (4), which is a beautiful yellow, becomes white in the sun, regaining its natural colour in the shade. I coated a piece of paper with this solution and dried it; the part exposed to the light became white while the part which was not exposed to the light remained yellow, but this solution absorbed too much of the humidity of the air, and I used it no more because by chance I found another substance simpler and better. A piece of paper coated with one or more layers of "rouille" or "safran de mars", exposed to the vapours of oxygenated hydrochloric acid (5) turns to a beautiful daffodil yellow and bleaches better and more rapidly than by the former process (iron chloride T.N.) I placed both in the camera and still the action of the light had no noticeable effect on either of them, though I was careful to change the position of the apparatus. Perhaps I did not wait long enough and I must make sure of this, because the substance was only slightly affected. I also believed as you did, my dear friend, that if one places in the camera a strong proof on paper, tinted with a fugitive colour or covered with the substance I employ, the image will appear on this paper in its natural colours (6), since the dark parts of the proof, being more opaque, intercept more or less the passage of the light rays, but without affecting the result. (7) I presume that the action of light is not strong enough and that the paper which I use is too heavy or, being too thickly coated, offers an insurmountable obstacle to the passage of the fluid; because I applied almost six coats of white. Such are the negative results which I have obtained. Fortunately they do not as yet disprove the value of the idea and I hope to take the matter up again and look forward to some measure of success.

"I have also succeeded in decolourizing black manganese oxide (8), that is to say, that a paper coated with this oxide becomes perfectly white when it is subjected to the vapours of oxygenated hydrochloric acid. If, before it is entirely decolourized, it is exposed to the light, it bleaches rapidly and, after it has bleached, if it is slightly blackened with the same oxide, it is again decolourized by the sole action of the luminous fluid. I think, dear friend, that this substance deserves further research and I intend to look into it more seriously. I also want to make certain whether the different vapours could fix the coloured image or modify the action of light by introducing them with the aid of a tube into the apparatus during the operation. I have only used the fumes of oxygenated hydrochloric acid, hydrogen and carbonic acid. The first decolourized the image; the second did not seem to produce any notice-able effect; while the third destroyed in a large measure the capacity in the substance employed of absorbing the light. This substance, though exposed for eight hours, coloured only slightly while subjected to the fumes and only in those parts which were most illuminated. I resumed these interesting experiments and tried several other vapours in succes-sion; especially oxygen, which, because of its affinity with metallic oxides and light, deserves special attention. I also have made new attempts to succeed in engraving on metal using mineral acids; but those acids which I used, that is to say muriatic and nitric acid, as well as the oxygenated hydrochloric acid, whether in the form of vapour, or in solution, only resulted in a blackish stain, more or less deep, according to the strength of the solvent. Oxygenated hydrochloric acid is the only reliable one, but it is only decomposed by the light when combined with water and in this state does not act on metals with sufficient energy to etch them perceptibly; for it does not produce any effervescence with them and oxidizes them as would liver of sulphur, which is not our object. But I am happy to have recognized that, with-out producing the troublesome agitation of other acids, it attacks the lithographic stone, which we use for engraving, sharply and cleanly. It attacks it slowly, as we require, in order that the influence of the light may be more sensible and the acid would etch the stone deeper, accord-ing to the different shades. Stopping everything, I turned to preparing one of these stones instead of paper on which the coloured images would be reproduced. I let it soak for some time in hot water and then I sub-jected it to the fumes of oxygenated hydrochloric acid which entered the apparatus, thus carrying out my method. I believe, with the aid of this manipulation, a decisive result will be obtained if, as we cannot doubt, the acid in question is decomposed by the light and, by this, the strength of the solvent is modified."

July 2, 1816 (9): "After repeated experiments, I recognized the impossibility of fixing the image of objects by the engraving process on stone by the combined action of acids and light. This fluid, it seemed to me, had no perceptible influence on the dissolving property of these chemical agents. I have, therefore, entirely given up their use."

December 11, 1816 (10): "I am very glad to finish the small apparatus for the experiments about which I told you, so that Isidore can inform you of the result . . . . If I can make my experiment today, Isidore will have the time to design and perhaps also make an engraving of the camera."

March 26, 1817 (11): "I have not yet been able to give an account of the process of which I told you for engraving on stone because the process has no bearing on the former, owing to the fact that I must employ another substance."

These quotations already permit a few conclusions. It has been shown how Niepce turned from lithography to the fixation of the images in the camera. Chemistry had nothing to do with it. But, as he explained in the unpublished introduction to which I referred in Chapter X of this book, after he had conceived the idea of designing by photography, he "searched among the substances of the three kingdoms for one which could best meet his requirements" and he "engaged in a great many experiments, thus losing a great deal of time." Therefore, chemistry, far from suggesting to him the idea of photographic design, showed him, on the contrary, what obstacles he would encounter. It is not surprising that he obtained little help from the works of the chemists of his time, who worked along entirely different lines. The chemical changes—blackening included—that light effected in substances had for them no other interest than the determination of the nature and the qualities of light. The blackening never meant to them more than an unimportant incident. None of these people had a thought of photography.

Nicéphore and Claude made use of the chemical dictionary of Klaproth (12), which was famous at that time. In the article on "Light", Klaproth states: "Silver muriate blackens in light." In his article on "Muriate", Klaproth writes: "Silver muriate blackens in air." Here is information which is very ambiguous and a blackening in which the chemists were little interested. Nicéphore had read, not only that well-known work, but also the original notes of the scholars cited in it. He speaks of a note by Vogel; he certainly knew the works of Scheele, of Senebier and of Humboldt. Thus, conversant with the recent works of the chemists of his time, he applied this acquired knowledge to his researches and endeavoured to discover new properties of light. We cannot sufficiently admire the sureness of the method with which he organized his experiments, without anyone who could guide him, carrying out a definite plan in which Claude shared.

And so his first attempts were direct photographs on paper, or engravings on stone or on metal, in the camera obscura by means of substances which the action of light colours, decolourizes or decomposes. They were unsuccessful. He continued this method until the middle of 1817, using gum guaiacum and finally phosphorus. "I was (13) at a loss to know of any other substance which I might substitute for silver muriate; then I read in a work on chemistry that gum guaiacum (14), which is a greyish-yellow, turns to a beautiful bright green when exposed to light. It acquires new properties through this and in that state a more pure alcohol is required to dissolve it than in its natural state." The change of colour took place; but it made no difference in the solubility whether the resin was acted upon by light or not, the image could not be fixed. Niepce gave up the use of guaiacum. He had discovered in Vogel's treatise that phosphorus (15) dissolved in hot water turns, by the action of light, a deep red and blackish and that in that state it is insoluble in Lampadius alcohol (carbon disulphide T.N.) which, on the other hand, dissolves white phosphorus. Further, that the phosphorus on which light had acted remained red and very stable; while phosphorus which the light had not touched changed spontaneously to phosphoric acid, which etches stone. Nicéphore deduced from this that he could obtain relief images, engraved on stone, in the camera. But phosphorus proved to be a rebellious material in these photographic experiments, and a dangerous companion. The inventor failed to produce an image in the camera and also burned his hand severely. (16)

EXPERIMENTS WITH DIFFERENT SUBSTANCES
REFERENCES: CHAPTER XV

1. Letter No.4 at Chalon.
2. Letter No.2 at Chalon, Fouque p.76.
3. Nicéphore affirms this statement many times.
4. The bleaching by the sun and its turning yellow again in the shade were observed by Bestucheff, in 1725, while making a preparation for a secret remedy which cured people at the time. The formula was purchased by the government of Empress Catherine of Russia. Klaproth, in 1782, investigated and explained these reactions. Niepce took his information from him.
5. Discovered by Scheele, in 1774, while investigating manganese. Berthollet studied the effetcs of light on this substance in 1783. (*Statique chimique*, 2-197).
6. For "colours" read "lights and shades".
7. The object of this is to obtain a positive by printing under a negative image which serves as a matrix. In 1816! Twenty-three years later Talbot received all honours for this discovery.
8. This had been employed a long time for bleaching glass while melting. Seguin, Thomson, Klaproth, Proust, studied the properties of black manganic oxide. Klaproth stated in his dictionary (*Dictionnaire de Chimie* by M.-H.Klaproth and F.Wolff, translated by Bouillon-Lagrange and Vogel, Paris, 1810): "Manganic oxide is used to release oxygen gas and for the manufacture of oxygenated hydrochloric acid. It is used to bleach glass and to coat cheap pottery. Boyle discovered a lode of manganese in England, Scheele analysed it and discovered manganese metal . . . . Black manganese oxide is found abundantly in nature."
9. No.3, 2nd series, at Chalon, Fouque p.81.
10. No.31, at Chalon, Fouque, p.84.
11. No.43 and 44 at Chalon.
12. *Dictionnaire de Chimie* by M.-H.Klaproth and F.Wolff translated from German with notes by E.-J.-B.Bouillon-Lagrange and H.-A.Vogel, Paris, 1810.
13. Nicéphore to Claude, April 20, 1817, No.47 at Chalon.
14. The influence of light on guaiacum was recognized and investigated by Hagemann, and by Senebier in 1782, and later by Wollaston in 1803.
15. Phosphorus was discovered in 1677 by Brandt, an alchemist at Hamburg. Shortly after Kunkel, professor at Wittenberg, who had tried to buy the secret from Brandt, succeeded in making phosphorus himself. Boyle in 1693 discovered a new way of making it. However, phosphorus was very rare. In 1737 Hellot published a process before the Académie des Sciences. Margraf, in 1743, and later Gahn and Scheele described practical methods for obtaining it. (Mémoires de l'Académie des Sciences, 1737). Still later phosphorus was studied by Beckmann in 1800; Ritter in 1801; Vogel in 1806.
16. Nicéphore to Claude, April 20, May 20, July 11, 1817. Nos.47, 50, 51, 54 at Chalon.

CHAPTER XVI

The Bitumen of Judea Process

WE have seen that Nicéphore advised his brother in March 1817 that he had changed his method which "because of the new substance employed was in no manner related to the former method". This new process attempted to reproduce an outline, serving as a resist, on stone, glass or metal, coated with light-sensitive varnish. Nicéphore, in the manner of the engraver, tried to etch through the varnish with acid more or less hardened by the action of light, and thus obtain a plate suitable for the printing press. At first he contented himself with reproducing engravings which had been made transparent, but, advancing in his process, he returned to his original idea to reproduce nature in the camera.

Our information on the period between 1817 and 1820 is incomplete because after Claude left for England (August 1817) the two brothers were very discreet in their correspondence. Their long negotiations and their experiences with bankers and business men had embittered them and made them suspicious. In some of the letters from Claude to Nicéphore, which are preserved, Claude is full of advice: "I beg of you, my dear friend (1), notwithstanding the interest which I take in reading the interesting details which you are good enough to write, omit the more intimate particulars because others might possibly profit by them . . . . This is my earnest advice prompted by our mutual interest, my dear friend, suggested by my consideration of your position."

Here are the passages where Claude alludes to Nicéphore's work. Claude to Nicéphore, December 31, 1818: "I earnestly desire that the new material that you have received from Paris will meet your requirements. I cannot imagine precisely what the substance may be, and I appreciate your discretion in not mentioning its name. If, as you are kind enough to say, the ingenious idea which you are working on belongs to us both, it is really yours because of your researches and your improvements in which I have been unable to participate."

August 24, 1819: "How I enjoyed reading the interesting details which you were good enough to give me about your new researches! How I desire that the promising hopes will not vanish in the air and that they will lead you to the desired realization which is, one might say, both beautiful and astonishing. I hope that this happy inspiration will lead you to this. We must agree that the substance which you employ, which I do not wholly guess, but one which I suppose to have the properties which you have indicated to me, and that I think it is best not to explain more fully. If then, I say, the result be attained, I must concede that it will excite curiosity and general admiration. What a source of satisfaction it must be to you, my dear friend, to have followed with so steadfast a devotion where all others would have been discouraged by the tremendous difficulties of the process. One must believe that you had a secret inspiration from above, which encouraged you to continue toward your goal."

December 11, 1819: "It seems, my dear friend, judging from what you have written about your interesting work, that you were fortunate enough to attain results which promise a complete solution of the problem which you have attempted to solve, although it seemed, by its nature, difficult to achieve."

January 22, 1820: "I believe that your ingenious process will surpass all others if the foundation will remain for a long time in the same state after the operation, because that is, I believe, where you will have to overcome the greatest difficulties. It seems, according to what you have been kind enough to tell me, that you have found the means which will certainly give to your substance the required effect, a precious property."

February 8, 1820: "I have read with the keenest interest of the new discovery you have made; if the renewed experiment, which you intend to make, achieves the same happy result as the first, I would regard that, just as you do, as the solution of the problem with which you are occupied."

February 25, 1820: "I notice with great pleasure that you have made new experiments which promise interesting results for your object . . . . Some day when you are assured that you have laid the foundation for the phenomenon which occupies you, you will then have realized the dream of my dear sister." (2)

March 17, 1820: "Let us speak first of the experiments on which you are working, which seem to lead rapidly to the end you desire, so difficult to discover and apparently as great as it is extraordinary. Receive then, my dear friend, the expression of my great satisfaction which I have experienced when reading and rereading the interesting details which you communicated to me. How much I wish that your splendid hopes may be realized, and that the process which you intend to try with the dark varnish, susceptible of yielding to the luminous fluid, by means of *l'h* . . . *oui* (3), which I remember very well and which, however, allows the impression to remain unalterable, will be successful! Without doubt the problem will then be solved in the most peremptory manner."

April 21, 1820: "Please accept my hearty congratulations on the fortunate discovery which you have made. Accept my affectionate thanks for the interesting and ingenious processes in which you are kind enough to include me . . . . I hope that the results that you have obtained have actually initiated you into the marvelous secret of nature's work."

These obscure passages (4) show the progress and the partial success of the inventor, but they do not acquaint us with the substance employed nor the manipulation. Isidore Niepce, fortunately, informs us on these two points: "From the end of 1815 (5) until March 29, 1821, during which period I sent in my resignation (6), I spent three months of each year with my family. At the time my father showed me the results that he had obtained on metal, on glass and on paper; either having printed a gravure on these different materials, previously coated with his varnish, or having obtained the image of nature in the camera on a pewter plate prepared with a varnish, according to the results of his experiments. Therefore I can only give the date of 1821 as the daily witness to my father's work. At first he worked on glass and used bitumen of Judea."

Where did Nicéphore get the idea of bitumen of Judea? From lithography. It came directly from gravure; Senefelder, who at first etched on copper with nitric acid, for economy's sake, thought of using stone. He discovered the lithographic process in the course of his different experiments; but, later, he returned to metal and used sheets of iron, zinc and especially pewter. Niepce, copying him, going further, employed also glass. With regard to bitumen of Judea, Isidore says that his father compounded for himself the varnish with which he coated the stones or the pewter which he wanted to etch. Now the varnishes, of which each engraver had a formula which he called his own, were almost all based on asphalt or bitumen of Judea. Rembrandt used a varnish composed of one part asphalt to one part mastic and two parts wax. Abraham Bosse used one part asphalt, two parts mastic and three parts wax. A common formula at the time of Niepce contained half asphalt; the covering varnish or *petit vernis* consists only of dissolved asphalt and lamp black. (7)

THE BITUMEN OF JUDEA PROCESS

Nicéphore, applying to heliography the investigations of resins (8) of Senebier, as we have seen, used the fact that the guaiacum changes colour in light. Logically following his experiments, he tried successively the different substances composing his varnishes. He dissolved the bitumen of Judea in petroleum, later in Dippel's oil (9); he finally recognized after many attempts that a thin dried coating of this solution, exposed to light, bleached a little (10) and, what is more important, is difficult to dissolve. The problem, says Claude, was solved.

Nicéphore spread a little of this varnish on a pewter plate and after it was dried he placed an oiled transparent gravure in contact with it and used it as a negative. After two or three hours of exposure to daylight the "gravure" appeared on the bitumen in the form of a dim whitish image. Having dipped the plate in petroleum, the parts affected by the light dissolved little, if at all, while the varnish underneath the blacks of the "gravure" and which the light had not hardened, completely dissolved. There remained then on the pewter a reversed image (contre-épreuve) of the gravure where the lights were represented by the white and hardened bitumen, and the blacks, by the plain metal, because the varnish had been washed away under these black parts. The first tests were hardly satisfactory. The solvent attacked the highlights more or less and the image did not stand out sharply. When he dealt with a "gravure" where the blacks were in absolute contrast to the whites, there was no trouble. But Nicéphore had two things in view: making copies of the "gravure" from transparencies, and obtaining photographs in the camera obscura. In these latter, in which the tones graduated into each other, the image remained confused; they were really printed by the light in the layers of coating, just as in the present bichromate process. In order to make the image appear visible and sharp, Nicéphore would have had to actually strip it since he needed to attack the coating from that side nearest to the metal and would have had to colour it with a pigment. These things were not discovered until many years after Niepce; but he discovered that the unsharp and barely perceptible image became perceptible when viewed as a transparency and that is why he adopted glass instead of metal as a support. It is easily seen that the different thicknesses of varnish carrying the print translate the gradations of the photographic image.

It was by this process that Nicéphore Niepce produced his first photograph, which was also the first photograph made in the world. In what year? In 1822.

HISTORY OF THE DISCOVERY OF PHOTOGRAPHY
REFERENCES: CHAPTER XVI

1. Claude to Nicéphore, October 29, 1818.
2. Nicéphore's wife. This shows the great interest she took in her husband's work. The Niepces had a sister, married in Paris, but she had died before this time.
3. This l'h . . . oui undoubtedly refers to Dippel's oil which Nicéphore used, as will be seen further on.
4. 31 letters from Claude to Nicéphore are preserved in the Museum at Chalon, partly known through Fouque's work: *La Vérité sur l'Invention de la Photographie.* It would be well to read them again.
5. *Unpublished manuscript of Isidore Niepce.*
6. From the Royal Guards. In the Annual of 1821, Isidore is mentioned among the Royal Military Household, rated as guardsman of the first class, with the rank of lieutenant in the army, consigned to the first company, which was in command of Lt.Gen.duc d'Havré et de Croy.
7. Klaproth's dictionary under "asphalt" states that this substance is used in the making of black varnish by the Chinese.
8. Senebier. *Mémoires physico-chimiques sur l'influence de la lumière solaire pour modifier les êtres des trois règnes de la nature,* Geneva 1782. Senebier investigated the changes effected by light on many resins, gamboge, gum ammoniac, guaiacum, mastic drops, dammar, sandarac, incense, etc. He does not mention asphalt.
9. Bone oil.
10. *Comptes rendus,* 1839, p.250, in Arago's notes.

96

CHAPTER XVII

The Date of the Invention of Photography

THE historians disagree as to this date. (1) Each one maintains his own conclusion; and the nationality of the writer often influences his choice. They would agree, however, more easily, if they would first agree to define what they mean by photography.

As far as I know, no one gives the name photography to anything but an image obtained in the camera on a surface sensitive to light and rendered permanent. Anyone insisting that these conditions are not essential for a photograph would astonish his hearers. It is easy to prove, and part of this proof has already been given, first that no one made a photograph before Niepce; second, that Niepce obtained a photograph, in the full sense of the word, in 1822.

We must distinguish, as the inventor himself always did, between copies by transparency (by contact T.N.) and true photographs, images in the camera. Niepce always called these images by a peculiar name, he named them "points de vue". We find this term "points de vue" used for our present word "photographs" in his letters to his son Isidore, to his brother Claude, to the engraver Lemaître, to his partner Daguerre, etc. His correspondents, in turn, use the same term when replying: the letters of July 19, 1822, February 24, and September 3, 1824, May 26, 1826 and February 2, June 4, July 24, and September 4, 1827, August 20, 1828, October 4, and 12, 1829. The same term, with its precise significance, is found again in the "Notice" written by the inventor on December 8, 1827 for the Royal Society of London and in the letter written on December 5, 1829 to his associate Daguerre. Everywhere the difference between "points de vue" and "copies de gravures" is emphasized. This explanation is essential in order that what follows may be understood.

Claude, on July 19, 1822, wrote from England to Nicéphore (2): "General Poncet must be very enthusiastic over the excellence of your discovery and your renewed success gives me great satisfaction. I have read and re-read the interesting details which you have been good enough to send me; I think I see you, my dear sister and my nephew, all eagerly following with your eyes this great work of the light; *I think I see, myself, one of your "points de vue" which I recall with great pleasure.*

How much I desire, my dear friend, that so great and interesting an experiment might have a complete and definite result both for you and for science." This letter, so clear, together with other statements, removes all doubt. The point in question here is a photograph, the words "points de vue" permit no chance for an error.

For lack of the "distinguo" (distinction), but a little subtle, I have stated that Fouque (3) and all the historians after him are mistaken as to the meaning of this letter when they repeat that Claude made here an allusion to a contact print from a steel engraving, the portrait of Pope Pius VII which Nicéphore presented to General Poncet. Claude, in fact, states this matter very precisely: *a "point de vue" which he remembered with great pleasure.* How can we believe that this was the portrait of Pope Pius VII? This vision of the past, which Claude in his exile conserved as a treasured souvenir, is not difficult to identify; for it is the yard, the bird house, the garden at Gras so often photographed in vain and now definitely fixed on glass coated with bitumen of Judea.

This image, was it permanent and fixed? As a matter of fact, Claude does not say how it was obtained. But we know from Isidore that his father used glass and bitumen of Judea at this time. "Employing this substance, he obtained in 1822 the wonderful reproduction of the portrait of Pope Pius VII which he presented as a gift to his relative, General Poncet de Maupas." (4) Claude, in his letter, precisely states that General Poncet was the host of the inventor at the time of this experiment, and that he received as a gift the copy of the "gravure" representing Pope Pius VII. The "point de vue" in question was obtained at the same time, by an identical process. It also was made on glass; bitumen of Judea was used for both. Moreover, Niepce used no other substance after this time. Now, we know that the portrait of Pope Pius VII was a permanent image. The happy owner in his enthusiasm took it to Paris, placed it between two glass plates and had it expensively framed by Giroux, stationer and publisher, on the rue du Coq-Saint-Honoré. The frail image was generally admired there until, by accident, someone dropped it and broke it beyond repair. (5)

The "point de vue" was not different from the gravure; the images made on bitumen of Judea are permanent, since some are still in existence. It is true that these are copies of "gravures" and are on metal. But the Société Française de Photographie has had for a long time in its possession a photograph on glass coated with bitumen of Judea made by Nicéphore Niepce at a date which it is impossible to establish exactly, which was presented to the Society by the grandson of the inventor in 1890. (6) The subject represents a table on which are placed vases, bread and bottles. Owing to circumstances unknown to us, this photograph no longer exists. The glass plate is so easily broken. But it is also possible that it has been lost and that some day it may be found in some collection. We must rely entirely on the reproduction which the Society had made in 1891, reproduced by halftone and through a very coarse screen. It is sufficient to enable us to judge the qualities of the original and to recognize the definition of the middle tones in the image without showing any retouching. This does away with all uncertainty as to the existence of photographs on glass by Niepce which were perfectly fixed, because this one has been preserved for more than seventy years and its disappearance is due to causes outside of photography.

I believe I have amply demonstrated that Nicéphore Niepce in 1822 obtained and fixed the images of the camera obscura. It is possible that he had done this successfully before this date, but we do not know that. No definite proof exists of any date before 1822.

In fact, this date is considered by Nicéphore himself as definite for his invention. It is also a tradition preserved in his family. In Isidore Niepce's papers I find the following: "With indefatigable perseverance, stimulated by some favorable results, he pursued his wonderful work, arriving finally in 1822 at a result which was the glorious reward for his physical sufferings and for his anxiety and bitter sorrows, all of which have their influence and effect on the physique of the man who devotes himself wholeheartedly to the research of the unknown. (7) All those who met the inventor and shared his confidence agree on this date 1822. It is inscribed on the monument erected on the property at Gras in order to commemorate the invention. The engraver Lemaître, intimately associated with Niepce and Daguerre, also gives the date as 1822. (8)

We must, therefore, establish the date for the invention of photography as the year 1822. This date is of such importance in the general history of civilization that it has seemed to me necessary to determine it exactly, even at the expense of some minute details.

1. *Bulletin de la Société française de photographie*, 1921, p.117. Note on the date of the invention of Photography.
2. The original is in the Museum at Chalon.
3. Fouque, p.106.
4. *Unpublished manuscript* of Isidore Niepce.
5. Fouque, p.107.
6. *Bulletin de la Société française de Photographie*, 1890, pp.146 and 148; 1891, p.423.
7. Note on J.-N.Niepce, inventor of photography, by Isidore Niepce (unpublished). At the beginning of a pamphlet published in 1841 under the title: *Historique de la découverte improprement nommée Daguerréotype* Isidore writes a note on the life and works of J.-N.Niepce. This remained unpublished among his papers, and, although published later, it seems more sincere than the first which was more of a polemic against Daguerre.
8. See *Bulletin de la Société Française de Photographie*, 1856, p.41 on the occasion of the Exposition in 1855, the speech of Durieu expressing Lemaître's opinion. Lacan also gives the date as 1822 and corrects Belloc who mentions 1824 (*La Lumière*, July 8, 1854).

CHAPTER XVIII

The Perfected Process

IN the years which followed, Nicéphore perfected his method and gave
it definite form. Isidore states: "The years 1823, 1824 and 1825 were
spent in various experiments, copying gravures on glass or metal. The
pewter plate now in the Museum of our town, which represents Christ
carrying His Cross dates from this period; the inscription made by me
on the metal carries the date 1825. (1) My father presented it to M.de
Champmartin. (2) It came back to us after his death at the request of
M.Jules Chevrier. (3) I presented it to the Museum. We have now
arrived at the year 1826. From this year I must date the reproduction
of Cardinal d'Amboise, a Minister of Louis XII. I was present during
the manipulation by which my father obtained this reproduction. He
used bitumen of Judea dissolved in Dippel's oil. This portrait(Lemaître's
first letter will approximately fix the month in which my father made it,
because two or three months later he sent it to this skilled engraver) (4)
was reproduced on a pewter plate, slightly etched by my father and
sent to Lemaître with the request that he add another deep etching of
the pewter by acid. Lemaître graciously acceded to the request of my
father. He pulled several proofs from the plate of the Cardinal's portrait, returned it, and my father gave the plate, I believe, to M.Chevrier.
I have sent the last proof which I had to my elder son at Paris at his
request. (5) M.Lemaître has another proof of it." (6)

We see here how heliography developed. In place of a print on glass
formed in the varnish and viewed as a transparency, the inventor
returned to his former ideas; he again took up metal as a base. Having
flowed his varnish (bitumen of Judea dissolved in Dippel's oil), the
plate was exposed under a gravure serving as a negative or at the back
of the camera in order to make a "point de vue". In the first case, the
exposure lasted two or three hours; in the second case, eight hours in
the full light of a summer day. The plate was then washed in petroleum
and a negative image appeared in relief, formed on the plate in layers of
varying thicknesses. Now Niepce became an engraver; he flowed his
plate with a weak acid solution, which etched the metal where the
varnish had been removed and, the inventor hoped, the plate also would
be etched proportionally to the varying thicknesses of the layers of

varnish which remained. After etching, the varnish was removed with alcohol.

A gravure, I repeat, consists of an image in black and white on paper without intermediate tones. The greys are lines more or less closed up. It will be noticed that by this etching the copies of gravures present a composition of incised lines where the metal had been bared, and of a surface, more or less extended, covered with the varnish, which corresponds to the whites. The action of the acid produced a plate with ridges which on the printing press again produce impressions reproducing the original. This does not apply to "points de vue" formed of continuous tones. The etching did not penetrate all the layers of the varnish or uniformly attack the metal. That is why Daguerre, with some malice, could state that Niepce never succeeded in etching (gravé) a "point de vue" (producing full tone images). (7)

The inventor again modified his method. The "point de vue" having been printed on the thick coating, Niepce, after having removed the excess of asphaltum, exposed the metal plate to the fumes of a few grains of iodine (8), the emanations of which darkened the image in proportion to the remaining varnish. It is easy to imagine that this process was precarious and the images so obtained were very weak. (9) But that does not matter. The Société Française de Photographie has a proof made by this method. It is true that this is only a copy of a gravure, because there are no photographs of Niepce in existence. Still, on this print, which is nearly a hundred years old, the smallest details of the design are visible. In the meantime it has remained almost unprotected and exposed to dust since its production, until I had it framed in 1912. I insist, therefore, that, contrary to everything that has been said, the "points de vue" of Niepce were complete and real photographs. It is deplorable that all of them have been lost.

In addition, we have the testimony of a man whose business qualified him as a competent judge and who saw one of these photographs. In October 1829, Niepce sent to Daguerre "a trial on a silvered plate" of a "point de vue" from nature made in the camera (10) which was taken from the window of the inventor's workroom. The subject can therefore be identified precisely: It is the yard, the barn and the garden. Niepce requested Daguerre to give him his opinion; at the same time he wrote to Lemaître asking him to go and see this print and to add his judgment to Daguerre's. The two experts, who were at first mistaken, took for an engraved plate that which was a photograph, darkened by iodine. But

Lemaître summed up their combined impressions as follows (12): "The background which appears in the center and which is the best portion, renders perfectly all the details of natural objects but it lacks entirely the tone values." This criticism is still made of today's photographs.

Thus photographs blackened by iodine not only did exist but they were complete and permanent images. It is necessary to bear this in mind in order to understand the sequence of later events better, because I have greatly anticipated, in point of time, in order to avoid returning to the technical details.

Niepce did not possess an intaglio press. In order to pull the proofs, he had to call upon a printer who had such a press. Unable to get satisfactory proofs at Dijon, he was introduced during the summer of 1825 (13), by his son's father-in-law to a skilled engraver in Paris named Lemaître (1797-1870). In the following years Lemaître printed many proofs from Niepce's plates and also gave him valuable advice.

We have seen that in these heliographic plates the whites of the picture were formed by the hardened bitumen and the blacks by the bare metal. The contrast, so little marked between the whites and the blacks, was increased if the plate was placed in front of a slate from which the light was reflected on it. Therefore the more the metal was polished, the darker the background appeared. It is on account of this particular rroperty that Niepce adopted pewter (14) and gave up copper. Lemaître advised silver plating the copper plates because such plates are harder than pewter. (15) The beginning of Daguerreotype can be traced directly to this. The heliogravure process above described was perfected around 1826 or 1827 and the inventor made no further change in it.

1. The plate is in the Museum at Chalon; Isidore's inscription follows: "*Dessin héliographique inventé par M.J.-N.Niepce, 1825.*"
2. Father-in-law of Isidore Niepce.
3. Chevrier was the custodian of the Museum at Chalon-sur-Saône.
4. Nicéphore obtained this plate in the summer of 1826; he wrote to the engraver Lemaître on February 2, 1827. Lemaître returned the plates on March 5th. Although the above details were published by Fouque in 1867 (p.123), the custodian Chevrier fixed the date of the production of this heliographic plate as 1824. Following the date given by the Museum at Chalon, the mistake was repeated by the Conservatoire des Arts et Métiers at Paris, and by the Société Française de Photographie, where the proofs from the plate of the portrait of Cardinal d'Amboise all carry the false date of 1824. See: *Bulletin de la Société Française de Photographie*, September 1919.
5. This proof on paper was presented by Eugène Niepce, the son of Isidore, on May 2, 1890 to the Société Française de Photographie where it is now preserved. (*Bulletin de la Société Française de Photographie*, 1890, p.148).
6. *Unpublished manuscript by Isidore Niepce.*
7. *Historique et description des procédés du daguerréotype*, etc., p.45, Note.
8. Iodine, discovered by Courtois in 1811, became known through the communications of Clément and Desormes in 1813 and was later investigated by Gay-Lussac.
9. This is what Daguerre asserted and, on Daguerre's assurance, what Arago accepted (Arago's Report to the Académie des Sciences. *Comptes rendus*, session of August 19, 1839; *Historique et description des procédés du daguerréotype*, etc.). The collection of heliographs of the Société Française de Photographie proves the contrary.
10. Letter from Niepce to Lemaître, October 4, 1829, *La Lumière*, March 30, 1851.
11. Niepce to Lemaître, October 25, 1829, *La Lumière*, March 30, 1851.
12. Lemaître to Niepce, October 12, 1829, *La Lumière*, March 30, 1851.
13. Niepce to Lemaître, January 17, 1827, *La Lumière*, February 16, 1851.
14. Niepce to his son Isidore, May 26, 1826 (Fouque, p.122). M.Cromer who owns the original of this letter, published a facsimile of it in the *Bulletin de la Société Française de Photographie* of 1922, p.69. Niepce to Daguerre, June 4, 1827; Isidore Niepce, *Historique de la découverte*, etc., p.23.
15. *Bulletin de la Société Française de Photographie*, 1856, p.69.

CHAPTER XIX

Daguerre Addresses Niepce

ONE day in January 1826 Niepce received a letter from an unknown correspondent; this was Daguerre, a Parisian artist, whose reputation was well-known; but Chalon was far from Paris in those days. Daguerre, who had made for a long time researches along the same lines, wrote that he would be happy to learn of the results of Niepce's work and gave detailed information about his own work which seemed fantastic. Niepce replied, polite and reserved. A year passed and in January 1827 came another letter from Daguerre; this time he asked to see a heliograph. Niepce, cold and suspicious by nature, inquired first of all from Lemaître, the engraver, for information about Daguerre. Lemaître answered: "You ask if I know M. Daguerre? For several years, without knowing him intimately, I have attended evening parties where I met him. Last Spring, having had an order from a publisher to make an engraving of one of Daguerre's pictures, which is in the Luxembourg Gallery (1), I called to show him the outline which I had made from it: that is how I made his acquaintance. I have not seen him since until I went to see one of his paintings at the Diorama. I also had to submit to him at the end of the month a proof of my "gravure" which is nearly finished. As far as my opinion of M. Daguerre is concerned, he has, as a painter, an excellent talent for imitation and an exquisite taste for the effects in his tableaux. I think he has a rare genius for anything relating to machines and for lighting effects. The amateur visiting his establishment is quite amazed. I know that for a long time he has worked to improve the camera obscura without, however, knowing the end for which he is working, such as I have heard from you and from the Comte de Mandelot, to whom, also, you have spoken of it." (2)

It was precisely a camera obscura which caused Daguerre to establish relations with Niepce. In the beginning of 1826 Nicéphore requested one of his relatives, Colonel Laurent Niepce, passing through Paris, to buy for him at the optician's, Chevalier father and son, a camera obscura equipped with a meniscus prism. (3) The Colonel mentioned Niepce's researches and also showed a copy of a gravure on metal. (4) Several persons were present at the time, among them the Comte de Mandelot, who were very much surprised. The Chevaliers were also interested because the painter Daguerre, one of their customers, had sought to interest them for more than a year in similar researches. They related the visit to him and gave him Niepce's address. Daguerre failed to understand the details; but a few days later Niepce received a letter from him. (5) This was the beginning of the relations between the two inventors.

Arago, in 1839, relates the above incident as follows: "It was the indiscretion of a Parisian optician which informed him (Nicéphore Niepce) that M. Daguerre was making experiments having also as their object the fixation of the images of the camera obscura." This strangely distorts the truth. Daguerre, who informed Arago, often had a short memory. (6)

DAGUERRE ADDRESSES NIEPCE
REFERENCES: CHAPTER XIX

1. *Galerie du Luxembourg: des Musées, Palais et Châteaux de France*, published by Liébert.
2. Lemaître to Niepce, *La Lumière*, February 16, 1851.
3. Revised by Charles Chevalier (1804-1859) in 1823. (*Etude sur la vie et les travaux de Charles Chevalier*, by his son, Arthur Chevalier, Paris, 1862.)
4. The subject was a young woman at a spinning wheel. This heliograph seems to have been lost.
5. *Etude sur la vie et les travaux de Charles Chevalier;* also Fouque, p.117, which gives Colonel Laurent Niepce's testimony.
6. See Chevalier, *Etude sur la vie*, etc., where he complains bitterly of Arago.

CHAPTER XX

Daguerre and the Diorama

NIEPCE'S life has been investigated down to the smallest details. It is not so with Daguerre, although he carried away the greater part of the glory.

We know hardly anything of this inventor, with the exception of a volume by Mentienne (1), other than the information printed in the journals at the time of his death. Perhaps even these may be discounted a little because it is the custom to heap flowers upon graves. I have given the bibliography of Daguerre and the sources in order that his history might be written more fully than it has been done up to the present. (2)

Daguerre was born in the small village of Cormeilles-en-Parisis (3) (Seine et Oise), November 18, 1787.

His father exercised the humble functions of a clerk in the local bailiff's office; his mother belonged to an old family at Cormeilles and, it is said, was of noble birth. In 1792, when the child was five years old, Daguerre, the father, moved with his family to Orléans where he had obtained employment on the royal estate, and there grew and was educated Louis-Jacques-Mandé Daguerre, who was afterwards so famous. In fact, his education was not what it should have been; his childhood lacked attention and his instruction was neglected. The times were difficult and his father was poor. Young Daguerre showed a strong inclination for drawing and his parents, who had hoped that he would enter the administration of the estate, placed him against their wishes with an architect at Orléans. Tradition states that he manifested a particular aptitude for architecture by drawing the caricature of his employer on the plans, prints, and other working papers. Three years later, after many requests, he succeeded in being sent to Paris and entered the studio of Degotti (4), a scenic painter who worked for the Opera. There, at once, the young man's talent was recognized; Degotti was an excellent teacher, but Daguerre was a still better pupil.

This alert and robust boy, acrobat, so said his friends (5), possessed "mens sana in corpore sano" (a healthy mind in a healthy body), quick to perceive, tenacious in his efforts, at the same time bold and persevering. His temperament enabled him to carry on his work with an energy which the others could not match. His intense devotion to his work, being sure of himself, and obstinate, made him the master of his destiny. This was the origin of all his success. He proved himself, moreover, to be unselfish, a friend worthy of confidence, generous, eager for glory; in short, an exceptional nature.

Thrown by his work and taste among people of the theatre, he became fond of their easy morals and their adventurous existence. It is not usual that one learns moderation and economy in a painter's studio. But this exuberance of youth did not prevent him from perfecting his insufficient knowledge and continuing to extend the study of his profession. In 1812, he married a young woman of English extraction, Louise-Georgine Arronsmith (6) whose brothers were his fellow workers. They had no children. About 1820, a brother of Madame Daguerre, dying, left a very young daughter born out of wedlock. The Daguerres decided to bring up this child and finished by taking her into their home and treating her as their own daughter.

Daguerre, although young, acquired enough reputation in a few years to be placed in charge of the decoration of the theatre Ambigu, and shortly after he worked for the Opéra-Comique. Degotti, having left the Opéra, Daguerre returned there no longer as a pupil but as a master. The decorative art of the theatre was at that time in its infancy and the method used extremely poor, especially the lighting effects. Oil lamps are not easy to manipulate, nor are they very efficient instruments for the change and distribution of light. Above all, Daguerre concerned himself with the introduction of new light effects. His decorations became the style and some of them created a sensation, according to his contemporaries. Such, for instance, were those of the "Vampire" at the Ambigu, a gloomy, dark melodrama wherein the stars of the night passed in the solitary sky painted on cardboard, with a dismal cemetery in the distance. Then again, there was a movable sun in the "lampe merveilleuse" at the Opéra. Such things had never been seen before. Then there were his paintings in the Machabées, the Belvéder, Calas, Klodie, the Forest of Senart, the Chapel of Glen-Korn, which had caused a revolution in the decorative art of the theatre. In fact, Daguerre was unique as a decorative artist. His sketches exhibited at numerous salons were always preparatory studies, more or less elaborate, of decorations for the Diorama. It is difficult for us to appreciate the talent of Daguerre, the painter, because there is nothing left of his real work, which was devoted to the decorative art of the theatre, and which we can judge only by what is left of the scenes he executed. Of his sketches, although

his contemporaries mention a great number, few remain. Our museums
have none; undoubtedly they are hidden in private collections. I know
of only one, belonging to Mentienne, representing a view of Mont Blanc,
made for the Diorama, painted with a great deal of care, correct, pleas-
ing in colour and showing an evident search by the artist to secure
atmospheric effects. The same care in the separation of distance of
receding planes is noticed in two small tableaux preserved by the Société
Française de Photographie (7), as well as another — a landscape in pastel
— which is rather mediocre. This quite accords with the estimate of
Daguerre by his contemporaries. (8) But his main work, by which he
gained his reputation, is the Diorama.

The Diorama was nothing but a variation of the panorama, thought
out, it is said, by Breysig and created in England by Robert Berker,
about 1793. The first seen in Paris was shown by Fulton in 1803. (9)
These show places were very popular during a long period. I have found
no less than eight open to the public in 1822; to which must be added
the Diorama, inaugurated July 11, 1822 in a building specially constructed after Daguerre's plans at No.4 rue Sanson. This street, laid out
on the grounds of the old palace of Sanson, the treasurer of the mint, ran
parallel to the faubourg du Temple, starting at the rue de Bondy, and
ended at the Boulevard Saint-Martin which was reached by some steps
at the Chateau d'Eau; it corresponds to the present rue de la Douane.
In that same street, at No.3 was the Vaux-hall d'été, opened in 1785,
where visitors found "a large garden, a dance hall, a café, and artistically
arranged fireworks." At the beginning of Boulevard Saint-Martin, if one
turned to the left, many theatres attracted great crowds: Lyrique,
Cirque Olympique, Folies Dramatiques, Gaîté, Funambules, Délasse-
ments comiques, etc. It was these which gave the Boulevard du Temple
the name of *boulevard of crime*, because of the tragedies that were staged
there. The Diorama was thus located in the center of the theatrical
attractions of the Paris of that time.

The spectacle, as in similar places, consisted of a landscape, sometimes a monument, where real objects, posed in the foreground, melted
in a harmonious manner with subjects painted to furnish the middle
planes, appearing on a canvas 13 m. high, 20 m. wide and 15 m. distant
from the audience. The whole thing gave an illusion of space and reality.
The lighting played an important part here, because it is the quantity
of vertical light falling between the spectator and the scene which produces the feeling of atmospheric perspective. A remarkable innovation

was added to these ordinary artifices: The tableaux permitted a kind of change of view obtained by means which completely mystified the astonished audience. I cannot do better than to quote the words of an eyewitness to a tableaux entitled: "A Midnight Mass at Saint-Etienne-du-Mont." "At first, it is daylight; we see the nave with its chairs; little by little the light wanes and the candles were lighted. In the rear of the choir, the church is illuminated and the faithful, arriving, take their places in front of the chairs, not hurriedly, as if the scenes were shifted, but gradually, quickly enough to amaze, but without exciting surprise. The midnight mass begins. In this reverent stillness the organ peals out from under the distant vaults. Now the daylight slowly returns, the congregation disperses, the candles are extinguished and the church with its chairs appears as at the beginning. This was magic." (10) I have made a list—undoubtedly incomplete—of the tableaux of the Diorama. They are as follows:

The interior of St. Peter's at Rome, by Bouton.

The midnight mass at Saint-Etienne-du-Mont, the first and one of the best tableaux of Daguerre.

A view of the Basilica of Saint-Peter and Saint-Paul outside the walls.

The Abbey of Roslyn in snow and fog (1824).

The chapel of Holyrood (1824) for which Daguerre was awarded the Cross of the Chevalier of the Legion d'honneur.

A view showing the vicinity of Naples.

The Saarnen Valley, in Switzerland.

The village of Unterseen, in Switzerland.

The Edinburgh fire.

The bridge of Thiers.

Mt. Saint-Gothard.

The cemetery at Pisa.

A view of Paris from Montmartre.

The tomb of Napoleon at St. Helena.

Mont-Blanc.

The Black Forest.

The central basin at Ghent.

The Goldau Valley.

The Church of Sainte-Marie, Montreal.

The port of Boulogne. (11)

July 28, 1830, at the City Hall, Paris.

The rise of the Flood, of which a sketch was shown at the Salon in 1840.

Solomon's Temple (1839), the last decorative painting by Daguerre for the Diorama.

The Diorama was not the work of Daguerre alone. He conceived the idea while he worked in the establishment of Prévost (1764-1823) from the panoramas painted by that artist. Daguerre, not sure of himself, although he had already become famous as a decorative painter, joined Bouton (1781-1853), an excellent painter of interiors; together they created the Diorama with the aid of a stock company. The partnership did not last long and Daguerre became the sole proprietor and had to purchase the shares held by the other stockholders. The profits amounted, it is said, in some years, to 200,000 francs, which is equal to a million francs today, because the Diorama was a remarkable success. According to the newspapers of the day, all Paris and all France visited it.

Such was the Diorama which, of itself, deserves lasting memory. For another reason the Diorama is of value to us. It was there that Daguerre made his researches and experiments; there he discovered the Daguerreotype. A fragment of the map of Paris in 1838 shows the site occupied by the Diorama. This quarter has undergone great changes on account of the opening of the Place du Château d'Eau in 1862; and from there the rue des Marais extends to the Faubourg du Temple. The Diorama comprised a theatre on the rue Sanson, a garden and a residence on the corner of the rue des Marais, where Bouton lived and later Daguerre. Today, one of the military barracks occupies this location at the end of the rue des Marais.

1. *La découverte de la Photographie en 1839* by Mentienne, Paris 1892. This partial book must be read with proper precaution in regard to everything that relates to the discovery of the daguerreotype. Mentienne knew Daguerre in his youth and received information from his father of many details about the inventor, which are important to us. See also Carpentier, *Notice sur Daguerre*, Paris 1855, a short but exact biography, written by a man who was Daguerre's intimate friend. The Société Française de Photographie also has a number of documents concerning Daguerre and his work. Other works are based only on hearsay.
2. In the *Bulletin de la Société Française de Photographie*, March, 1920: "Sur les débuts de la photographie."
3. His birthplace still exists there.
4. Desgotti; this is the name given in Bottin's Directory: Desgotti, scene painter, Barrière Poisonnière, aux cinq moulins; Carpentier spells it Dégotis; Mentienne, Degotis; Degoty, according to Robertson. He arrived in Paris about 1790 with letters of recommendation from Comte d'Artois (*Mémoires récréatifs, scientifiques et anecdotiques*), Paris, 1831, 1-70.
5. *Magasin pittoresque de 1868*, vol.36; p.250.
6. Born in 1790, died in 1857, Mentienne (in the work cited above) writes Arronsmith. A niece of Mme. Daguerre was good enough to furnish me with additional information on the spelling of her name, Arronsmith. The name inscribed on the tomb at Bry-sur-Marne is Arrowsmith. The Directory of Painters of Siret also prints: Arrowsmith (Charles) who was Daguerre's brother-in-law.
7. Regarding the relics of Daguerre, see *Bulletin de la Société Française de Photographie*, March 1920 and April 1920.
8. See addresses delivered at the dedication of Daguerre's monument in 1852. Mentienne, p.116.
9. Robert Fulton (1765-1815), famous engineer, was first a designer and painter. Robertson states in his memoirs that he himself about 1802 undertook to produce a panorama on the site of the old Capucine convent. He had a view of Paris made by Fontaine and Bouton, taken from the terrace of the Tuilleries. But Robertson was evicted by Fulton who acquired the site and the painting and who took the place of the originator (E.-G.Robertson: *Mémoires récréatifs, scientifiques et anecdotiques*, Paris, 1831, 1.322).
10. Manuscript belongs to the Société Française de Photographie.
11. This and the following items have been given me by Cromer who owns reproductions of them in his valuable collection.

CHAPTER XXI

Daguerre and Photography

ON a summer's day in 1823, in the studio of the Diorama, Daguerre noticed the image of a tree projected through a very small hole in the shutter, closed on account of the heat, on a tableau which he had finished. The next day by chance, examining this painting, he was surprised to see that the image remained. That gave him the idea of trying to fix the image of the camera. After many unsuccessful trials to reproduce this phenomenon, he at last remembered that he had mixed iodine with his colours when painting his tableaux; here began his researches in the sensitivity of iodine and the iodides. This statement, although coming from the inventor himself, seems to me like a legend (1); it contradicts the recollection of Chevalier and it is certain that Daguerre did not begin his experiments with iodine.

Charles Chevalier (2), in his *Souvenirs*, says that Daguerre lived in the rue de Crussol at the time when he made the decorations for the Ambigu (before 1822), and that Daguerre came into his store almost every week and spoke incessantly of fixing the image of the camera. One day, he cried out: I have found it, but he had no image to show, and talked of it no more. The truth is that Daguerre, strange as it seems, used the camera obscura for making drawings. The idea thus came to him, after Wedgwood, after Niepce, to seek to make permanent these fugitive images. He had equipped a laboratory in the Diorama where, all alone, he devoted himself to mysterious experiments which, it seems, came to nothing. "I had a glimpse into that laboratory" said Chevalier (3) "but neither I nor any others were permitted to enter. Mme. Daguerre, Bouton, Sibon, Carpentier can testify to that." The celebrated chemist, J.-B. Dumas, who was a witness and was perhaps familiar with Daguerre's experiments, told the following story: "In 1827, when I was still young, I was told that someone wished to speak to me. It was Mme. Daguerre. She came to consult me on the subject of her husband's researches, which she feared would be a failure. She did not hide her anxiety for the future and asked me if there was any hope that her husband might realize his dream and, timidly, whether there was not some way to have him declared incapable of managing his affairs. (4)

Daguerre, in fact, surrendered himself with ardour, aye, with frenzy

114

to anything which caught his interest for the moment. Oblivious to time, he shut himself in his workroom for several days, bolting the food brought to him, without sleep, obsessed by his idea, until he had discovered some mechanical contrivance or until he had finished a particular decoration. (5) While Daguerre, under these conditions, made his experiments on light, dreaming only of them, speaking of nothing else and refusing conversation on any other subject, the optician, Chevalier, gave him Niepce's address.

1. Mentienne confirms having heard Daguerre relate this.
2. *Etude sur la vie et les travaux de Ch.Chevalier* by A.Chevalier, his son, Paris, 1862, p.140.
3. A.Chevalier, work cited.
4. Mentienne, p.127: This incident is reported by Félix Hément in *Paris-Photographe*, April 25, 1891, as related by J.-B.Dumas at the dedication of the monument at Cormeilles in 1883. J.-B.Dumas had told this anecdote at the Société d'Encouragement in 1864 without mentioning Mme.Daguerre's name. *Bulletin de la Société d'Encouragement pour l'Industrie Nationale*, 1864, 2nd series, vol.XI, p.194.
5. Manuscript notes of Carpentier belonging to the Société Française de Photographie. *Bulletin de la Société d'Encouragement pour l'Industrie Nationale*, 1864, p.194.

CHAPTER XXII

Niepce's Visits to Paris and London

I HAVE mentioned that Daguerre had written twice to Niepce, in January 1826 and in January 1827 and that Niepce, having made inquiries, had learned that the unknown correspondent was a talented painter and the founder of a famous establishment. Daguerre asked to see a proof; Niepce refused. (1) With unwearied patience, entirely contrary to Daguerre's character, he renewed his attack and offered to Niepce "a little design in sepia, very elegantly framed, and finished by means of his process". This design, which represented an interior, was quite effective, although it could not be determined whether it was photographic or if the work of a brush had been added. And Niepce adds, speaking to Lemaître, "perhaps, Monsieur, you already know this sort of a design, which the author calls "dessin-fumée" and which can be bought at the shop of Alphonse Giroux." (2)

It seems certain—judging from the text of Niepce's letter—that Daguerre represented this proof as having been made in part by the aid of the photographic process. The "dessin-fumée" cannot be called "photographic" as far as can be affirmed. Hamman states (3) in his work on the graphic arts: "The Abbé Soulacrois in 1839 also used this solution (10 gr. of white gum lac in 100 gr. of alcohol) for making designs produced with the carbon of a candle to which he added a few touches of sepia, and emphasized the highlights with twisted pieces of paper in order to give them all the verve of a wash drawing. The real inventor of the "dessin-fumée" seems to be Mandé Daguerre." We must add to this passage Mentienne's statement: "When death stopped him, he (Daguerre) had occupied himself equally with a new process of monochrome painting of which his niece, Mme.de Sainville, whom he had adopted as his daughter, possessed splendid specimens. This painting was executed on glass and was viewed from the other side. The glass served him as varnish. They were made with a black pigment, which gave the effect of incomparable strength. The lights were obtained by means of the transparency of the more or less thick coating of this black pigment, and by placing a white material behind the picture. These exquisite, strong, original effects were not produced with the brush, but with the finger. What a firm and expert hand was required to achieve these new results! He has left behind him no indication of the means he used to attain them." (4)

Whatever these "dessin-fumée" might be, Niepce felt himself under obligations and, on the 4th of June 1827, he sent to Daguerre a heliograph and the following letter: "Sir, you will receive practically at the same time as my letter a box containing a pewter plate engraved by my heliographic process and a proof of this same plate which is defective and very weak . . . . Will you be good enough to tell me what you think of it. This is not one of my most recent results, it dates from last spring. (5) Since then I have been diverted from my researches by other matters. I shall take this work up again today because the countryside is in its full splendour and lends itself more than ever for the copying of "points de vue" from nature . . . . You will probably ask why I engrave on pewter instead of on copper. I have used copper as well; but in my first attempts I had to prefer pewter . . . because the clear whiteness of this metal tends to render more exactly the image of the object which it represents." (6) Daguerre made a sharp criticism of the plate sent to him. This is at present preserved in the collection of the Société Française de Photographie. It is the kind of a criticism from which anyone today may judge the judge.

The matter might have rested there if Niepce did not find it necessary to go to England, owing to an alarming report about the health of his brother Claude. Nicéphore and his wife started on this journey towards the end of August 1827; remained for a few days in Paris, owing to the necessary passport formalities. While there, they visited Lemaître and Daguerre, and Daguerre showed them the Diorama. Nicéphore communicated some of his impressions to his son in a letter which is one of the rare documents informing us about the first photographic work of Daguerre. (7) "I had frequent and long interviews with M. Daguerre. He visited us yesterday and stayed for three hours. We shall have to return his visit before we depart, and I am not certain how long we will stay with him because this will be the last time and the conversation we shall have on this subject in which we are both interested is verily endless. I must repeat to you, my dear Isidore, what I have told M. de Champmartin. I have not seen anything here that impressed me more, or gave me as much pleasure as the Diorama. M. Daguerre conducted us personally and we had the opportunity to observe everything, taking our time to see the magnificent tableaux which are there exhibited. The interior view of Saint Peter's at Rome, by M. Bouton, is certainly an admirable work and produces the most complete illusion. Nothing is finer than the two views painted by M. Daguerre, one of Edinburgh, taken by moonlight during a fire; the other of a Swiss village, looking down a wide street, facing a mountain of tremendous height, covered with eternal snow. (8) These pictures are so real, even in the smallest details, that one believes oneself actually seeing rural and primeval nature, with all the fascination which the charm of colours and the magic of light and shade endow it. The illusion is even so great that one is tempted to leave his box in order to wander in the open and climb to the summit of the mountain. I can assure you there is not the least exaggeration on my part. The objects, moreover, were, or seemed to be, of a natural grandeur . . . . But let us return to M. Daguerre. I must tell you, my dear Isidore, that he insists that I am further advanced than he in the researches which we are both pursuing. One thing is fully demonstrated, this is that his process and mine are entirely different. His process is a marvelous thing and he accomplishes his results with a rapidity which we might compare with that of the electric current. M. Daguerre has arrived at a point where he can add to his chemical substance some of the coloured rays of the prism. He had already reunited four and he is now at work to reunite the other three, in order to have the seven primary colours. But the difficulties which he encounters constantly grow in proportion to the modifications which the mentioned substance must undergo in order to combine several colours at the same time. His greatest obstacle, and that which mystifies him completely, lies in the fact that these different combinations result in entirely opposite effects. Thus, a strong shadow projected through a blue glass onto the mentioned substance will produce a lighter tone than the same shade when viewed in the direct light. On the other hand, this fixation of elementary colours results in tints so fugitive and feeble that one does not see them at all in daylight; they are only visible in darkness and this is the reason: the substance in question is like the *Bologna stone* and like *pyrophore*. It absorbs the light eagerly but cannot retain it for any length of time, because the action of this fluid, when prolonged, ends by decomposing it. M. Daguerre also does not pretend to be able to make the coloured images of objects permanent by this process, even though he could succeed in surmounting all the obstacles which he encounters; he was able to apply this method only as an intermediate step. After what he told me, there is little hope of his success and his researches can hardly have any other object than that of pure curiosity , . . . He requested that I make some experiments with coloured glasses, in order to ascertain whether the impression produced upon my substance would be the same as on his. (I have ordered five glasses from Chevalier Vincent, such as he already has made for M. Daguerre . . . . M. Daguerre's chemical compound is a very fine powder, which does not adhere to the material on which it is projected, which necessitates using the plate on a horizontal plane. This powder, on the slightest exposure to light, becomes so luminous that the camera obscura is entirely illuminated by it. This process is very analogous, as far as I can recall, to *sulfate de baryte* or the *Bologna stone*, as both have the same property of retaining certain of the prismatic rays." (9)

Without discussing this letter any further, we must conclude that in 1827 Daguerre's photographic discoveries amounted to nothing, because he had not succeeded in obtaining an image. But his talent, his reputation, his great establishment, and without doubt his superior personality had impressed Nicéphore Niepce.

NIEPCE'S VISITS TO PARIS AND LONDON
REFERENCES: CHAPTER XXII

1. Letter from Niepce to Daguerre, February 2, 1827, published by Isidore Niepce in the *Historique de la Découverte improprement nommée Daguerréotype*.
2. Niepce to Lemaître, April 3, 1827 in *La Lumière* of March 9, 1851. The stationer Giroux was a relative of Mme. Daguerre.
3. *Des Arts graphiques* by J.-M.-H. Hammann, Geneva, 1857.
4. Mentienne: *La Découverte de la Photographie en 1839*, p.111; Carpentier (work cited, p.23) gives the same details.
5. This fixes the date when the proof was obtained: The Spring of 1827.
6. Niepce to Daguerre, June 4, 1827 in the *Historique de la Découverte*, etc. p.23. This letter is not at the Museum at Chalon.
7. Nicéphore Niepce to Isidore, September 2 and 4, 1827, No.57 at the Museum at Chalon.
8. La Société Française de Photographie has a sketch of this tableau of the Diorama made at Unterseen by Daguerre in 1826.
9. Carpentier in *Notice sur Daguerre*, confirms all these details and Daguerre's lack of confidence in the final success. On phosphorescence and its history, see Chapter XXIV.

CHAPTER XXIII

Niepce's Visit to England

NIEPCE and his wife arrived at Kew, one of London's suburbs, in October 1827 and found Claude desperately ill. Desperate also was the condition of his affairs and full of cruel disappointments. "I want to spare your feelings and ours, my dear Isidore," writes Nicéphore, "by refraining from the sad details. Our troubles are lessened by seeing my poor brother indifferent to his condition and more occupied with agreeable illusions which hide from him his true condition . . . . He has been ill for some time — for five or six years, we have been told — and without our knowledge! We were also unaware that *the great news and the success of perpetual motion* were nothing but a dream, the vain delusions of a delirious brain. As far as we can see, his illness is without remedy . . . . As far as the pyreolophore and the hydraulic machine are concerned, I do not know what we can do about it; we have no intention to risk any further expense on these two ventures . . . ." (1)

What a catastrophe! Thirty years of work, protracted efforts, loans which they could not repay, exceeding their fortune, their whole existence threatened by this machine and, at the end, nothing left of their hopes but smoke which vanished! What a bitter result! But nature had made Nicéphore an inventor. Distressed about the future, afflicted by the condition of his tenderly beloved brother, terribly disappointed, he still had no doubt of his own invention, this heliography, which thus far had not produced any great results. He made use of his stay in London to display there his designed and engraved plates. (2) He also solicited an audience with the King and a presentation to the Royal Society.

A note (3) written for this purpose did not contain the details of his manipulation, because Niepce intended to guard his secret. This created an obstacle and, because of this, the presentation to the King and to the Royal Society did not take place. Since the inventor did not wish to make known in what his discovery consisted, his plates were returned to him, together with his memoir and the matter ended with that. Nevertheless, the propaganda which he made in England was not fruitless. An English scientist, Francis Bauer, whom Niepce knew through his brother Claude, made himself the champion of heliography and twelve years later contributed valuable testimony to the memory of Niepce. A fact still more important is that, among the persons who then saw the proofs and the memoir of Niepce was Fox Talbot.

HISTORY OF THE DISCOVERY OF PHOTOGRAPHY
REFERENCES: CHAPTER XXIII

1. Nicéphore to Isidore Niepce, November 5, 1827. This letter is not in the Museum at Chalon.
2. Made by contact and others made in the camera. T.N.
3. Published for the first time by Fouque in 1867. It contains nothing of particular interest.

CHAPTER XXIV

Niepce's Association with Daguerre

NIEPCE and his wife returned to France in January 1828, several days before Claude died. The difficulties which followed did not prevent a realization of a project which had been anticipated by Niepce during his earlier stay in Paris. Because from that moment, the inventor had contemplated the possibility and perhaps the desirability of an association with Daguerre. In 1828 Niepce was 63 years old and very much embarrassed financially. He asked himself whether he could not, by exploiting his discovery, recover the fortune, dissipated in the development of his invention. He was unfamiliar with affairs, having lived in retirement in the country since he was twenty-six years old, in debt, getting old, not knowing any other branch of industry in which to engage. On the other hand, here was Daguerre, young, famous, engaged in the same work, moreover an artist, a determining factor for Niepce, who was convinced that only an artist could succeed in heliography. Daguerre must have seemed to him to be the ideal associate. Nevertheless two more years passed, two years of negotiations, two years of hesitation on the part of Niepce, during which, however, he kept up a regular correspondence with Daguerre.

Hardly anything remains but the package sent by Niepce on October 4, 1829 containing a photograph taken — as always — from the window of his room, which Daguerre and Lemaître criticized so severely, as I have related. (1) The draft of the Introduction, of which I have given the unpublished text on page 64, must be ascribed to this period. There is an allusion to Phosphorescence and to Daguerre's experiments and a mention of the voyage to London. Meanwhile, Niepce decided to publish the manipulation of his process. Thus this work preceded his association with Daguerre, which had an exactly opposite purpose and was one of the various projects which made Niepce hesitate. Urged at the same time by the desire for publicity, that is, for immediate fame or for financial gain, which required secrecy, the poor inventor chose the money.

So, toward the end of October 1829 Niepce offered to Daguerre to "cooperate with him for the purpose of perfecting the heliographic processes and to combine their advantages, which might result in a complete

125

success." Niepce, somewhat naively, it seems, made the same offer to Lemaître who accepted "with thanks". But Lemaître does not appear in the subsequent negotiations. Daguerre, no doubt, thought that there were enough associates. The agreement which bound Niepce to Daguerre was signed on December 14, 1829. The text has been published several times (2) and is here again reproduced, because it is essential that the reader peruse the original documents.

(On pp.136, 137, 138, 139 in M.Potonniée's book there is reproduced in facsimile: "Bases du Traité Provisoire" (Basis of Provisional Agreement), T.N.) (3)

We read in this document that "*Monsieur Daguerre invites Monsieur Niepce to join him in order to obtain the perfection of a new method discovered by Monsieur Niepce, for fixing the images of nature without having recourse to an artist.*" The Society took the title Niepce-Daguerre. The term of the partnership was fixed at ten years. In case of the death of Niepce, his son Isidore was to replace him. Niepce contributed "as his part, his invention, representing the value of half the yield which the Society is capable." Daguerre contributed, "a new adaptation of the camera obscura, his talents and his labour, equivalent to the other half of the above-mentioned yield." Here are two halves very unequal. As compensation for the invention of which Niepce divulged the secret only very hesitatingly, Daguerre furnished an improvement of the camera obscura — a questionable one — and an uncertain engagement to perfect heliography and to make it of practical utility. It really did not exist at this time, which does not detract from the merit of the inventor, because we must distinguish between the commercial value and the scientific value of a discovery. Who made any money out of colour photography by the interference method? No one. Nevertheless, would anyone dare to challenge the right of Lippmann to be called an inventor?

Fortunately, aside from the items mentioned above, Daguerre contributed valuable assets, although they are not mentioned, namely: his name, and the reputation which attached to it, his confidence in himself, his habitual success and the great advantage of presumably having the future before him, because he was only forty-two years old. Of his discoveries in photography, nothing appears in the contract and justly so because the name of the firm was "Niepce-Daguerre", inasmuch as Niepce furnished everything and Daguerre nothing.

As a consequence of this contract, Niepce communicated to his associate the detailed description of his process in the form of a note, written

126

in duplicate, which both signed. Niepce's copy is now in the possession of the family; I do not know (4) where Daguerre's copy can be found.

NOTE ON HELIOGRAPHY BY M.Jh-Nre NIEPCE
The discovery which I have made and designate by the name *Heliography* consists in the *spontaneous* reproduction, by the action of light, with their gradations of tones from black to white, of the images obtained in the camera obscura.

FUNDAMENTAL PRINCIPLE OF THIS DISCOVERY
Light, in the state of combination and decomposition, reacts chemically on substances. It is absorbed by them, combines with them, and imparts to them new properties. It augments the natural density of some substances, it even solidifies them and renders them more or less insoluble, according to the duration or intensity of its action. This is, in a few words, the principle of the invention.

FIRST SUBSTANCE — PREPARATION
The first substance or material which I use, the one which makes my process most successful and which contributes more directly to the production of the effect, is *asphaltum* or *bitumen of Judea*, prepared in the following manner. I fill half a glass with this pulverized bitumen. I pour, drop by drop, essential oil of lavender on it until the bitumen will absorb no more and it has been entirely penetrated by it. Then I add enough of this essential oil so that it stands about three lignes above this mixture, which must then be covered and left in a moderate temperature until the added essence is saturated by the colouring matter of the bitumen. If this varnish is not of the required degree of consistency, it is allowed to evaporate in a dish in the open air, protecting it against moisture which would change it and finally decompose it. This mishap is particularly to be feared during the cold, and humid season when making experiments in the camera. A small amount of this varnish, applied cold to a highly polished silvered plate with a very soft leather ball (tampon), gives the plate a beautiful ruby colour and spreads itself over it in a thin and uniform coating. The plate is then placed on a hot iron plate covered with several layers of paper, from which the moisture has been previously removed; the varnish is now no longer tacky, the plate is withdrawn for cooling and is finished by drying it at a moderate temperature, protected from contact with moist air. I must not forget to call attention to the fact that it is principally in the application of the varnish that this precaution is indispensable. In this case, a thin disk, in the

center of which a short stick held in the mouth is fixed, is sufficient to arrest and condense the moisture of the breath. A plate prepared in this manner can be exposed immediately to the action of the luminous fluid; but even after having been exposed long enough to ensure that the effect had been obtained, nothing indicates that the image really exists because the impression remains invisible. It is, therefore, a question of bringing out the picture, and this can only be accomplished by the aid of a solvent.

SOLVENT — MANNER OF PREPARATION

Since the solvent must be adjusted according to the result to be obtained, it is difficult to determine exactly the proportions of the composition. But, all things being equal, it had better be weaker rather than too strong. The mixture I preferably employ is composed, by volume not by weight, of one part of essential oil of lavender to six parts, same measure, of white oil of petroleum. The mixture which at first shows quite milky, becomes perfectly clear at the end of two or three days and can be used several times in succession, losing its desolvable property only when it approaches the saturation point which is recognized because it becomes opaque and of a very turbid colour; but it can be distilled and rendered as good as before.

The plate or varnished tablet, having been removed from the camera, is put in a tinned dish, an inch deep, longer and wider than the plate, and is covered by a considerable quantity of solvent until entirely immersed. When the plate is plunged in this liquid and is viewed at a certain angle in indirect light, the impression will appear, revealing itself little by little, although still veiled by the oil, which floats on the surface, more or less saturated with varnish. The plate is then removed and placed in a perpendicular position, in order that it may be well drained of the solvent. When the plate is completely drained, I proceed to the last operation, by no means the least important.

WASHING — MANNER OF PROCEDURE

It is sufficient for this to have only a very simple apparatus, composed of a board four feet long and wider than the plate. On the long side of the board two strips are nailed, which form a ledge two inches high. The ledge is fastened by hinges to a support at the top, which permits it to be inclined at will, in order to pour the water on to the plate as rapidly as required. At the lower end of the board is a vessel for catching the water which flows off. The plate is placed on the inclined board and prevented from sliding by two small hooks, which, however, must not be higher than the plate. It is necessary at this season to use lukewarm water. It is not flowed directly on the plate but from above, in order that, falling on it, it will carry away the last particles of the oil adhering to the varnish. The image will now be completely developed and will show everywhere perfect definition, if the operation has been well done, and especially if one has a perfected camera at one's disposal.

APPLICATION OF THE HELIOGRAPHIC PROCESS

Since the varnish can be applied equally to stone, metal, and glass, without change of manipulation, I shall confine myself to the method of application to silvered plates and glass, however noting that in engraving on copper there may be added without inconvenience to the varnish mixture a small quantity of wax, dissolved in lavender oil.

Up to now silvered plates seem to me best for the production of images, owing to their white colour and resplendency. There is no doubt that the result obtained will be satisfactory, after washing, provided the image is quite dry. It would be desirable, however, if, by blackening the plate, all the gradations of tone from black to white could be obtained. I, therefore, devoted myself to this object by using at first a solution of potassium sulphide (sulfure de potasse liquide). When used in concentrated form it attacks the varnish, and if diluted with water, it only turns the metal red. This twofold defect compelled me to give up this medium. The substance which I am now using with greater hope for success is iodine, which has the property of evaporating at ordinary temperature. In order to blacken the plate by this process, it is only necessary to place the plate against the inner side of a box open at the top, and to put a few grains of iodine into a small groove in the opposite side on the bottom of the box. It is then covered with a glass, in order to judge the effect which, if it operates less rapidly, is, on the other hand, more certain. The varnish can then be removed with alcohol and not a trace remains of the original image. Since this process is still quite new for me, I shall confine myself to this simple modification, until experience has enriched me with more information on the exact details. Two attempts in making a "point de vue" on glass, made in the camera obscura, have presented results which, although still faulty, seem to me necessary to record, because this method of application can be more easily perfected and therefore may later become of very particular interest.

In one of these experiments, the light, having acted with less intensity, uncovered the varnish in such a manner that the gradations of tones showed more clearly so that the image seen by transmission reproduced, up to a certain point, the well known effects of the Diorama. In the other experiment, however, where the action of the luminous fluid was more intense, the parts most illuminated, not having been affected by the solvent, remained transparent and the difference of tones resulted solely from the proportionate thickness of the greater or lesser opacity of the varnish. If the image is received by reflection in a mirror from the varnished side, and held at a certain angle, it produces a striking effect, while, if viewed by transmission, it presents only a confused and colourless image and, what is more astonishing, it seems to affect the local colours of certain objects. Meditating on this remarkable fact, I was led to believe that I might draw certain conclusions from it, which would permit me to connect them with Newton's theory on the phenomenon of coloured rings. It would be sufficient for this purpose to suppose that such a prismatic ray, the green for instance, acting on the substance of the varnish and combining with it, gave it the necessary degree of solubility, so that the layer which had formed by this method, after the double operation of the developer and the rinsing, would reflect the green colour. Finally I have made this observation merely in order to determine the truth of this hypothesis and the matter seems to me of sufficient interest to provoke a continuance of the research and deserves a more profound examination.

REMARKS

Although undoubtedly there is no difficulty in the method which I have explained, the result may not at first be completely successful. I believe, therefore, that it is advisable to start in a small way by copying engravings in diffused light according to the following very simple method:

The engraving is varnished on the reverse side only, in order to make it thoroughly transparent. When completely dry, the engraving is placed, right side down, on the varnished plate under a glass, diminishing the pressure by inclining the plate at an angle of 45 degrees. In this manner, several experiments can be made in the course of a day, using two engravings, thus prepared, and four small silvered plates. This can be done even in overcast weather, providing that the room is protected against cold and especially against moisture which, I repeat, deteriorates the varnish to such a point that it will come off the plate in layers when immersed in the solvent. This prevented me from using the camera obscura during the inclement season. Repeating the experiments of which I have spoken will soon enable one to carry out the manipulation of the process in its entirety. Concerning the manner of applying the varnish, I must recall that it can be used only in a consistency thick enough to form a compact and as thin a coating as possible, so it may better resist the action of the solvent, and at the same time become more sensitive to the action of light.

Concerning the use of iodine for blackening the images on silvered plates, as well as regarding the acid for etching the copper, it is essential that the varnish, after rinsing, be used just as described in the report given above in the second experiment on glass; because it becomes thus less permeable, both in acid and under the iodine vapours, particularly in those parts where it has preserved its full transparency, for only under these conditions can one hope, even with the best optical apparatus, to arrive at a completely successful end.

Executed in duplicate at Chalon-sur-Saône November 24, 1829.

J.-N. NIEPCE.

ADDITIONS

When the varnished plate is removed for drying, it must be protected not only against moisture, but care must be taken to shield it from exposure to light. In speaking of my experiments made in diffused light, I have not mentioned those experiments on glass. I add this in order not to omit a specific improvement. It consists simply in placing a piece of black paper under the glass, and interposing a border of cardboard on which the engraving has been tightly stretched and glued between the plate on its coated side and the engraving. This arrangement results in the image appearing much more vividly than on a white background, which will contribute to the acceleration of the action; in the second place, it will prevent varnish from being damaged by close contact with the engraving as in the other process, a mishap which is not easy to avoid in warm weather, even when the varnish is quite dry. But this disadvantage is quite compensated by the advantage which the images on the silvered plates offer, in resisting the action during the rinsing while it is rarely that this operation does not more or less damage the images on glass, a substance to which the varnish adheres less easily, owing to its nature and its highly polished surface. It would be necessary, therefore, in order to remedy this disadvantage, to etch the varnish more, and I believe that I have achieved this, at least insofar as I may be permitted to judge after new and numerous experiments.

This new varnish consists of a solution of bitumen of Judea in Dippel's animal oil, which is allowed to evaporate at the ordinary atmospheric temperature to the required degree of consistency. This varnish is more greasy, tougher and more strongly coloured than the other, and it can be exposed to light as soon as it is applied, and it seems to solidify more rapidly because of the great volatility of the animal oil which causes it to dry more quickly.

Executed in duplicate December 5, 1829.

J.-N. NIEPCE.

Duplicate of this note
received from M. Niepce.

DAGUERRE.

(On pp. 146, 147, 148, 149 in M. Potonnée's book the facsimile of essential passages in Niepce's note is reproduced. T.N.)

During the following days, photographic demonstrations were made in order to acquaint M. Daguerre with the technique of the process, after which Daguerre returned to Paris and never again saw his partner. Each pursued his labours alone and we know nothing of their progress: Daguerre remained silent on the matter. We only know that in 1831 he invited Niepce to experiment with iodine in combination with silver as a light-sensitive substance. Niepce remained lukewarm, remembering his lack of success in 1816 with the muriate and also with silver iodide. (5)

We must conclude from this that since Daguerre proposed iodine two years after Niepce had advised him of its use for the blackening of heliographic images, that his (Daguerre) experiments with iodine cannot be dated as early as 1824.

NIEPCE'S ASSOCIATION WITH DAGUERRE
REFERENCES: CHAPTER XXIV

1. Twenty-five years later the engraver Lemaître, moved by the memory of his old friend Niepce, spoke with almost exaggerated enthusiasm of the same proofs which he had formerly criticized so severely. See *La Lumière*, March 1851 and *Bulletin de la Société Française de Photographie*, 1855, p.185; 1856, p.41.
2. The two originals of this famous document had diverse fortunes. The first is preserved in the Niepce family, who always have had it in their possession and which I showed at the meeting of the Société Française de Photographie in March 1920 (*Bulletin de la Société Française de Photographie* 1920, p.55.) The other is now preserved in the Argentine Republic (see Footnote 4 below). It was sent by Daguerre to Arago in 1839 for use in making his report, and was retained by Arago. In 1890 Dr.Arata, of Buenos Aires, purchased from a bookseller in Frankfurt the collection of Arago's works in seventeen volumes, published between 1854 and 1862 by J.-A.Barral, under instructions from Arago. The Doctor was surprised to find that he had acquired the unique collection gathered by and for Barral and that it included thirty documents or letters from notables of the period, among which was item No.9:
   Two letters from Niepce to Daguerre: February 2 and June 4, 1827.
   The partnership contract of which we speak here.
   Two additional contracts of 1835 and 1837, which will be discussed later.
   See: Arata, *Documents historiques relatifs à la découverte de la photographie*, Paris, 1892.
3. See *Brit.Jour.Phot.* Nov.14, 1930, p.684.
4. The documents referred to in Footnote 2 and the one quoted here are not the same. Footnote 2 above cites the agreement signed December 14, 1829 while the reference here is to the Notice on Heliography. It is this Notice of which one example seems to have been lost.
5. Letters of Niepce to Daguerre of June 24 and November 8, 1831, January 29 and March 3, 1832 are published in *Historique et Description des Procédés du Daguerréotype et du Diorama* by Daguerre, Paris 1839. This correspondence shows that Niepce used iodine and silver before Daguerre. "I have made studies of these before we became acquainted", he states. (June 24, 1831).

133

CHAPTER XXV

Death of Nicéphore Niepce

IN the midst of his labours about which we are so poorly informed, Niepce died. He suffered an attack of apoplexy on July 3, 1833 and he died on the 5th, in his house at Gras, in the same room where we have seen him make all his experiments and at the very moment, it is said, when he was about to attain the most complete success. He was buried in the cemetery at Saint-Loup-de-Varenne, aged sixty-eight years and four months.

So runs the history of this inventor, unknown for a long time, and worse than that, misjudged, and so it is still today, notwithstanding the statue which was erected to him in the town of Chalon. He was a persistent and patient seeker, a genius, who was able to disentangle the terms of a particular problem, so obscure that no one had preceded him or could show him the way; an astonishing personality who, starting at the birth, with nothing to help him, created this marvel which has become photography.

A troublesome liquidation followed Niepce's death. The son and the widow calculated his productive results and what they had cost. A cruel inventory, which showed no return for the many ruinous experiments. In thirty years everything had been dissipated and they were reduced to poverty. They were compelled to sell the domain at Gras, the mill, the vineyards, the inn, and all their properties. The house in the rue de l'Oratoire at Chalon, given to Isidore as a dowry when he married Mlle. Eugénie de Champmartin in 1825, sold before 1830 to a locksmith.

The property at Gras, which was first bought by a native of Chalon, was cut up and later owned by three different persons. It faced the main road from Chalon to Lyons; a garden separated it from the buildings which looked out on the court, the dovecote, and that part of the garden which Nicéphore described so often in his letters and which is illustrated in his heliographic plates. Behind these was the barn, the stable, the dog kennel, and a field which now borders on the railroad track. It is in the second of these three buildings that we find the attic room where Niepce made his experiments, and the window through which he pointed his apparatus. (1) But the many changes which these buildings underwent hardly permit one to recognize this famous attic today.

DEATH OF NICÉPHORE NIEPCE

Twenty-two years after the death of the inventor, on July 26, 1855, his widow, Agnès Roméro died at the age of ninety-five. The Municipal Council at Saint-Loup granted to the couple in perpetuity the plot where the two sleep side by side. This narrow plot is situated in the cemetery of Saint-Loup-de-Varenne, where the two headstones are enclosed in a grille.

One grave bears the inscription:

Here reposes
Antoinette-Marie-Catherine
Agnès Reparade Romezo (2)
wife of Joseph Nicéphore
Niepce
inventor of photography
died at Chalon-Sr/S.
July 26, 1855
aged 95 years

The other grave:

Here reposes
M. Joseph-Nicéphore Niepce
a model of all the virtues
father of the poor
a man of profound genius
to whom science owed discoveries
both beautiful and important
Modest to excess his life passed peacefully
in the bosom of his family
from which he parted
July the 3rd 1833 (3) at the age of 69

Meanwhile, four years before Madam Niepce, Daguerre died in 1851, and the Société libre des Beaux-Arts erected a monument to him in the cemetery at Bry in 1852. (4) It was then that a Chalon municipal councillor, Boissenot, proposed to honour the memory of Niepce by the erection of a monument. This was again proposed in 1855 by Chevrier and Fouque. The municipal Council decided to open a public subscription to which it contributed 5,000 francs, and requested the necessary authorization from the government. This was refused; "since", stated the head of the office charged with the inquiry, "it is not certain that Niepce invented photography, it is not necessary at present to erect a monument to him." Fouque irreverently called this honourable official an ass. (5) The same request, renewed in 1862 and several times afterward was always rejected.

While this was going on, Chevrier visited in 1861 the old home of Isidore Niepce at Lux, a village situated midway between Saint-Loup and Chalon, and found abandoned in an attic the apparatus, cameras, stands, retorts, press, etc. which Nicéphore had used. The owner consented to present them to the Société d'Histoire et d'Archéologie at Chalon which deposited them in the town Museum after its establishment in 1866. (6) Chevrier, the custodian of the Museum, searched also for any heliographs which might still exist. Isidore Niepce presented some of them; others were in the possession of Nicéphore's old friends. In this manner the Museum collection was established.

In 1866, a friend of the Niepce family, Dr. Lépine, caused a tablet to be erected at his expense alongside the railway bordering the old property at Gras, with the following inscription: "House where J -Nicéphore Niepce discovered photography in the year 1822. Propter veritatem et posteros inscripsit (7) Doctor Lépine, 1866."

However, in 1877, after a renewed request of the Municipal Council at Chalon, a presidential decree of November 19, 1877, authorized the town of Chalon to open a public subscription for the erection of a statue to the inventor of photographv. Slow at first, the subscription with the support of the Société Française de Photographie became international in scope. On June 21, 1885, the statue was dedicated in the Square Port-Villiers, at Chalon. It is the work of the sculptor Guillaume. Austria, Germany, Portugal, Belgium, Denmark, Spain and Mexico contributed only a small part, France subscribed the balance of the fund. (8)

DEATH OF NICÉPHORE NIEPCE
REFERENCES: CHAPTER XXV

1. Fouque on pp.15, 247 and following, described the state of these properties in 1867. He also gave the names of the persons who owned them.
2. The name was not spelled correctly.
3. Niepce died on July 5th. This is an error which could easily have been corrected because the tombstone shows the date as July 3rd.
4. Lacan (*La Lumière*, July 20 and November 3, 1851) desired to have Niepce included with Daguerre in this monument and felt hurt by the refusal of the Société libre des Beaux-Arts.
5. Unpublished correspondence between Isidore Niepce and Fouque.
6. Jules Chevrier. *Archéologie et Photographie*, Chalon 1861. *Musée de Chalon-sur-Saône*, Chalon 1866. I am also indebted to MM.Gallas and Pierre Besnard of Chalon for a part of these details, to whom I hereby express my thanks.
7. Inscribed in the name of Truth and Posterity. (T.N.).
8. Landa. *Rapport au Conseil municipal de Chalon*, Chalon 1877. *Bulletin de la Société Française de Photographie* 1884, p.203; 1885, pp.177, 180, 253, 287 and also in the manuscript report owned by the Society. The total subscription amounted to 24,584 francs.

CHAPTER XXVI

Relics of Nicéphore Niepce

TODAY (1923) the memory of Niepce is recalled to us by his grave at Saint-Loup-de-Varenne; by the engraved tablet in the field on the old property at Gras; by the statue erected at Chalon in 1885. At Chalon, in the quarter of Saint-Côme, a street is named after Nicéphore Niepce. The Gras domain divided, is partly destroyed or changed. (1) The birthplace of Niepce at Chalon belongs to the family who acquired it in 1867, who had bought it from the locksmith Muard, who in turn had purchased it from Isidore Niepce.

The present owner, a wine merchant, owned the adjoining house; he joined the two houses by tearing down part of the old ramparts (8 meters thick), which served as a retaining wall and made important changes in the interior. But the exterior was not changed and the shop could still be seen where the locksmith had plied his trade. The number of the house is 9 de la rue de l'Oratoire and that street remains in its former state, at least that part where Niepce's house is located. No memorial tablet recalls the fact that here the author of one of the greatest inventions of humanity was born.

The Museum at Chalon possesses:

Correspondence

Sixty letters from Nicéphore, thirty-one letters from Claude to his brother, a page from the expense account book of the Niepce household, the Introduction, the text of which I have given in Chapter X. All these items were presented by Eugène Niepce, the inventor's grandson, to the mayor of Chalon, June 21, 1885, the day of the dedication of the statue of Niepce.

Heliographs

A. A view of the Pantheon, on a silvered copper plate, inscribed: "Heliographic proof made by Isidore Niepce, son of Nicéphore, 1839."

B. A view of the Quai Voltaire, Paris, on a silvered copper plate, 0.22 m wide, 0.16 m high, bought by the Museum in 1874. The proof is inscribed: "Gift of M.Niepce, the son, proprietor of Lux, near Chalon, who told me that it was one of the first photographs, made on the Quai Voltaire, Paris."

"Acquired from M.Routy, former pharmacist at Chalon-sur-Saône, to whom it was given by Isidore Niepce as a remembrance of the late Nicéphore Niepce, one of his former friends." Note by the custodian, October 1875, J.Chevrier.

These two proofs are not by Nicéphore Niepce. They are two daguerreotypes. The first was made by Isidore after the publication of the daguerreotype, in August 1839. It is utterly impossible that Nicéphore made the second, inasmuch as he was only in Paris in 1827 and no mention can be found in his letters of any attempt to make photographs of the streets. Moreover, it would have been impossible for him to obtain in 1827 a photograph of that sort. This must certainly be a photograph given by Daguerre to Isidore, as a proof of the new process originated by him, after the modification of the agreement which they signed in 1837. This is one of the oldest daguerreotypes known.

The proofs that follow are veritable heliographs:

1st. "Heliograph on a silvered copper plate. Reproduction of a gravure, (a monk and a young man are leaving a house; a woman with hands clasped.) M.Isidore Niepce and his wife certify that this reproduction was made by Nicéphore Niepce in May 1829. Gift of M.Grozellier, proprietor at Lux, in 1874, 0.045 m (sic) wide, 0.06 m high".

2nd. "Heliograph on silvered copper plate. Reproduction of a lithograph (a Greek man and woman). Gift of Isidore Niepce, 0.07m wide, 0.09m high."

This proof is in very bad condition, hardly visible.

3rd. "Heliograph on zinc plate. Reproduction of a gravure (Christ carrying His Cross) 0.08m wide, 0.11m high. On the back of the plate this inscription is scratched with the point of a penknife: "Heliographic design, invented by M.J.-N.Niepce, 1825." Gift of M.Isidore Niepce."

Proof in bad condition. The inscription was engraved by Isidore on the back of the plate shortly after he obtained it. (2)

4th. "Heliograph on zinc plate. Reproduction of a gravure (landscape with figures), made in 1825, circular 0.12m in diameter. Gift of Isidore Niepce."

5th. "Heliograph on zinc plate. Reproduction of a gravure (landscape) made in 1823, 0.07m wide, 0.06m high."

6th. "Heliograph engraved on pewter plate. Reproduction of a gravure (Cardinal d'Amboise) (3), 0.13m wide, 0.17m high. This proof carries on the back the scratched inscription: "obtained by J.-N.Niepce in 1824. Gift of Isidore Niepce."

(It was necessary to observe the greatest care as to the dates when these plates were made as given above by the curator of the Museum. I do not know who made this last inscription, but the date given is wrong, as stated in Chapter XVII. This plate was obtained in May or June of 1826 and etched by Lemaître in February 1827. I have discussed this subject in the *Bulletin de la Société de Photographie* of September 1919.)

7th. "Heliograph on pewter plate, similar to the preceding plate and obtained at the same time, as is shown in the letter from Niepce to Lemaître, February 2, 1827."

8th. "Heliograph on pewter plate, 0.19m wide, 0.23m high. Reproduction of a gravure (Holy Family). Gift of Isidore Niepce."

This proof dates from 1827. The inventor sent a similar plate to Daguerre, June 4, 1827, adding that he had made it in the preceding Spring. It must be noted that Niepce usually pulled two proofs of every subject. See his *Note* under: *observations*.

9th. "Heliograph on pewter plate. Reproduction of a gravure (landscape) 0.18m wide, 0.12m high. Gift of Isidore Niepce."

The Museum, then, possesses nine heliographs on metal.

Proofs on Paper

From the above-mentioned plates, a certain number of proofs have been pulled on paper (4), of which two are in the Museum.

1st. Proof on paper of Cardinal d'Amboise (heliograph No.6) "printed in 1824 from the heliographic plate. Gift of Jules Chevrier."

This is the same remark as that given for the date on the plate; as a matter of fact, the print was made by Lemaître in February 1827.

2nd. Proof on paper; same as the above, but this was printed in 1864 by Jules Chevrier. A certain number of proofs pulled in 1864 have been found. The Museum originally possessed two of them, but the Conservatoire des Arts et Métiers, Paris, which until recently had none, exhibits one of these today; I suppose this must be one of the Chalon proofs.

The Museum in addition has four engravings which have been used to make the above heliographs and which have been rendered transparent by means of a varnish.

Apparatus

1st. A camera obscura 0.30m square.

2nd. A camera obscura of the same size, pierced with round openings, closed with corks, which permit a view of the interior.

3rd. A camera with a bellows of 0.30m extension and with an opening for the lens.

4th. A camera 0.40m square, furnished on the inside with a movable apparatus and equipped with a diaphragm 0.11m in diameter.

5th. A camera 0.65m wide and 0.36m high.

6th. A square bellows consisting of wooden frames, held together by leather and which could be fitted to cameras.

7th. A frame equipped with a roller and handle; Sundry debris and an ink roller. This frame seemed to have been a rudimentary intaglio printing press.

All these objects were presented by the Marquis d'Ivry, who had bought Isidore Niepce's house at Lux, as mentioned above.

In 1913, Mme. Louis Poizat presented to the Museum a draisine which formerly had belonged to Nicéphore. (5)

The Société de l'Histoire et d'Archéologie of Chalon-sur-Saône preserves in its lecture hall, a camera and various glass utensils, which Niepce used.

The Société Française de Photographie, Paris, has in its collection:

1st. "A heliograph engraved on pewter plate. Reproduction of a gravure (Holy Family) 0.18m wide, 0.21m high. This plate is engraved on the back: Heliography by J.-N. Niepce. The author to M. Daguerre."

This plate was made in 1827 and sent to Daguerre by Niepce on June 4, 1827, as I have mentioned above. It was acquired by the Society in 1875.

2nd. "A heliograph on a metal plate. Reproduction of an engraving (a man standing, ruffled hair, jacket with lapels, in soft boots), 0.105m wide, 0.150m high. This plate was presented to the Society by Eugène Niepce in 1890."

3rd. "A proof on paper printed by the engraver Lemaître in February 1827 from the plate of Cardinal d'Amboise, No.6 in the Museum at Chalon. It carries the false date of 1824 and was presented to the Society by Eugène Niepce in 1890."

4th. "A proof on paper similar to the last mentioned, but printed by Jules Chevrier in 1864. The proof bears these two remarks: "First result obtained in 1824, printed from the original plate in 1864 by Jules Chevrier of Chalon. "Gift to the Société Française by Niepce de Saint-Victor." It was presented to the Society by Niepce de Saint-Victor in 1865."

5th. "A proof on paper representing the Holy Family, printed by order of the Société Française from the heliographic plate mentioned above (No.1) in 1875.

6th. In addition the Society has possessed for a long time a heliograph on glass from nature (mentioned in Chapter XVI), representing a table on which there are several objects. Nothing remains of it but a reproduction in halftone, executed by order of the Society in 1891. Eugène Niepce, the donor, has given the date of its production as 1823 or 1825, but it is probable that this photograph was obtained after 1829. Niepce never called photographs in his letters anything but "points de vue", never "natures mortes". (still life). On the contrary Daguerre photographs this kind of subject exclusively in his first attempts; his experiments as a painter pointed out to him their advantage and one may suppose that Niepce was guided in his choice by his associate. This conjecture is somewhat hazardous and I give it only as such.

At the Conservatoire des Arts et Métiers, Paris, there are exhibited: Two prints on paper of Cardinal d'Amboise, erroneously dated 1824, one printed by Lemaître in 1827 and the other printed by Chevrier in 1864.

A recapitulation shows that there remain of Niepce's works eleven heliographs on metal plates, etched or photographed, and seven images on paper, printed from these plates (six of Cardinal d'Amboise, three in 1827 and three in 1864; also one of the Holy Family). I do not know of any others. That others existed, however, may be traced in the text. Niepce sent to Daguerre on October 4, 1829 a photograph on metal blackened with iodine, of his courtyard and his bird house, which must be regarded as lost. The engraver Lemaître owned a certain number of heliographs and extra copies of proofs on paper which he had printed. He showed them and has spoken of them several times. (6) Arthur Chevalier mentions several times (7) that a heliograph offered to him in 1829 by Nicéphore (8) had been deposited in the archives of the Institute "in order to establish France's priority to the invention, which was claimed by England". At the time of the discussion raised by the advent of the daguerreotype, Charles Chevalier sent this proof (Christ carrying His Cross, similar to the proof No.3 at Chalon) to Arago who showed it at the Académie des Sciences on February 11, 1839. Chevalier believed that it had been deposited in the archives. It is not there. A search of the archives of the Institute, made at my request, in 1919, proved that the plate was not there. Arago, during the same session of February 11, 1839 (9), states that "M. de Laguiche owned a plate of the same kind which he also had obtained from M. Niepce."

At the time of his trip to England, Niepce offered some of his helio-graphs to the naturalist, Francis Bauer, who still owned them in 1839. (10) One of these was the first photograph obtained by Niepce, con-sequently that of 1822. Niepce also offered a heliographic plate (a copy of an engraving) to a Sir Cussell, who lived at Kew. This heliograph was found and bought after the death of its first owner by Joseph Ellis, a photographer at Brighton, who still owned it in 1862. (11) Where are these plates now? I do not know.

Considering the eagerness with which the early proofs pertaining to printing and engraving are sought at the present time, we may well suppose that the initial attempts at photography, scorned and wasted by us, will become precious in their turn, after we and they have passed on and following generations will seek to gather them with the same zest for the collections of the future. It is for those to whom I seek to render a service that I have collected these lists, but particularly I have sought to aid those who may later wish to reassemble the relics in honour of the memory of the inventor of photography.

The portraits which we have of Niepce, are they at all authentic, and do they resemble him? All the portraits of Niepce, engraved, sculptured or painted are derived from a bust modeled by Isidore during the life of his father and which was said to closely resemble him. In 1867, this bust was photographed by Bourgeois, a photographer at Chalon, for an illustration of Fouque's book: *La vérité sur l'invention de la photographie.* Dujardin reproduced this photograph by heliogravure, using Garnier's process, but the heliogravures were not ready when the book went to press and the first copies of the book were illustrated with photoprints by Bourgeois, later copies contained heliogravure prints by Dujardin.

The original bust is in the museum at Chalon, and was used as model for a portrait painted by Léonard Berger in 1853 (12), for a clay model by Rougelet (13), for a bust modeled by Barré in 1855 (14), and finally for the statue erected at Chalon in 1885. Isidore also drew a crayon portrait of his father, which Lacan reproduced in *"La Lumière"* of July 6, 1851. We have no other contemporary portrait of Niepce.

It may be interesting to some of my readers to learn that the infor-mation which we possess concerning Niepce is contained in a small number of documents which are enumerated herewith:

A. *Documents originating with the inventor himself.*

1st. A note on heliography, written in 1827, intended for the Royal Society of London; published for the first time by Fouque in 1867.

2nd. A more elaborated note than the preceding on the definite processes of heliography written at the end of 1829 in two copies, one of which was sent to Daguerre; the second is preserved by the Niepce family. It was published for the first time by Daguerre in his *Historique et description des procédés du daguerréotype et du diorama*, Paris, 1839.

3rd. The letters which Nicéphore wrote to his brother Claude, to his son Isidore, to the engraver Lemaître and to the optician Chevalier. The first were used and in part published by Fouque. The letters addressed to the engraver Lemaître were given by him to *La Lumière*, which published them in February and March 1851. Those addressed to the optician Chevalier, which contain very little of interest, were included by him in the work: *Etude sur la vie et les travaux de Charles Chevalier* by A.Chevalier, his son, Paris, 1862.

4th. The article entitled *Introduction* which is in the Museum at Chalon and the text of which is published for the first time in Chapter X of this work.

B. *Documents originating with those who knew Nicéphore Niepce and his works.*

1st. The letters written to Nicéphore both by his brother Claude and his son Isidore were also used and published in part by Fouque. All this correspondence was found by Isidore between the years 1857 and 1867, after he made a search at the request of Fouque.

2nd. The testimony of witnesses of Niepce's work, written or oral. Recollections of Isidore published in *Historique de la découverte improprement nommée Daguerréotype*, Paris, 1841. Also souvenirs of Isidore written at Fouque's request and preserved by the family Niepce. Those of Francis Bauer, in a letter addressed to the *Literary Gazette* in 1839. Those of Daguerre, of Lemaître, of Chevalier, scattered through many publications and which, if consulted, may aid the historian. The manuscripts in the possession of the Niepce family must be added to these.

C. *Heliographs executed by Nicéphore Niepce*

No one has used or studied these heliographs. I have made a list of them above which I hope is exact, if not complete. It is probably advisable to note here that Niepce was not the only one who made heliographs. (15)

RELICS OF NICÉPHORE NIEPCE
REFERENCES: CHAPTER XXVI

1. A memorial was erected in 1933 at Saint-Loup-de-Varenne, at a location easily seen from the road and the railway Paris-Marseille, and a tablet was affixed on the family house in Chalon.
2. Unpublished manuscript of Isidore Niepce.
3. Engraved by Briot, see Belloc: *Les quatre branches de la photographie*, Paris, 1855.
4. According to Eugène Niepce there were only five proofs of Cardinal d'Amboise printed in 1827. One was given to the Museum at Lyons, one to the Museum at Chalon, one to Lemaître, one to de La Blanchère, and the last to the Société Française de Photographie. *Bulletin de la Société Française de Photographie*, 1890, p.148. The Museum at Lyons reports that this proof is not in its possession.
5. "La draisienne" (Webster: draisine) was quite in style about 1818. It was an improvement over the invention by Civrac in 1690, thought out by Drais de Sauerbron for the acceleration of locomotion. The handlebar was movable.
6. *La Lumière*, April 20, 1851, May 28, 1853; *Comptes rendus*, May 23, 1853. *Bulletin de la Société Française de photographie*, 1855, pp.41, 185; 1856, p.37; 1857, p.252. *Catalogue des Expositions de la Société Française de Photographie*, Paris, 1862, p.20.
7. Ch.Chevalier, *Nouvelles instructions sur le daguerréotype*, Paris, 1841, p.6. Arthur Chevalier, *Etude sur la vie et les travaux scientifiques de Charles Chevalier*, Paris, 1862, p.20.
8. Arthur Chevalier published an appendix to his *Etude sur la vie, etc.* It is dated January 12, 1829.
9. *Comptes rendus*, 1839, 1st semester, p.207.
10. *Comptes rendus*, March 11, 1839. Bauer's letter of February 27, 1839 to the *Literary Gazette*.
11. *The Photographic News*, July 11, 1862.
12. At the Museum at Chalon.
13. At the Museum at Chalon.
14. At the Société Française de Photographie.
15. *Bulletin de la Société Française de Photographie*, 1885, pp.183, 258 (note).

CHAPTER XXVII

The Beginning of the Experiments of Daguerre

AFTER Nicéphore's death, his son Isidore succeeded him in the partnership, according to the Agreement of December 1829. Isidore, born in 1795, was then thirty-eight years old. He lived, after his resignation from the army in 1821, at Saint-Loup just as at Chalon, in idleness and elegance as a man-about-town. His marriage, in 1825, with Mlle. de Champmartin made no change in his manner of living; but the death of his uncle Claude, the failure of their expectations and the liquidation which followed Nicéphore's death made his existence difficult. Isidore does not seem to have been very familiar with the work of his father, and he had no great opinion of the experiments which had turned out so disastrously. It was not until much later that he became enthusiastic about them. He took no part in the researches of his associate, contenting himself with the hope that the exploitation of the process would reimburse him for a part of the losses which they had suffered. Fortunately Daguerre, generous, and at that time wealthy, made him more than one advance of money. Daguerre worked hard at this time, and it was said that, always a hard worker, he attended more than ever to his work.

We know very little about the nature of Daguerre's photographic researches before he knew Niepce. At any rate, his results were nil, because there is no mention of them in the Agreement of 1829. We know that Daguerre in 1827 entertained Niepce with his experiments with the colours of the spectrum; Carpentier confirms this: "Daguerre" he says (1) "is much preoccupied with obtaining coloured images. He told us about the results of his experiments: he had succeeded in finding substances which have the property, when spread on strips of paper fixed on cardboard, to absorb separately the three primary colours: red, yellow and blue. In a room entirely darkened he made a small opening in the wall which could be closed. He exposed these cartons together to the sunlight and after a few minutes he entered the dark room and closed the opening. What was his surprise! The three substances which had absorbed the red, yellow and blue rays became luminous. It showed, he said, in this dark room a luminosity equal to that of the solar rays which had acted on it." Notwithstanding these statements, Daguerre avowed

146

that he never had any chance of success, "because it was impossible so to combine the substances that they would selectively absorb as many particles of the red ray, the yellow ray and the blue ray, as were necessary in order to obtain the millions of shades and colours offered by natural objects (or the nature of objects) according to the formation and disposition of their molecules, which determines their infinite variety of colours and shades, in numbers truly incalculable." (2)

Arago (3) gave, as the date of these experiments, 1824; but he confines himself to the conclusion that Daguerre seemed to have rendered sulphide of baryte more phosphorescent than his predecessors.

But this was nothing new. (4) Without repeating the fables of antiquity and of the medieval age, and not mentioning a well-known book by Conrad Gesner (5), I have called attention to the discovery of phosphorus, toward the end of the seventeenth century (Chapter VIII). Seventy-five years earlier, in 1602 or 1603, a Bolognese artisan who dabbled in alchemy, Vincenzo Casciorolo, having found a very heavy stone which he thought contained silver, calcinated it. He was surprised to find that it glowed in the dark after it had been exposed to light. (6) This discovery attracted much attention, but was soon forgotten. The Bolognese physician, Ovide Montalbani, in 1634, the Angers physician, Pothier, in 1635, especially Licetus (7), in 1640, described the invention, preparation and properties of the Bologna stone. Nevertheless, when Homberg, a half century later, visited Italy at the place where this was discovered, nobody could tell him anything about it. Either they had not heard about it, or they believed that the secret of its composition had been lost.

Mentzelius (1675), Count de Marsiglii (1698), also published the method of treating Bologna stone. Powdered, moistened, calcinated, this substance emits in the dark an orange light, sometimes blended with yellow and bluish light.

In the meantime, Brandt (1677) discovered phosphorus, which had been investigated also by a number of other chemists. In 1675, Baudoin recognized that the nitrate of limestone (phosphore de Baudoin) glowed in the dark. Homberg recognized the same property in calcium chloride (phosphore de Homberg) and, in 1711, he discovered potassium sulphide which ignites in the air and which is called pyrophosphore or pyrophore. Lemery made analogous preparations. Dufay in 1730 (8) demonstrated the phosphorescence of a great number of calcinated stones, shells and calcinous concretions. He exposed them to the action of light under different coloured glasses without the tints of the phosphorescence being affected. Beccarius (9) (1744) at first believed the contrary; but he drew the wrong conclusions, owing to imperfect experiments. Shortly after, Zanotti (1748) proved that the action of the different coloured rays of the solar spectrum had no effect on the phosphorescent colour of the Bologna stone.

Canton, in 1764, discovered a new substance—Canton phosphorus, which could be prepared easily. It was produced from pulverized oyster shells mixed with one-fourth part of sulphur and subjected to red heat for an hour. This mixture, having been exposed to the light, emitted yellow or green light in the dark. Wilson (1776-1780) pursued this question of the colour of phosphorescence. He observed that the layers of calcinated oyster shells showed sometimes red and sometimes yellow or bluish green. These layers emit respectively the shades of their own colour; but whatever may be the colour of the light to which the phosphorescent powder is exposed, this never emits any but its own colour of light unchanged. The rays dispersed by the prism have no action on the colour of the phosphorescent bodies. Michel de Grosser, in 1782, confirmed these experiments, which were made again in 1815 by Grotthus who obtained the identical results.

Did Daguerre simply separate red, yellow and blue powders which, affected by white light, respectively reflected red, yellow and blue; or was he more fortunate than the chemists mentioned and did he find phosphorescent substances which take on the colour of the light which they absorb? We cannot know this. The fact that no one saw these experiments; that Daguerre gave no indication of the nature of the powders employed by him, and moreover, that he subsequently never spoke of this matter, would lead us to believe that these results are to a great extent to be attributed to his imagination. At any rate, it cannot be denied that in these experiments he dealt only with the chemistry of light and not with photography. (10)

Biot (11) had also given the formula of a paper sensitive to silver chloride (muriate d'argent) which Daguerre employed in 1826; but again Daguerre does not tell us whether he obtained images in the camera obscura and the blackening of silver chloride in light was well known and an old story in 1826.

BEGINNING OF THE EXPERIMENTS OF DAGUERRE
REFERENCES: CHAPTER XXVII

1. Carpentier, *Notice sur Daguerre*, Paris, 1855.
2. Did Daguerre have a vague idea of photography in colours, later realized by Ducos du Hauron in 1869? Undoubtedly he knew the work of the painter Leblond (*L'Art d'imprimer les tableaux*, Paris, 1757) who described colour printing with four plates, following each other, the blue, yellow and red of the image, reinforced by a black plate. At any rate, the only thing he proved was the impossibility of achieving the result.
3. *Comptes rendus*, 1839, 1st semester, p.243.
4. E. Becquerel, *La Lumière*, Paris, 1868, 1st vol.
5. Conradis Gesneri, *De raris et admirandis herbis quae, sive quod noctu luceant, sive alias ob causas, lunariae nominantur commentatoribus; et obiter de aliis etiam rebus quae in tenebris lucent. . . .*, Tiguri 1555. (On the rare and wonderful plants which, whether because they shine at night or for other reasons, are called moon-plants by the commentators; and incidentally about some other things which shine in the dark. T.N.).
6. Barium sulphate is changed by calcination to sulphur.
7. *Litheosphorus sive de lapide bononiensi.* (Lithophosphor or Bologna stone. T.N.).
8. *Mémoires de l'Académie des Sciences*, 1730.
9. *De quam plurimis phosphoris. . . .*, Bologna 1744. (Jacopo Bartholomeo Beccari T.N.).
10. This paragraph is questioned by M.L.-P. Clerc insofar as the statements as to phosphorescence are concerned because all "phosphorescent bodies are almost colourless" and because "phosphorescence always gives light of a greater wave length than that of the exciting rays". T.N.
11. *Comptes rendus*, 1839, 1st semester, p.246 and on the phosphorescent powders, p.250, in Arago's report. The note in which Arago speaks of a mixture of three powders used by Daguerre and which turns red in red, blue in blue and green in green, is not very explicit and only confirms the doubts expressed above.

CHAPTER XXVIII

Daguerre's Work in Photography

IT may be said, without fear of distorting the truth, that the serious attempts of Daguerre began only after he learned Niepce's secret. Whoever examines heliographs and daguerreotypes together will be struck with their close resemblance; it is evident that the two are related to each other and spring from the same source and this conviction grows stronger as the details of manipulation are observed: it is there that the daguerreotype departs from heliography. Niepce's Note sent to his associate described the manipulations of the daguerreotype process, in which only the substances were changed.

What lines did Daguerre follow in progressing from one to the other of these two processes? We know nothing about it and Daguerre is silent on the matter. At the most, he gave Arago some incomplete explanations. (1) But I believe that we may speculate on these matters which he did not wish to discuss. We recall that Niepce subjected the polished plate to iodine vapours. Daguerre recognized that silvered plates fumed with iodine were sensitive to light. Because if a silvered plate coated with iodine was exposed to daylight, it turned black in time. If it remained in the camera obscura for a sufficient length of time, the image recorded itself first as a negative, later as a positive. (2) For this reason, Daguerre, in 1831, having been the first to observe these facts, suggested to his associate that he experiment with silver iodide. (3) Neither of them was able to produce anything by this first method; the success of the daguerreotype was due to the recognition of the fact that when the image on silver iodide, before it becomes visible, is subjected to mercury vapours, even for a short time, it appears at once as a positive.

Now, in the heliographs, the blacks of the image were formed by the bared metal. In order to increase the contrast between the blacks and the whites, which was too weak, the plate was placed before a black board from which the light was reflected by the brilliant parts of the metal plate; when the images are thus examined, they appear much stronger. It was thus found to be advantageous to operate on a polished surface, a veritable mirror. For this reason Niepce abandoned copper for pewter, and pewter for silver, and for the same reason, Daguerre turned to mercury; doubtless this is where he got the idea of mercury and its use as an amalgam with silver. In the course of the "innumerable" attempts which he made (4) he used mercury, sometimes before, sometimes after the plate had been exposed to light and he saw the latent image become visible. This is only a conjecture, but it is probably close to the truth. Daguerre also stated that he used mercury before he knew of the latent image. (5) He made this discovery in 1835 and the story runs as follows: A plate which had been exposed was locked up in a chest containing various chemicals, and sometime later Daguerre noticed that there was a complete image on it. Eliminating one after the other of the chemicals lying near the plate, he finally succeeded in repeating the experiment by using mercury. So runs the story, which undoubtedly may be placed alongside the other, when in his imagination he saw a tree designing itself on his tableau (see p.114 T.N.).

However that may be, Daguerre had obtained in 1835 the following result: on Niepce's silvered copper plate he spread the iodine with a tampon (like printers' ink-balls T.N.), or by placing the plate over some iodine flakes. This plate was placed in the camera obscura and, after exposure, taken out before the image became visible. It was then placed above a vessel containing heated mercury. The mercury was deposited on the whites of the image which presently appeared as a positive. But the image was not permanent. It could not be examined in daylight without the silver iodide continuing to be affected and soon becoming completely effaced. Whereupon, with his usual assurance and that self-confidence which he always displayed, Daguerre advertised his triumph prematurely. The *Journal des Artistes* of September 27, 1835 contains this passage: "He (Daguerre) found, so it is said, a means to obtain on a plate prepared by him the image produced in a camera, such as a portrait, a landscape, any view, which is projected on his plate in the ordinary camera obscura. This image leaves its imprint in light and shade, presenting also the most perfect of all pictures. A preparation applied to this image will preserve it indefinitely." The inventor had not then, nor two years later—two years of research and intense work—found anything which, even if successful, would seem simple to us. By washing the plate in a hot solution of cooking salt, he removed the iodide not affected and the image became permanent, or at least did not change for a long time. Here again, as Chevalier states (6) "the good fortune which accompanied him in all his undertakings did not fail him." We may perhaps add that Daguerre's keen intelligence and persistence aided his good fortune for, while searching for a medium of fixation, he moved in an unknown world: at best he was influenced by the fact that iodine comes from salt water.

REFERENCES: CHAPTER XXVIII

1. *Comptes rendus de l' Académie des Sciences*, 1839, 2nd semester, p.423.
2. *Comptes rendus*, 1842, 2nd semester, p.119.
3. Niepce to Daguerre: June 24 and November 8, 1831, January 29, March 3, 1832 and *Comptes rendus*, 1839, 2nd semester, p.423. Gaudin (*Traité pratique de Photographie*, p.4) states having learned from a reliable source that this discovery was an accident. A spoon left without intent on a heliographic plate, blackened by the iodine, left its imprint under the action of light. Daguerre, according to Mentienne, frowned when this anecdote was related and treated it as a fable.
4. *Comptes rendus*, 1839, 1st semester, p.243.
5. *Comptes rendus*, 1839, 2nd semester, p.412.
6. Charles Chevalier, *Souvenirs historiques*, p.147.

CHAPTER XXIX

Daguerre's Association with Isidore Niepce

WE have seen how little Isidore Niepce, since 1833, contributed in comparison with the diligent Daguerre. The latter chafed under the fact that his associate wholly benefited by the association, and since 1835 after having found the use of mercury, he made up his mind that the name of the firm should be changed. It became Daguerre-Niepce, instead of Niepce-Daguerre, which it had been. After the process became perfected and definite, the demands of Daguerre increased; he thought that his name alone should figure in the contract and the name of Niepce should be omitted. Daguerre called Isidore to Paris, showed him the results which he had obtained—probably the view of the Tuileries which is in the Museum at Chalon—but did not communicate to his associate the details of his process. He contented himself with informing him that he had discovered something new and that, in case of his refusing the proposed modifications, he would publish and exploit his invention without Isidore. The latter protested, he was indignant, he said, but fearing to lose everything, he finally consented and signed. (1) Isidore's protestations were probably not so vehement as he would like to have us believe. It must be noted that the financial clauses were not to be modified. The profits were to be divided equally. For this Daguerre must be given credit, who showed himself more eager for glory than for gain. At any rate, Daguerre died poor, leaving his widow not quite 40,000 francs, certainly a small amount considering the enormous profits of the first years of the Diorama. It is true, he was a spendthrift, but he was also generous and unselfish. The financial question was important to Isidore Niepce for another reason. His sole income was derived from his father's invention; from 1833 until 1839 he was in debt to Daguerre; presumably he easily consented that the name of his father be effaced as soon as he found that the financial clauses were not to be changed. The name of Niepce was, therefore, erased and thus the invention took the name of Daguerreotype.

The two associates stipulated in the contract that the discovery should be exploited by means of a public subscription, or sold for a price of not less than 200,000 francs. But the subscription offered by a notary from March until August 1838, was unsuccessful. Photography in its beginning did not appeal to a speculator as worth risking one cent on its future; it did not seem the kind of business which would return any profit. However, Daguerre, as we may easily suppose, showed his plates, talking noisily as possible about his discovery; he had requested and obtained permission to make daguerreotypes of the monuments of Paris with a bulky and heavy apparatus: more than one hundred pounds of crude paraphernalia, according to Chevalier. (2) This was mounted on a truck. The exposures took place in the street for a half hour, often longer, in the midst of crowds, and accompanied by what comments! The Parisian of today can easily imagine the character of these comments because he has a chance to hear similar remarks daily. This was good publicity, but Daguerre jealously kept the details of the operation to himself, and this hindered the negotiations. And so passed the year 1838. Although business men kept aloof, scientists became interested. Daguerre showed his images to J.B. Dumas (1800-1884), to Biot (1774-1862), to Arago (1786-1853) to the lithographer Grevedon (1776-1860), to the publisher Giroux, to de Cailleux, the curator of the Louvre, and undoubtedly also to others. If Mentienne (3) is to be believed, the novelty spread far: England, Russia, Prussia and the United States made splendid offers to the inventor. I have never been able to find any proof of this. But it is almost certain that England offered to buy the secret of the process for 200,000 francs. (4) This created discord between the associates. Isidore wanted to accept the offer without waiting longer; Daguerre was of the opinion that the matter should be submitted first to the French government, and his advice prevailed.

Daguerre then turned to Arago who reported the matter to the Academy. Humboldt, Biot and Arago, as a committee of the Academy, called on Daguerre and he showed them a series of plates listed here: a view of the Cité with the towers of Notre Dame, a view of the Seine with several of the bridges and views of some of the Capital's gates. At the session of January 7, 1839, Arago reported to the Academy on this visit. "M. Daguerre" he said, "had discovered a special ground upon which the optical image leaves perfect imprint. The whole world, having admired the images produced in the camera obscura, regretted that they could not be preserved." (5) . . . . "The extreme sensitiveness of M. Daguerre's preparation (eight or ten minutes in sunlight, at noon in summer) does not constitute the only characteristic by which this discovery differs from the imperfect attempts which formerly were made by producing silhouettes on a silver chloride surface." Arago ends his report with this information, which must have been given to him by Daguerre: "The invention of M. Daguerre is the fruit of researches extended over several years, during which he had as collaborator his friend, the late M. Niepce of Chalon-sur-Saône." (6) Nothing could be further from the truth.

Biot, knowing of these images for a long time, confirmed Arago's statement, who announced that he would propose to the French government the purchase of this process, which could not be kept secret, as soon as Daguerre "would furnish him with the proof that the results were economical, easy to obtain and that the process could be available to travellers everywhere."

Arago's report caused an enormous sensation among the public interested in this matter. "I will always remember," writes Abbé Moigno (7) "the astonishing effect which was produced, first among the academicians, and then throughout all France, when the verbal report of M. Arago was made at the session of January 7. The fame of this discovery, so unexpected and marvelous, was on everybody's tongue and the name of Daguerre became the best known of his time in Europe." "When we were told for the first time," states the academician Turpin, "of M. Daguerre's results, we could hardly credit them and we would have rejected this novelty as a fable invented for our pleasure, if the learned and capable men who had seen it had not assured us of its reality." (8) "Few discoveries produced so vivid a sensation as the daguerreotypy" says Belloc. (9) Many other witnesses could be cited.

Most of the scientific journals of France and foreign countries reproduced Arago's report. Of course, Daguerre knew better than anyone the value of publicity. On the evening preceding the day when Arago was to speak, the *Gazette de France*, in giving the news of the novelty to its subscribers, presented the inventor with this timely publicity, which I hope was gratuitous. Jules Janin, on the other hand, in a famous article (10), extolled the daguerreotype to artists and invented details of which he was seemingly ignorant, with more audacity than success. *Le Technologiste*, *l'Echo du Monde Savant*, *le Moniteur* and other periodicals opened their pages to Daguerre and he brought them some of the views he had made. Jules Janin cites: The Louvre, the Institute, the Tuileries, the Pont-Neuf, Notre Dame de Paris, the Hotel de Ville, the Panthéon. We note that some of the views are not the same as enumerated by Arago.

Such was the enthusiasm or, at least, the lively interest that was aroused by the discovery of the daguerreotype. This is evidenced by the claims which soon arose. The announcement of the discovery had hardly been published before the English scientist, Fox Talbot (11) wrote to Arago and Biot (January 29th) to "make a formal claim of priority in, 1st: the fixation of images of the camera obscura and, 2nd: for the subsequent preservation of these images even when exposed to sunlight." The letter irritated Arago who vigorously defended Daguerre: "The first idea of fixing the images of the camera obscura" he wrote (12) "belongs neither to M. Daguerre nor to M. Talbot. We are going to make researches to know if M. Charles, a member of the Académie des Sciences, who made silhouettes during his public lectures, preceded or followed Mr. Wedgwood. In any case, the first attempts of M. Niepce were made in 1814. We shall prove that M. Daguerre, while his friend, who died on July 5, 1833, was still alive, was already in possession of this entirely novel process which he uses today, and that some of the pictures which the public had so much admired existed at that time." Arago's zeal carried him somewhat too far, for some of his assertions are inexact.

At any rate, there was no cause for such alarm. The photographic pictures of Talbot were only prints made by contact on sensitive paper. It was not until a little later (February 20th) that Talbot gave details of his manipulations and had found a paper sufficiently sensitive for use in the camera obscura. In March he indicated thiosulphate of soda as the fixing agent, an improvement by which Daguerre profited. Other inventors, or some who called themselves such, also suddenly awakened to their rights to the discovery of photography and claimed them either before the Académie des Sciences, or in the public journals. I will refer to them later when I discuss the work of Talbot. The daguerreotype images, moreover, seemed so perfect that the public refused to believe that they could be improved, even when confronted with the evidence. In June 1839 Bayard, as will be seen, exhibited photographs on paper which were at least as good as the daguerreotypes and to which no one paid any attention.

Among the claims which followed those of Talbot, there is one worth citing for its generosity, and that is the one of the English scientist, Francis Bauer. It will be remembered that Bauer, who lived at Kew in 1827, knew Niepce and had received his confidences. Niepce, on the advice of Bauer, had written his memoir for the Royal Society and gratefully gave to his good counsellor several heliographs which Bauer still possessed. The English scientist protested against the partiality of

Arago who attributed to Daguerre alone the merit for the invention and recalled that, a good many years previously, "his respected friend" had produced true and perfect images. (13) An act of courage which should appeal to others. At Paris, the optician Chevalier sent to Arago a heliograph on metal which Niepce had presented to him in 1829, and requested him to deposit it in the archives of the Académie des Sciences in order to establish the priority of the discovery. (14)

HISTORY OF THE DISCOVERY OF PHOTOGRAPHY
REFERENCES: CHAPTER XXIX

1. *Historique de la Découverte improprement nommée Daguerréotype*, pp.47-53. The two contracts were signed May 9, 1835 and June 13, 1837.
2. Chevalier, *Nouvelles Instructions sur l'Usage du Daguerréotype*, Paris, 1841.
3. Mentienne, *La Découverte de la Photographie en 1839*, pp.16,137.
4. Session of June 15, 1839 of the Chamber of Deputies in exposition of the underlying reasons for the preliminary draft of the law presented by the Minister of the Interior. Mentienne say 10,000 pounds sterling and a life pension of 1,000 pounds.
5. This is not in accordance with the facts, and few persons regarded it in this manner.
6. *Comptes rendus*, January 7, 1839.
7. Abbé Moigno, *Repertoire d'Optique*, Paris 1847, 2nd part, p.692.
8. *Comptes rendus*, 1840, 1st semester, p.587.
9. Belloc, *Annales de la Photographie*, Paris, 1855, p.XXV.
10. *L'Artiste*, January 27, 1839.
11. On Fox Talbot, see Chapter XXXIV.
12. *Comptes rendus*, 1839, 1st semester, 170.
13. *Comptes rendus*, 1839, 1st semester, p.361. Isidore Niepce, *Historique de la Découverte improprement nommée Daguerréotype*, p.61.
14. I have mentioned this heliograph in Chapter XXVI.

CHAPTER XXX

The French Government Acquires the Photographic Process

MEANWHILE, in the midst of these discussions, and with all the noise caused by this extraordinary discovery, the negotiations of Daguerre and Niepce's son with the French Government continued through the intervention of Arago. (1) The inventors demanded the sum of 200,000 francs which they proposed to divide equally; such was the desire of Niepce. Arago proposed an annuity for life for each. The payment of a fixed sum, he said, gave the contract the shabby character of a trade; a pension is a national reward; it will return less profit but more honour. Daguerre—who had no children—accepted the pension. He deserves especial merit because he had suffered a great misfortune. The Diorama, which he had directed for seventeen years, to which he had consecrated so much thought and care, and which constituted his whole fortune, because he had used all his savings to repurchase the interest of the stockholders, was destroyed by fire on March 3, 1839 and by one stroke Daguerre was ruined. (2) A stagehand, having carelessly approached a newly varnished decoration with a lamp, set it afire and in a few hours the building, filled with scenery, became a mass of cinders.

This somewhat modified the clauses of the contract. The Diorama having disappeared, there existed no further reason for maintaining the secrecy concerning the processes but, on the contrary, it now became necessary to draw some profit from them. Of course, after seventeen years of exploitation, the novelty of the Diorama had worn off. It was agreed that Daguerre would describe his processes at the same time as that of the daguerreotype and the pension was set at 6,000 francs for Daguerre and 4,000 francs for Isidore Niepce. These matters having been agreed upon, the Minister of the Interior, Duchâtel, presented to the Chamber of Deputies on June 15, 1839 the draft of the following law:

"*Louis Philippe, King of the French, to those present and to come, greetings!*

"We have commanded and do command that the draft of a bill, the contents of which follow, be submitted in our name to the Chamber of Deputies by our Minister, Secretary of State for the Department of the Interior, whom we order to explain the underlying motives and to support the negotiations.

"ARTICLE I.

"The provisional agreement made on June 14, 1839, between the Minister of the Interior, acting for the State, and MM. Daguerre and Niepce, the son, a copy of which is joined to the present law and approved.

"ARTICLE II.

"To M. Daguerre is granted an annual pension for life of 6,000 francs; to M. Niepce, the son, is granted an annual pension for life of 4,000 francs.

"ARTICLE III.

"On the passage of this present law these pensions shall be recorded in the Records of civil pensions of the Public Treasury, with their enjoyment to begin on the promulgation of the present law. They shall not be subject to the prohibitive law of accumulation. They are to be revertible, half and half, to the widows of MM. Daguerre and Niepce.

"Given at the Palais of the Tuileries, June 15, 1839."

The convention added to the first article of the law in question says that Daguerre and the son of Niepce have ceded to the State the process of M. Niepce the father, with the improvements of M. Daguerre and of the last process of M. Daguerre, used to fix the images of the camera obscura; in addition "the processes of painting and the physical means which characterized the invention of the Diorama" and finally, the improvements which Daguerre might make on his discoveries in the future.

Arago was entrusted with the duty of verifying the correctness of Daguerre's claims. He had already done this. Since January the inventor had taken Arago into his confidence, in fact, he had done more. Arago himself had experimented with the process, using Daguerre's apparatus, and he had been able to obtain a view of the Boulevard du Temple which was perfectly successful. (3)

Under such conditions it was not difficult to convince the Deputies. The Minister contented himself with recounting the history of the invention as related to him by Arago, who in turn had received the information from Daguerre. "Gentlemen" he exclaimed, "you know that after fifteen years of persevering and expensive researches, M. Daguerre has succeeded in fixing the images of the camera obscura . . . . The possibility of fixing, momentarily, the images of the camera obscura has been known since the last century . . . . M. Niepce, the father, invented a method of rendering these images permanent but, although he had solved this difficult problem, his invention, nevertheless, remained very imperfect. He obtained only a silhouette of the objects (4), and it required at least twelve hours to obtain any kind of design. *Following an entirely different road, and putting aside the experience of M.Niepce,* Daguerre has arrived at admirable results of which today we are the witnesses . . . . *The method of M.Daguerre is his own; it belongs to him alone and it differs from that of his predecessor as well in its cause as in its effects* . . . . However, before his death, M.Niepce, the father, and M. Daguerre, signed an agreement by which they engaged mutually to share all the profits which would accrue from their discoveries; since this stipulation extended to Niepce, the son, it is impossible today to deal with M.Daguerre alone, even as far as this process is concerned, which he had not only perfected but invented. Moreover, it must not be forgotten that M.Niepce's method, although it remained imperfect, might be susceptible of some improvements; it might also be usefully applied under certain circumstances and it is, therefore, important for the history of science that it should be made public at the same time as that of M.Daguerre . . . . We hope that you will approve the motives which have dictated this contract and the conditions upon which they rest. You will thus become associated in an idea which has already excited general sympathy, and you will not suffer that we shall allow foreign nations the glory of presenting to the scientific and artistic world one of the most marvelous discoveries which honours our country."

One cannot help but conclude that the immense development of photography has shown that the enthusiastic words of the Minister were not far from the truth. His debut is less admirable. I have italicized the passages which alter the truth most boldly. Alas! These official errors have become the fashion and have been repeated time and time again despite the evidence. The project was taken under consideration, Arago was charged with the making of the report. The law was adopted by the Chamber of Deputies at the Session of July 3rd; by the Chamber of Peers July 30, 1839. Gay-Lussac—who passes Niepce over in silence —made the report to the Peers. A few days later, the Minister wrote to Arago: "My dear Sir and Colleague, the law which accords a national reward to M.Daguerre has received the sanction of the King, and it becomes my duty to make his discovery public. I thought that the best and most convenient means would be to communicate it to the Académie des Sciences. Please inform me if the Académie will be prepared to receive this communication at the Session of next Monday (August 19th), to which might be invited the members of the Académie des Beaux-Arts.

1. *Comptes rendus*, 1839, 2nd semester, p.250.
2. Daguerre's loss was several hundred thousand francs, according to Mentienne, work cited, p.137.
3. *Comptes rendus*, February 4, 1839. The preliminary draft of the law presented by the Minister, the report by Arago to the Deputies, that of Gay-Lussac to the Peers, were published in the beginning of a brochure, printed at the expense of the government: *Historique et Description des Procédés du Daguerréotype et du Diorama* by Daguerre, Paris, 1839.
4. The heliographs, reproduced in the French edition, demonstrate the contrary.

CHAPTER XXXI

Photography is Made Public

A ND so before the most brilliant assembly, before the two Académies des Sciences and des Beaux-Arts, and an audience which comprised all the famous artists, scientists and literary men of our country,
Arago on August 19, 1839, made public before the Académie and by it,
Urbi et Orbi, to the town and to the Universe, the method of obtaining
the daguerreotype. (1) This report, ever celebrated, always consulted
and quoted, thus became, as it were, the official birth certificate of photography. However, we do not know the exact terms today, because we
find the following note in the *Comptes rendus:* "In the absence of any
guide for finding not only the expressions used by the Secretary of the
Académie, but also the sequence of his discussions, we believe, after
some hesitation, that it is necessary to reproduce the principal passages
of the written report which M.Arago presented to the Chamber of
Deputies, as explaining today those passages in the notes which evidently remained unspoken before the Chamber."

There were many errors in the document; some unimportant made by
Arago and others furnished by Daguerre. Arago attributes to Porta the
invention of the camera obscura and the construction of the hand camera. He states: "Let us begin with the germ of the invention and show
its progress." He cites Fabricius who, in 1566, speaks in his treatise on
metal *"of a silver mine called 'argentum cornei' and which when exposed to
the light changes from a yellowish grey to violet and that, after more prolonged action, to almost black"*, and emphasizing this, *"a peculiar property of silver chloride discovered by the old alchemists."* He mentioned the
experiments of Charles, without giving the precise date nor their detail;
he had read Davy's Memoir of 1802, but he thinks that the Wedgwood
in question was the celebrated English potter, although the matter concerns one of his sons, and finally arrived at Niepce's experiments.

"M.Niepce" he says, "went to England in 1827. In December of the
same year he presented a note on his photographic work to the Royal
Society of London. The note was accompanied by several specimens on
metal produced by methods already discovered by our countryman. At
the time of the claim for priority, these specimens, still in good condition, were loyally lent from their collections by different English scientists.

They prove without a doubt that, *in order to obtain photographic prints from engravings* (2), M.Niepce knew in 1827 the means of obtaining the relations of shadow to shadow, half tone to half tone, lights to lights, and that he knew, moreover, once his prints were made, that it was necessary to protect them from the subsequent blackening action of the solar rays . . . . In our remarks made above, one undoubtedly will note these restrictive words: *for photographic prints from engravings.* In effect, after a great number of fruitless attempts, M.Niepce also had almost abandoned the reproduction of the images of the camera obscura, because the preparations which he used did not turn black fast enough under the action of light; because he required ten or twelve hours to produce the image; because during this long interval the shadows of the objects were much displaced; because by a method so defective all the effects resulting from the contrasts of light and shade were lost; because in spite of all these immense disadvantages, one was never sure of success; because after taking infinite precautions, inexplicable and accidental causes intervened, sometimes giving a passable result, sometimes an incomplete image was obtained which showed here and there empty spaces and because finally, when exposed to sunlight, the sensitive coating, upon which the images are received, if it did not blacken, would become brittle and scale off.

"If one takes the opposite of all these imperfections, one has an almost clear picture of the merits of the method which M.Daguerre discovered and achieved after laborious, delicate and costly experiments . . . . In the process to which a grateful public has given the name of Daguerreotype, the coating of the plate or the surface on which the image is received is of a golden-yellow colour with which the plate is covered while placed in a horizontal position with the silvered surface facing downward in a box at the bottom of which some grains of iodine are left for spontaneous evaporation. When this plate is taken out of the camera obscura, one sees absolutely no trace of the image. The yellowish layer of silver iodide which has received the image seems of the same uniform shade all over. When, however, this plate is exposed in a second box to ascending vapours of mercury rising from a capsule of liquid heated by a spirit lamp to 75°C., these vapours produce at once the most curious effect. They deposit abundantly on those parts of the surface of the plate which the light has most affected; they leave unchanged those parts representing the shadows. In short, they are precipitated on the spaces which represent the middle tones in varying degree proportionately as the intensities of these middle tones graduate into the light or dark parts. By using the weak light of a candle, the operator can follow step by step the gradual formation of the image. He can see the mercury vapours, like an extremely delicate pencil, marking each part of the plate with its proper tone. The image of the camera obscura thus produced must be protected in order that the light will not affect it. M. Daguerre arrives at this result by placing the plate in hyposulphite of soda and then washing it with hot distilled water . . . . The rapidity of the method has probably astonished the public most. In fact, scarcely ten or twelve minutes are required even in the dull weather of winter for taking the view of a monument, of a town quarter or a scene. In the summer sunlight, the time can be reduced by half. In the southern clime, two or three minutes will certainly be sufficient (3) . . . . It is necessary to add the time required for unpacking and mounting the camera, the preparation of the plate, and the short period needed to protect the image after exposure from the action of light. All these manipulations together may occupy thirty minutes or three-quarters of an hour. Those who imagine, at the last moment before starting on a journey, that they can employ every moment while the coach slowly climbs the hill by taking views of the country, will be disappointed in their expectation. No less will we be disappointed when struck by the curious results obtained from the reproduction of manuscripts or (4) the illustrations of ancient works, or when dreaming of being able to reproduce and multiply photographic images by lithography . . . . When such images are rubbed or even slightly tamped, and they are submitted to the action of a printing press or a roller, they are destroyed beyond redemption . . . . It will be asked, after having obtained in the daguerreotype the most wonderful gradation of tones, if it will be possible to reproduce the colours, to substitute, in a word, pictures like engravings in aquatints as they are made now. This problem will be solved on the day when a substance will be discovered which alone and of itself will reproduce the red rays in red, yellow rays in yellow, blue rays in blue, etc. M. Niepce has already pointed out effects of this nature (5) in which, if I am correct, the phenomenon of coloured rings played a role. Perhaps this is the same effect of the red and violet which Seebeck obtained simultaneously on silver chloride at the two opposite extremities of the spectrum. M. Quetelet has informed me of a letter in which Sir John Herschel announces that his sensitive paper, having been exposed to a very bright solar spectrum, resulted in all the prismatic colours with the exception of red . . . . We will endeavour, gentlemen, to set forth everything of interest that M. Daguerre's discovery offers . . . . We are striving to make you share our convictions because they are vivid and sincere, because we have examined and studied everything with religious scruples, in keeping with the duty imposed upon us by your votes, because if it were possible to misjudge the importance of the daguerreotype and the position which it will occupy in the esteem of men, all doubt would have vanished when we saw how eagerly foreign nations set themselves to pounce upon an erroneous date, on a questionable fact, and on the slightest pretext in order to support questions of priority, endeavouring to add the brilliant ornament which the photographic process will always contribute to the crown of unequalled discoveries . . . . If it were necessary, it would not embarrass us at all to produce here the testimony of the most eminent men in England and Germany, and before which our most flattering utterance on the discovery of our countryman would completely pale. France has adopted this discovery and from the first has shown her pride in being able to generously donate it to the whole world."

It must be admitted that Arago, insufficiently informed on the study which preceded the daguerreotype, was singularly clear-sighted about its future. The importance of photography did not escape him and he foresaw at once its consequences—consequences unknown until then in the history of humanity—of an automatic reproduction, the work of an optical apparatus.

We, who have been able to contribute to the development of the discovery and to record its continuous progress, can only admire the penetration of the scientist. But since the daguerreotype for which Arago predicted so great a future was only a transitory process, we wonder why this scientist did not realize that photography did not begin with Daguerre, but perhaps with Wedgwood, who had an obscure presentiment of it, and assuredly with Niepce, the marvelous genius who made it a reality. How great Arago's error, for he did not say that the daguerreotype was only an improved heliograph!

PHOTOGRAPHY IS MADE PUBLIC
REFERENCES: CHAPTER XXXI

1. *Comptes rendus*, August 12 and 19, 1839, pp.227 and 250. See the enthusiastic report made by Gaudin on the day's proceedings. *Traité pratique de Photographie*, Paris, 1844, pp.5 and following.
2. These words are italicized in the original text.
3. The time of exposure for the daguerreotypes of 1839 which are preserved is generally twenty to thirty minutes.
4. Process is described in the *Comptes rendus*, 1839.
5. Note sent to Daguerre in December 1829.

CHAPTER XXXII

Daguerre Acclaimed

IT is difficult to imagine with what impatience and excitement artists and scientists awaited Arago's communication both in France and abroad. (1) From the time that the details of the obtaining of images by the daguerreotype became known, immense acclamation and its loud echo resounded the name of Daguerre over the whole world. Opticians, artists and chemists, eager to penetrate the astonishing secret, made many experiments and tried at all hazards to produce a material similar to that of Daguerre. After some indiscretions, whether true or not, which had lately been committed, the optician Chevalier introduced a camera and different accessories for making daguerreotypes: and on the 21st of August, the second day after the publication of the process, his client Captain Richoux and he obtained a daguerreotype image on a plate which, if it still exists, is certainly the oldest in the world, with the exception, of course, of those made by the inventor and by Arago. (2)

In the days that followed all the world could make daguerreotypes; that is, after the excitment had passed from specialists to the general public and, under the influence of researches made by all sorts of enterprises, the process was quickly modified and the exposure became so short that it was expected that portraits could be made, which aroused great enthusiasm. The process having been made public, all scientific instrument makers turned to selling the apparatus; but, of course, those recommended by the inventor were specially favoured. Daguerre placed his apparatus for sale through Susse Frères, Place de la Bourse, and through Giroux in the rue du Coq-Saint-Honoré. The optician Chevalier in his ire parodied a celebrated phrase: "When an optician is needed, a stationer is chosen." (3) However, Giroux was not chosen on account of his stationery business, but because he was a relative of Mme. Daguerre. Six months before the publication of the process, Giroux had received so many orders for the apparatus, to be filled in the future, that he did not know how he could deliver them.

At any rate, the two rival stores were besieged by the public. One found exhibited there plates side by side with the camera, a mercury box and mysterious flasks, to all of which was given the name pharmacy. Everyone wanted to see this extraordinary novelty. There was crowding and jostling until the police had to be called in to control the crowd and they formed the good Parisian public in line. It was the event of the day. A lithograph by Mourisset caricatured the craze from its first appearance.

How they enjoyed making fun of all these photographers of the first days! The exposure, so short, thirteen minutes without sun; the machine recalling the tortures of the Middle Ages, in order that the patient should not move; the portable apparatus, heavy as a house, nothing lacked. One saw also the fear expressed which the infant photography inspired in the minds of the artists. The opinion was unanimous that photography would destroy and take the place of all arts of design. As for the engravers, the gallows were ready to be rented, and at a low price. But the fear was unfounded: photography destroyed no one.

The specialists, however, were disappointed, because they expected that Daguerre himself would give the necessary explanations and make a plate before the Academy. The scientific terms employed by Arago terrified the artists. Jules Janin (4) expressed their fears that it contained only some complicated chemical terms, and that the daguerreotype was not as difficult as had been expected. In order to overcome this impression, Daguerre hastened to invite well-known personages to visit him and see him operate at home on the third floor of No.17 Boulevard Saint-Martin. He lived there after the burning of the Diorama. He wrote a pamphlet during the summer: "*Historique et Description des Procédés du Daguerréotype et du Diorama par Daguerre, Peintre, Inventeur du Diorama, Officier de la Légion d'Honneur, Membre de plusieurs Académies, etc., etc.*" (5) which minutely describes the manipulations of the daguerreotype and became the vade mecum and gospel of the early photographers. This small volume, published at the expense of the government (6), was sold beginning with August at the shops of Susse and Giroux and went through several editions. (7) Every Thursday, from 11 to 3, during the month of September Daguerre gave a public demonstration of his process at the Conservatoire des Arts et Métiers.(8)

The excitement over the invention was probably greater abroad than in France because the news became exaggerated on its way. From the beginning until Arago's report became known in January 1839, artists, scientists and manufacturers of all countries came to Paris. The optician Claudet came from London; and from England came, as I have said, Herschel, Watt and other scientists. England, however, is nearby; among those who took great trouble to come from a distance, I must cite Prof. Ettingshausen, who came as the official representative of

Austria, the art dealer Sachse from Berlin, and Morse from America. They brought to Daguerre official honours, the testimony of their admiration, or simply business propositions. I append here an unpublished letter from the famous physicist Morse.

"New York, May 20, 1839.
"TO M. DAGUERRE.

"DEAR SIR,
"I have the honour to enclose you the note of the Secretary of our Academy (9), informing you of your election, at our last Annual Meeting, into the Board of Honourary Members of our National Academy of Design. When I proposed your name, it was received with enthusiasm and the vote was unanimous. I hope, my dear sir, that you will receive this as a testimonial, not merely of my personal esteem, and deep sympathy in your late losses (10), but also as a proof that your genius is, in some degree, estimated on this side of the water.

"Notwithstanding the efforts made in England (11) to give to another the credit which is your due, I think I may with confidence assure you that throughout the United States your name alone will be associated with the brilliant discovery which justly bears your name. The letter I wrote from Paris, the day after your sad loss (12), has been published throughout this whole country in hundreds of journals, and has excited great interest. Should any attempt be made here to give to any other than yourself the honour of this discovery, my pen is ever at your service.

"I hope before this reaches you, that the French Government, long and deservedly celebrated for its generosity to men of genius, will have amply supplied all your losses by a liberal sum. If, when the proper remuneration shall be secured to you in France, you should think it may be to your advantage to make an arrangement with the Government to hold back the secret for six months or a year, and would consent to an exhibition of your *results* in this country for a short time, the exhibition might be managed, I think, to your pecuniary advantage. If you think favorably of the plan, I offer you my services gratuitously." (13)
"SAML F. B. MORSE, *President N.A.D.*"

I do not believe anything came of Morse's proposition but the recognition accorded to Daguerre's invention conferred upon him a sort of distinction and it is said that it was Morse who, with his associate Professor Draper, made the first daguerreotypes in America. However, Sachse (14) asserts that the first American daguerreotype was made by

DAGUERRE ACCLAIMED

Joseph Saxton, in Philadelphia, October 16, 1839: Daguerre's formula having reached that city on September 25th and New York only October 14th.

I have read in one of Vogel's works (15) that a dealer in objects of art to the Court of Berlin, Sachse, came to Paris in April 1839 and approached Daguerre with a proposition to represent him in Germany. On April 22nd (see Vogel) Daguerre is supposed to have confided to Sachse the secret of his invention. I do not believe a word of this; Daguerre was too clever to do that. With the exception of Arago, he had hidden his process from everybody, even from his associate Isidore Niepce. It is certain that Niepce and Daguerre hoped to exploit their discovery in the several countries of Europe and in America, and that they intended to give the process gratuitously only to France. Among Isidore's papers I have found a contract in which the two associates demanded a third of the proceeds of the sale and the exploitation of their process in England, where they had taken out a patent August 14, 1839. This agreement is dated February, 1840. Daguerre and Niepce tried to exploit their discovery in Germany and in Austria. They soon found this impossible. The Government had bought the secret without reservations and had presented it to the world. Even the sale of the apparatus by the inventor, which is the only thing that might have been left to him, brought no great profits because these apparatuses were rapidly surpassed by those built by makers trained in the construction of scientific instruments.

At any rate, the first German to make a daguerreotype was not Sachse. Sachse knew Daguerre from his dealings in objects of art. Attracted by the novelty of the extraordinary discovery, he visited the inventor in April 1839, saw the daguerrean images and the camera obscura which Daguerre was in the habit of exhibiting to everyone, and sought the rights for the exploitation of the process in Germany. Daguerre, who was negotiating with the French Government, did not commit himself. In July, Giroux, having the sales privilege, informed Sachse of it and took his order for six *daguerreotypes* which he was to forward as soon as the process became public. But Arago's Report traveled faster than the apparatus. It became known in Berlin August 31st and the daguerreotypes did not arrive until September 6th. With them came the necessary accessories, prepared plates, and an original example made by Daguerre, with six explanatory pamphlets. Unfortunately, Giroux had packed the merchandise so badly that it arrived broken to such an

171

extent that Sachse, after all kinds of efforts, was unable to obtain a daguerrean image until September 20th. Some days previously, how-.ever, several daguerrean images could be seen but they were so horrible that they created a doubt of the value of the invention.

On September 20th Sachse photographed a part of the Jaegerstrasse which adjoins the avenue Unter den Linden. A few days later, on September 30, 1839, commanded to present himself at the Royal Castle of Charlottenburg, he took five views of the Royal Park in the presence of King Friedrich Wilhelm III. This aroused such enthusiasm that Sachse in six weeks sold more than six hundred daguerreotype plates at the average price of from one to two frederics d'or (a frederic d'or was worth about frs. 20.80; sh.16.3; $3.96). When the pictures sent by Giroux came from Paris they cost as much as fr. 120; Giroux being too busy, shipped only very few of them.

The daguerreotypes with their accessories cost Sachse 425 francs each in addition to considerable expense of transport, which was about 100 francs per apparatus. He resold them for 30 frederics d'or (about frs. 625). The first to buy them was the Royal Institute of Arts and Industry, Humboldt, Doctor Lucanus (16) and later Korsten, Moser, Nörremberg and Mme. Misterlich. (17)

I have not sufficient information as to who were the first in each country to make the first daguerreotype images and this would probably be an impossible task. But what happened in Berlin gives an exact idea of the reception which photography met with abroad.

Among the photographers of the first days, Ettingshausen in Austria might be mentioned who also claims to have been in Daguerre's confidence, Martin, Pohl, Endlicher, Schultner, Wawra; in Bavaria, Steinheil; in Italy, Jest, of Turin; in Switzerland, the engraver Hamann of Geneva, and the painter Isenring of Saint Gallen; in Belgium, the lithographer Jobard.

We recall that Claudet (18), a Frenchman living in London, obtained from Daguerre a license for England. Before the daguerreotype was made public only the name of Claudet appears on the agreement of which I have spoken above.

In August, as soon as the law of acquisition was voted, daguerrean images were sent to the different sovereigns of Europe by courtesy of our Minister of Foreign Affairs. The impressions made when these pictures were received and the curiosity which they excited in high society changed this from an act of courtesy to one of clever propaganda. The daguerrean images sent from France were considered first-class everywhere.

Daguerre received in return flattering distinctions. The King of Prussia presented him with the Order of Merit of Prussia. The Emperor of Austria sent him a snuff box decorated with diamonds, a gold medal and a letter full of praise. (19) The Emperor of Russia also honoured him with a present. The Academies of Vienna, Edinburgh, Munich and New York considered it an honour to elect him an honourary member. (20) King Louis Philippe had already promoted him to the rank of Officer of the Légion d'Honneur, having been a Chevalier of the Légion since 1824.

It is almost impossible to enumerate the first photographers in France; there are too many. However, the first, aside from the inventor, to make a daguerreotype is certainly Arago, because this scientist made a view of the Boulevard du Temple in February 1839, being the only one who shared with Daguerre the secret of the invention. He also made pictures of the Boulevard Saint-Jacques. Chevalier and Richoux were the second to succeed in making a daguerrean image on August 21st. Doctor Donné joined them and also obtained a plate on the 22nd. (21) Among the operators of 1839 who are still to be remembered, because of their fame, are scientists such as Biot, Jean-Baptiste Dumas, Séguier, Regnault, Donné, Gaudin, Foucault; artists like Horace Vernet and his pupil Goupil, the engravers Lemaître, Hurliman, Martens, the lithographer Marquier, Nadar, the brothers Bisson, and the opticians Chevalier, Soleil, Cauche, Lerebours and Vaillat. Also the amateurs such as the architect Hubert who was helped by Daguerre, and Baron Gros, diplomat, who, learning of the discovery of the daguerreotype in South America where he lived, improved the first daguerreotype apparatus which was operated on that continent. Baron Gros later became one of the most expert operators of our country. The brothers Montmirel assert that they made the first portraits in Paris (22) but the optician Richebourg claims the same and names his models: the portrait of a lady and that of Doctor H.B. which he exhibited to the public towards the end of 1839.

HISTORY OF THE DISCOVERY OF PHOTOGRAPHY
REFERENCES: CHAPTER XXXII

1. *Rapport sur le Daguerréotype* by Macédoine Melloni, Paris 1840, pp.11, 40, 42.
2. Ch. Chevalier, *Nouvelles Instructions sur l'Usage du Daguerréotype*, Paris 1841, p.7. *Traité pratique de Photographie* by M.A.Gaudin, Paris 1844, p.5.
3. *Nouvelles Instructions sur l'Usage du Daguerréotype by* Ch. Chevalier, Paris 1841, p.22. The memoirs of the Duchess d'Abrantès show that Susse and Giroux had the two most frequented stationery shops in Paris. Daguerre's pamphlet: *Historique et Description, etc.*, published by Giroux in 1839, mentions that the apparatus manufactured by Alphonse Giroux & Co. are "The only ones made under the personal direction of M.Daguerre, the only ones carrying his signature."
4. *L'Artiste*, August 25, 1839.
5. History and description of the daguerreotype process and the Diorama of Daguerre, painter, inventor of the Diorama, officer of the Légion d'Honneur, member of several academies, etc., etc. (T.N.).
6. *Comptes rendus*, 1839, 2nd semester, p.411.
7. The library of the Société Française de Photographie has three editions of 1839.
8. *Comptes rendus*, 1839, 2nd semester, p.425.
9. National Academy of Design. Morse (1791-1872) was then president. The famous inventor of the electrical telegraphic instrument which carries his name was a painter; he did not interest himself in physics until about 1832. See: *Samuel F.B.Morse; His Letters and Journals*, Boston 1914, Vol.II, pp. 141-143. (T.N.).
10. Allusion to the Diorama fire.
11. The vindication of Talbot was upheld in England as a national affair.
12. The Diorama burned on March 3, 1839. This determines the date of Morse's presence in Paris.
13. The original of this letter belongs to the Société Française de Photographie.
14. On the beginning of photography in America see *American Journal of Photography*, 1892, pp.241, 306, 355, 403, 451, 543; 1893, p.369. *Early Daguerreotypy Days, an Historical Reminiscence*, by Julius F.Sachse.
15. H.Vogel, *La Photographie et la Chimie de la Lumière*, Paris 1876, p.12. Germer-Baillière, 17 rue de l'Ecole de Médicine. Vogel was Professor at the Polytechnic Academie, Berlin. This book was written by Vogel in French and is not a translation.
16. *Photographische Mitteilungen* . . . . H-W.Vogel, Berlin, August and September 1889, pp.150, 165, 181.
17. Vogel, *La Photographie et la Chimie de la Lumière*, Paris, 1876.
18. Claudet (1797-1867) married an English woman in 1821 and established himself in England in 1827. On the advice of his friend, the optician Lerebours, he came to Paris in the summer of 1839 in order to acquaint himself with the daguerreotype process and, like many other opticians here, returned to London in order to make heliographic portraits. He was elected a member of the Royal Society of London on June 2, 1853.
19. Eder, *Geschichte der Photographie*, p.198.
20. Mentienne, *La Découverte de la Photographie en 1839*, p.137. The originals of most of these letters belong to the Société Française de Photographie.
21. *Nouvelles Instructions sur l'Usage du Daguerréotype* by Chevalier, Paris 1841, p.5.
22. *Le Daguerréotype mis a la Portée de tout le Monde* by E.T. and E.Montmirel, Paris, 1842. On these different specimens see: *Comptes rendus*, 1839, 2nd semester, p.539; 1840, 1st semester; pp.41, 628; 2nd semester, p.824 and *Nouveau Manuel complementaire pour l'Usage pratique du Daguerréotype*, by Richebourg, Paris, 1842.

CHAPTER XXXIII

Claims for the Priority of the Invention

ALL great men have their detractors; many claimants arose against Daguerre. I have already mentioned Talbot's claim of January 1839. The *Comptes rendus de l'Académie des Sciences* enumerates others. At the meeting of February 11th, Desmarest deposited in a sealed envelope *A Process for the Fixation of the Images of the Camera Obscura*, of which nothing further was heard. Lassaigne, on April 8th, described a *photogenic process* giving direct images, which, with those of Bayard, will be dealt with later. Lassaigne, however, never obtained pictures in the camera obscura, which Biot confirms. (1) Gaumé, a photographer of Mans, had attempted in 1827, when he was a pupil at the college of Château-Gontier, to obtain photographs by a bleaching process. (2) Charles Chevalier tells us of an unknown person who visited him in 1826 at his store and entrusted him with photographs on paper, together with a flask containing a brown solution from which Daguerre was unable to get any result. Chevalier believed that this young man, unable to succeed, owing to his poverty, met with a tragic end. The world was romantic then. (3) After Ibbetson (4), Professor Gerber of Bern attempted, long before 1839, to fix the images of the camera obscura. As soon as the news of the discovery of the daguerreotype became known in Italy, Bonnafous wrote from Turin that a work by Antonio Cellio, published at Rome in 1686: "*Descrizione di un nuovo Modo di trasportare qual si sia Figura disegnata in Carta, medianti i Raggi solari*" (Description of a new means of reproducing an illustration designed on paper by the medium of solar rays T.N.) which seems to describe Daguerre's process rather closely; and there were many writers who insisted that Daguerre had simply copied Cellio. This matter is thoroughly covered in the *Dictionnaire de la conversation;* Libri felt obliged to deny this hoax. (5) Jobard of Brussels (6) relates in 1839 that, in an old booklet discovered in Berlin, it was found that photography had been described more than three hundred years before. In 1863 there were shown in England (7) photographs made prior to 1791. After a long controversy, it had to be admitted that these proofs were made in 1842 by Talbot and from daguerreotypes of the same period. In 1851, before the Heliographic Society, Delécluze (8), a former pupil of David, who had become an art critic, expressed the opinion that the gravure prints made by a certain Gonord, dated 1805, were photographs. Poitevin (9) relates that the fixing of the images of the camera haunted him during his adolescence, until he learned that Daguerre had found the solution of the problem. I have said that De La Blanchère (10) gave the precise date of the birth of photography: *"photography saw the light of day in the seventeenth century. In 1670 Tiphaigne de La Roche discovered the method of fixing the luminous rays."*

Unfortunately for these innovators, one seeks in vain for any one among them who, before the year 1839, showed images fixed in the camera or even announced his intention of doing so. In England also, there are a certain number who claimed precedence. Robert Hunt published his experiments in detail in his work: *"Researches on Light"* in 1844. Towson, who assisted Hunt in his experiments, asserts that he produced, in 1838, a photographic print on glass which he sent to Herschel. (11) Hunt made a claim against Talbot, and J.B.Reade joined Robert Hunt. (12) Reade had employed, in 1836, an infusion of gallnuts for an intensifier and hyposulphite of soda for fixation; but he had no thought of photography; he only wanted to continue the experiments of Wedgwood and Davy, of which he had read in the Memoir. Sutton (13) asserts that Mungo Ponton made photographs, in 1838, by means of a paper impregnated with potassium and sulphate of indigo. Draper in America is also listed among those who made photographs before 1839. I see only that all these scientists intended to create a method of drawing in the camera by the aid of chemistry; what they did was photo-chemistry — not photography. Herschel, who for years had known of the action of light and of hyposulphite of soda on silver, which Daguerre and Talbot lacked for the completion of their processes, is a typical example. On this account he is numbered as one of the "predecessors". The fact is that, after Daguerre had produced his marvelous daguerreotypes, the idea of drawing by means of the camera obscura, the automatic fixation of the ground-glass image, entered many minds, especially those of chemists, and established itself there as a simple and permanent idea. But the academician Turpin (14) exactly expressed the general impression when he said: "If we were told for the first time of M.Daguerre's results, it would be difficult for us to believe them and we would reject this novelty as a fairy tale invented for our entertainment. However, the testimony of learned and worthy men who have seen them assure us of their being a fact." When the discovery of Daguerre was made public in Europe, the terms used by the scientists of every country express everywhere the thoughts and almost the very words of Turpin. Melloni stated before the Academy of Sciences in Naples: "Who would have thought, a few months ago, that light, being penetrable, intangible, imponderable, would be deprived in totality of all its properties as matter and that it would assume the role of a painter, drawing with the most exquisite talent these ethereal images which art itself had struggled in vain to make permanent?" (15)

No doubt, since Wedgwood and Niepce, time had passed. The idea of photography was no longer a novelty. For fifteen years Daguerre had talked about it in public. I do not know whether the study of the nature and properties of light gave birth to the idea in the minds of scientists; but they had no idea of photography. In particular, Niepce's visit to England in 1827, his report to the Royal Society, the plates which he left there, greatly influenced the mind of the student and showed the road to follow. This was the case with Talbot, for of all the inventors who appeared after the invention, two of them must be set apart, Talbot and Bayard.

1. *Comptes rendus*, 1839, 1st semester, p.547—1840, 1st semester, p.374.
2. *Bulletin de la Société Française de Photographie*, 1881, p.58.
3. *Souvenirs historiques* in *Etude sur la Vie et les Travaux scientifiques de Charles Chevalier* by Arthur Chevalier, his son, Paris, 1862.
4. Exposition of the London Photographic Society, reported in the *Atheneum*, 1853 and *La Lumière* of January 22, 1853.
5. *Comptes rendus*, 1st semester, p.714; 2nd semester, p.289.
6. J.-B.-A.-M.Jobard. *Rapport sur l'Exposition de 1839 à Bruxelles*.
7. *The Photographic News*, November 13, 1863.
8. *La Lumière*, April 20, 1851.
9. *Traité de l'Impression photographique sans Sels d'Argent*, by Alphonse Poitevin Paris, 1862.
10. De La Blanchère, *Repertoire encyclopédique de Photographie*, Paris 1863, I-472.
11. *Bulletin de la Société Française de Photographie*, 1858, p.280.
12. Letters from Rev.J.B.Reade to Robert Hunt and to Talbot. *La Lumière*, May 2 ,1854 and June 24, 1854.
13. *Photographic Notes*, November 1858.
14. *Comptes rendus*, 1840, 1st semester, p.587.
15. *Rapport sur le Daguerréotype* by Macédoine Melloni, Paris 1840.

CHAPTER XXXIV

Talbot

WILLIAM HENRY FOX-TALBOT was a well-to-do English amateur who devoted his leisure to the study of sciences. He was born in 1800 (1), was educated at Trinity College, Cambridge and, while still a young man, published numerous articles on mathematics. During a tour in Italy, in 1823, he had made drawings with the aid of the camera obscura (2) but soon discarded this unsatisfactory method. Niepce's memoir, in 1827, modified his ideas. At Lake Como, in 1833, he again employed the camera obscura and then thought "to retain the image formed by the light in this apparatus". He made a note of this, intending to begin some experiments as soon as he returned to England. He returned in January 1834 and the first attempts were made in the spring of the same year.

The silver chloride was not sufficiently sensitive to be affected in the camera obscura; he then used silver iodide. Many experiments, however, showed that silver chloride becomes more sensitive when it contains an excess of nitrate and that, on the contrary, chloride in excess greatly reduces the sensitiveness. He finally obtained an image in the camera, in 1835, on paper soaked successively in baths of salt and silver. The exposure lasted ten minutes. The fixation with potassium iodide or with sodium chloride was uncertain, which Talbot himself recognized because he says that the whites of the image showed a weak lilac tint.

At any rate Talbot, after this, made only photographic prints by placing in contact with his sensitive paper laces, leaves, drawings or other transparent objects, and it seems that he was unable to repeat his success of 1835. Finally he abandoned all his photographic experiments. In the meantime, he had published quite a number of articles on light, on the nature of light, on the chemical changes of colours, on the silver iodides and on mercury. He was familiar in 1838 (4) with Davy's Memoir (published in 1802) on Wedgwood's work, and this perhaps reawakened his hope of being able to fix images in the camera. Talbot meanwhile made no other attempt until after the beginning of January 1839 when Arago's communication appeared. In two identical letters, addressed to Arago and to Biot on January 29th, Talbot at once claimed the priority for the invention: 1st "of obtaining images in the camera obscura"; 2nd, "of the subsequent permanence of these images to such a degree that they could withstand full sunlight". At the same time he exhibited some of his *photogenic drawings* at the Royal Institution of London and read a communication before the Royal Society (January 30th).

These photogenic drawings were nothing but contact prints on sensitive paper and the report to the Royal Society gives no details as to the method by which they were obtained. It was not until several days later (5) that Talbot indicated his method of manipulation in two letters addressed to Biot. In the interval between the two letters, the inventor discovered two improvements on his process. In order to render his paper more sensitive, Talbot coated it with a solution of silver nitrate, then with a solution of potassium bromide, and again with another solution of silver nitrate, drying the paper before a fire after each operation. The paper so treated gave images in the camera with an exposure of six to seven minutes. Talbot advised for the fixation of images, in addition to a solution of sea salt and that of potassium iodide, also a solution of potassium ferrocyanide. But the surest method of fixation, which has been employed ever since, he learned from his friend Herschel. "The fourth method" says Talbot, "which far excels all the others, consists in washing the picture with hyposulphite of soda. This process naturally presented itself to the mind of Herschel, because it was he who discovered hyposulphites and established the principal properties, among which he remarked as very important that hyposulphite of soda easily dissolved silver chloride . . . . Some of the references in which Herschel describes the properties of hyposulphites will be found in: *Brewster's Edinburgh Philosophical Journal*, vol.I, pages 8 and 396; vol.II, page 154, 1819 and 1820."

It must be recalled that in all his processes Talbot obtained a reversed image translating the highlights of the copy into blacks and the shadows into whites. In order to obtain a true image, or a positive as we call it today, he printed his negative picture anew on a second sensitive paper. We must not think the fact of obtaining a negative, from which an unlimited number of positives could be produced, was considered at first a fortunate accomplishment. Talbot thought this, as did the whole world (6), only an inferior result of his process and renewed more than ever his efforts to obtain direct images, in which he succeeded a little later.

The first photogenic drawings of Talbot were defective. Herschel who was quite familiar with them, while passing through Paris in May 1839, together with other scientists, Forbes, Watt, Murchison and others, expressed a desire to see Daguerre's images. Arago conducted him there. "This is a miracle" he murmured, when he saw the daguerreotypes, and he added: "*Talbot's drawings are child's play compared with these.*" (7) Biot in February 1840, presenting Talbot's drawings to the Academy, considered only one of them as good, and even this one he compared unfavorably in favor of Bayard. (8) We are no longer able to judge his images. I do not know the present state of specimens in the collection of the Photographic Society of London, but those which Talbot presented to the Société Française de Photographie have become invisible and entirely black, notwithstanding that they were protected against dust and air and were kept in a soft light. At any rate, his method was in the beginning so uncertain that the inventor did not apply for a patent and did not complete the specifications until February 1841. (9) We see from this patent that Talbot, after having described how the positive picture was obtained in the printing frame under a negative, points out as an improvement the method of producing positives directly in the camera. Notwithstanding everything, Talbot's process never succeeded. A few photographers who employed his process were disappointed; the manipulations were difficult, the result uncertain and the image unsatisfactory. (10) The process was given up.

Talbot in his patent forbade all exploitation of his process in England. In 1852, he used for the first time bichromated gelatine in a photogravure process. At any rate, he did not confine his activities to photochemical and photographic works, but he published several learned works: *Hermes, or Classical and Antiquarian Researches, The Antiquity of the Book of Genesis;* these two works were published in 1839, and *English Etymologies* in 1846. Talbot must also be given credit for the first book illustrated by photography: *The Pencil of Nature,* a serial published in 1844 by subscription and of which only five numbers appeared. In 1845 he published 23 views of Scotland, in the form of an album, illustrated with photographs but without text.

He died in 1877, full of glory and honours.

HISTORY OF THE DISCOVERY OF PHOTOGRAPHY
REFERENCES: CHAPTER XXXIV

1. On Talbot see: Richard Cull, *A Biographical Notice of the late W.H.Fox-Talbot*, London 1879 and *British Journal of Photography: Sketches of Eminent Photographers*, July 1, 1864, p.220— August 5, p.278— August 19, p.303— September 9, p.340— October 21, p.412. These articles are attributed to John Traill Taylor.
2. *Bulletin de la Société Française de Photographie*, 1881, p.52: *Notes communiquées* by Sir Henry Talbot (his son); and *Bulletin de la Société Française de Photographie*, 1878, p.13: *Obituary* by Perrot de Chaumeux.
3. *Comptes rendus*, February 25, 1839, p.302.
4. *Bulletin de la Société Française de Photographie*, 1881, *Notes* by Sir Henry Talbot.
5. *Comptes rendus*, February 25, p.302; March 4, 1839, p.341. The letters from Talbot are dated February 20, 21 and March 1, 1839.
6. Biot, *Comptes rendus*, February 18, 1839, p.246.
7. *Comptes rendus*, 1839, 1st semester, p.838.
8. *Comptes rendus*, 1840, 1st semester, p.247.
9. The patent applied for at Westminster, February 8, 1841, was made public in France the following June 7. It is published in the *Bulletin de la Société Française de Photographie* of 1857, p.222.
10. "The talbotype was made public prematurely and was at first incomplete; the process, given up almost as soon as it was started, remained dormant for some years . . . . Not until 1849 and for the first time, portraits on paper imported from Germany, appeared on the Parisian boulevards . . . . The usual fickleness of the public was all that was necessary to start a reaction in favor of these poor Talbotype images which could be compared only to the worst kind of a lithograph." *Les quatre Branches de la Photographie*, by A.Belloc, Paris 1855, p.74. "Spots were frequent, so frequent, that they seemed to be a part of the process itself." Perrot de Chaumeux. *Bulletin de la Société Française de Photographie*, 1878, 13.

CHAPTER XXXV

Bayard

HIPPOLYTE BAYARD was born at Breteuil-sur-Noye, a small town in the department of Oise, on the 30th nivôse in the year IX, corresponding to January 20, 1801. (1) For some time he was a clerk in a notary's office and while still young went to Paris where he entered the Ministry of Finance. His father was a Justice of the Peace, the first elected at Breteuil, according to the decree of July 1790 (2) which created this judicial office.

The few biographies existing of Bayard relate how he made early and modest attempts at photography. While a child, he had seen his father obtain silhouettes and initials by means of stencils on fruit ripening in the sun. Imitating his father, having more experience, he exposed to the light under stencils papers coloured with safflower. While the sun bleached the paper, those parts covered by the stencil preserved their original colour. From these experiments he tried to work out a photographic process about 1837, but did not succeed.

We see in these recitals the tendency of writers to make photo-chemistry the necessary prelude to photography; this is an error. These experiments on the colouring and bleaching action of the solar rays on vegetable matter were common at the beginning of the nineteenth century. Senebier and Ingenhousz had made the details of these experiments public twenty years before. (3) In 1810, amateurs in the provinces looked upon this as a pastime. When Bayard interested himself in photography, he was thirty-seven years old and had long since forgotten the amusements of his youth.

While living in Breteuil, Bayard had as a fellow clerk in the same office a young man by the name of Edmond Geoffroy. The two friends came to Paris together in order to try their fortunes but they followed different paths. While Bayard entered the employ of the government, Geoffroy became an actor at the Comédie Française. Bayard, who liked to draw, became acquainted through his friend with some artists. His papers, preserved by the Société Française de Photographie show that he was acquainted with Gavarni, Charlet, Grevedon and others. Dupuis, an actor at the Théâtre-Français, painted with a good deal of taste, so did Geoffroy. Dupuis studied with Amaury Duval, a pupil of

Ingres. In this artistic company, very much impressed in 1837 by Daguerre's persistent agitation in behalf of his discovery, Bayard became acquainted with and interested in photography. I cannot find any trace either in his writings or in his talks that he made experiments or researches at this period; but he allowed these things to be said without protest. In any event, he commenced a new series of experiments on January 20, 1839. This was immediately after Arago's report on Daguerre but before Talbot's communication became known. Sixteen days later, on February 5th, he showed images, imperfect it is true, to Desprets, of the Institute. On March 20th, he had completely solved the problem and showed his prints to Saint, to Grevedon, and to others. The exposure required about an hour. He brought to Biot on May 13th and to Arago on May 20th positive photographs on paper obtained directly in the camera. At a charity bazaar in the auction rooms on June 24th, Bayard exhibited to the public thirty photographs, most of which are still preserved and in perfect condition. They aroused public admiration and the exhibition is reported in the *Moniteur* (July 22, 1839), the *Constitutionnel* (August 3rd), the *Capitole*, etc. In short, at this period there existed no other photographic prints than those of Bayard and Daguerre, because the method of operation was not yet known. Bayard took no trouble to hide his process and freely showed it to those about him. But he presented no official communication because Arago earnestly requested him not to publish anything about his discovery, in order not to prejudice that of Daguerre. (4) Bayard received from the Minister of the Interior a subsidy of 600 francs for the purpose of buying a suitable camera and lens. Two months later the Daguerreotype process was made public. In the meantime, the Académie des Beaux-Arts remembered Bayard's photographs on paper and instructed Raoul Rochette to make a report on the matter. (5) The Academy declared the superiority of paper over metal, expressed its satisfaction and recommended the inventor "to the interest and generosity of the government". (6)

Bayard did not publish his process officially until the beginning of 1840, and then only because he feared that the merit of his discovery might be disputed. He wrote to the Académie des Sciences on February 24, 1840 (7): "I have deferred until today the publication of the photographic process of which I am the author in order to first render this process as perfect as possible. When, however, I could not prevent some of the information leaking out, and since the credit for the honour of my discovery might be disputed, I felt compelled not to wait any longer in the publication of my method. The time is short. Here is a summary of my process: "Ordinary letter paper having been prepared according to M. Talbot's method and blackened by light, I soak it for several seconds in a solution of potassium iodide, then putting the paper on a piece of slate, I place it in the camera. After the image is formed, I wash this paper in a solution of hyposulphite of soda and again in pure hot water and dry it in the dark." This is not the formula which he gave later. (8) He soaked his paper in a two percent solution of nitrate of silver, and dried it again in the dark. When dry, the paper was exposed to light until it was completely blackened. Immersed in a four percent solution of potassium iodide, it was put while still moist on a slate and placed in the camera obscura; the light bleached the paper in those parts containing the image, thus presenting the positive in the end. Bayard then thoroughly washed it and fixed it with a solution of potassium bromide.

Bayard rightly apprehended that the credit for his discovery would be disputed, for on the same day Vérignon brought to the attention of the Académie a similar process. Some days later, Lassaigne recalled that he had presented this process a year earlier to the Académie. There ensued a controversy in which Biot and Arago took part. At the meeting of March 16, 1840 Arago lectured on his *Historical Note on Photography* (9): "The processes presented by MM. Vérignon and Bayard" he said, "in no way differ from that of M. Lassaigne which, on the other hand, Mr. Fyfe conceived and communicated to the Society of Arts of Edinburgh on April 17, 1839. Both effectively employed paper coated with silver chloride or silver phosphate and soaked in a solution of potassium iodide. Both advised that the paper be used while still moist . . . . Mr. Fyfe made experiments with the same paper in the camera obscura; he also used silver chloride. All these details may be found in a memoir published in June 1839. As far as M. Lassaigne is concerned, his process is published in the *Echo du Monde savant* of April 10, 1839." (10)

Arago seems to forget that Bayard showed his specimens before March 1839 and only kept his process secret because of Arago's own request. It is undoubtedly due to this lack of goodwill, as well as to an excessive timidity on his part, that the clumsiness of the explanations given above by Bayard must be attributed. I cannot understand how Lassaigne, Fyfe and Bayard conceived an identical process at practically the same time. It is possible that they may have borrowed from the same source.

I have no information about the photographs made by Fyfe; Lassaigne did not succeed in making any and, of the three inventors, Bayard is assuredly the first. We may justly affirm that he preceded Talbot, not in his experiments, but in his accomplishment of a photographic process on paper, since Talbot did not make his process definite until September 1840 and did not publish it until 1841. (11)

A short debate then ensued between these two inventors. We know that Daguerre applied a thin layer of iodine to a silvered metal plate. Placed in the camera obscura, after a sufficient exposure, this plate was exposed to the vapours of mercury; the picture, invisible until then, suddenly appeared. The essential innovation of daguerreotypy consisted, then, in revealing the latent image, the invisible image, under the action of a chemical agent. Bayard, inspired by Daguerre, applied this principle at once to photography on paper, and deposited his method in a sealed envelope with the Académie des Sciences on November 11, 1839. In the beginning of 1841 Talbot informed Biot that he had found the method for rendering visible the image, which was still invisible on the paper when taken out of the camera, and that he would soon publish his process. At once Bayard claimed the priority of this invention and demanded that the sealed envelope which had been deposited fourteen months previously be opened.

On opening this envelope it was found to contain a photograph and the following explanation: "The enclosed photographic image was obtained on October 24, 1839 in eighteen minutes from 11:00 to 11:18 in the forenoon by the following process: Soak the paper in a weak solution of sodium chloride; after it is quite dry, coat this paper with silver nitrate dissolved in six times its weight of water; the paper, having become almost dry, must be protected from all light-action, exposed to the fumes of iodine, then placed in the camera obscura, then subjected to mercury as in M. Daguerre's process; finally, it is washed in a solution of hyposulphite of soda. After the paper has been taken from the camera obscura, the outlines of the picture can only be barely distinguished, after the condensation of the mercurial vapours on the paper, the images are seen to develop, the same as on metallic plates, with this difference that the images are produced in a contrary direction, as in Talbot's process. Paris, November 8, 1839."

The priority was evident; Talbot did not press the point. How is it then that under these conditions Talbot became famous, while Bayard remained unknown? Different circumstances are the cause of this. First of all, in the years that followed 1839, Daguerre's invention was so much the vogue, the name of Daguerre had such acclaim, that the rival processes were relegated to the background without any chance of success. Bayard and Talbot, ignored by the general public, plunged fraternally into the same oblivion. Their processes were inferior to daguerreotype. Talbot's photographs were defective, without refinement, coarse, the grain of the paper was exaggerated by the twofold impression of positive under negative. Bayard's process was much slower. It required twenty minutes for the average exposure and could not be used in portraiture, although his other images were excellent. Bayard, excessively modest, did nothing to spread his method, detesting advertising or clamour on his behalf. He even refused to exploit his process or to draw from it any profit whatever. When he divulged it, it was done with such self-effacement that, even twenty years later, his process was thought to be secret and its publication was practically unknown.

Talbot's method was not a success. In 1846, Blanquart Evrard again took it up and perfected this process; he made it practical and obtained very fine specimens. English writers, remembering Talbot, naturally claim for their country the credit for the discovery of photography on paper. Thus Talbot knew glory. To us who had Daguerre, Bayard was undoubtedly superfluous. The Académie des Beaux-Arts, his sole protector, having appealed to the government in November 1840, recalling the report addressed to them a year previously, and the attainments of Bayard, again demanded that he be compensated; to which no response was made. Bayard abandoned his process. (12)

This process was not without merit: far from it. It would be wrong to consider it merely a laboratory experiment, outside of present photographic practice. The Société Française de Photographie has in its collection almost six hundred prints made during 1839 and 1840. These images, eighty-three years old, seemingly ageless, perfectly preserved, are rich in middle tones, beautifully harmonious, and justly admired.

Moreover, the most fervent partisans of the daguerreotype warmly recognized Bayard's merits; Hubert, friend, pupil and assistant of Daguerre, stated in 1840 (13): "The discovery of the method of obtaining images on paper aids immensely in eliminating reflections and offers designs which can be carried without damage by rubbing; it avoids the uncertainty of exposure and the images can be seen during their development; already the process has overtaken its predecessor, which, operating on metal, is affected by unsurmountable barriers while the nature and texture of the paper are not opposed to the strength of the chemical

reagent used . . . . Let us hope that M. Bayard's perseverance, and
that of other leaders who have already obtained so promising a success
for the future, will soon be able to surmount the last of these barriers
before which up to now we have been forced to halt."

When the album containing Bayard's proofs is examined, it will be
seen that the author at first obtained negative images and then turned
to substitute positive images, obtained directly in the camera. This is
an error which he committed in company with all the workers of his
time, including Talbot. If Bayard was probably the first to print a positive in a printing frame, under a negative obtained in the camera, he
was also the first who made a positive, in June 1839. Although this print
is on paper, it is mounted to be viewed as a transparency without any
apparent grain, producing a very fine effect.

Many of the first prints by Bayard represent still life; but the Parisian scenes which he photographed are full of interest and are the earliest we have. They serve and will continue to serve to perpetuate the
vague details of that Paris which has now disappeared, for instance, the
windmills of Montmartre photographed in 1842, and they will assist the
students of today. The artists of that time did not regard them very
highly. Bayard made his own portrait on paper, although rather late; it
certainly is not a masterpiece.

After he had abandoned the work of an inventor to become Chief
Clerk of the Ministry of Finance—a more secure profession—he still
remained a photographer. To the end of his life he practised the methods
of the time, including the daguerreotype, and contributed many improvements. Certain of his images which I exhibited in 1913 (14) astonished all who saw them and those who were not familiar with the degree
of perfection photography had reached about 1855. Bayard was one of
the founders of the Société d'héliographie in 1851, the oldest photographic society in France and, in 1854, he was also among those who
started the Société Française de Photographie, of which he became the
honorary secretary, a position of which he was very proud, his tombstone bearing this simple inscription: "*Here lies Hippolyte Bayard,
chevalier of the Légion d'honneur, one of the first inventors of photography,
honorary general secretary of the Société Française de Photographie 1800-
1887.*" (15)

He was made chevalier of the Légion d'honneur on January 24, 1863
and, having retired, spent the rest of his life in the peaceful little town of
Nemours. Some of his friends were attracted to the place, among them

Geoffroy, the friend of his youth, Dupuis, and two or three others including Amaury Duval, who made a beautiful crayon portrait of Bayard. All these, including Bayard, had a taste for painting and Nemours was always a well-known resort for artists, who were attracted by the enchanting riverside of the Loing. Bayard died at Nemours (at No.25 Quai des Fossés) on May 14, 1887, aged more than eighty-six years. Shortly after his death, all the specimens which he left behind, about nine hundred pieces, came into the possession of the Société Française de Photographie and are classified there today. At different times (1855, 1860, 1863, 1887), the Society has celebrated the accomplishments of Bayard and his inventions. His colleagues, who were his friends, who knew his work, and honoured his unselfishness, recalled the immense services which he had rendered to photography. From all this, he gained no great success. Bayard died and so did those who knew him. The years went on, and oblivion has slowly shrouded the memory of the man and his work.

However, in 1913, these old matters came to light again; memories were awakened in the minds of men who perhaps had known the inventor and, having come together, they formed in Breteuil an association, supplied the necessary funds, a sculptor, and decided to erect a monument to the memory of Bayard, in the shape of a bust in front of his birthplace. Everything being ready in the early months of the following year, the dedication was set for August 2, 1914. This was the day when the general mobilization preceding the war was decreed, unexpected as a thunderbolt from a clear sky.

The disorder was so great, while everyone was hastening to join their posts or returning to their homes, that the specimens of 1839, which had been prepared by the Société Française de Photographie to be exhibited at Breteuil on that day, were forgotten on a table. There they remained for more than three months, bathed each day in the full summer sunlight, until I found them, towards the end of November, without the slightest alteration that I could perceive, a new proof of the complete stability of these images.

Misfortune followed Bayard even after his death. The proposed dedication did not take place and the pedestal without the bust remained forgotten for several years while Breteuil was devastated by the war. The bust was finally erected on July 14, 1922 and, I regret to say, without any participation of the photographic world. (16)

HISTORY OF THE DISCOVERY OF PHOTOGRAPHY
REFERENCES: CHAPTER XXXV

1. The date on the tombstone is engraved by mistake as 1800.
2. *Moniteur*, July 8, 9 and 10, 1790.
3. Ingenhousz published his work in England in 1779. A French translation of his experiments on vegetable matter was published in Paris in 1780. Senebier's work dates from 1782.
4. This fact was reported by Lacan in *La Lumière* of September 2, 1854. Bayard in his manuscript notes, which belong to the Société Française de Photographie bitterly complains of it.
5. The report of Rochette was published in the *Moniteur* of November 13, 1839 and reprinted in *La Lumière* (September 30, 1854) and in the *Bulletin de la Société Française de Photographie* of 1855, etc.
6. Meeting of November 2, 1839.
7. *Comptes rendus*, 1840, 1st semester, p.337.
8. *Bulletin de la Société Française de Photographie*, 1860, p.293.
9. The report rendered does not give the name of the author of this historic note; but the table of contents indicates that it was "communicated by M. Arago".
10. *Comptes rendus*, 1840, 1st semester, pp.336, 337, 374.
11. *Comptes rendus*, 1841, 1st semester, pp.225 and 305.
12. *La Lumière*, September 30, 1854; La Société d'Encouragement pour l'Industrie Nationale bestowed on him in 1842 a prize of 3,000 francs. *Bulletin de la Société d'Encouragement*, 1842, p.124.
13. *Le Daguerréotype considéré sous un Point de Vue artistique, mécanique et pittoresque* (The Daguerreotype regarded from the viewpoint of art, mechanics and picturesqueness) by an amateur. Paris 1840. This pamphlet, without the name of the author, is by Hubert, which is proven by the Report of Melloni. See also: *Traité pratique de Photographie* by M.A.Gaudin, Paris 1844, p.180.
14. *Bulletin de la Société Française de Photographie*, 1913, p.366.
15. In the cemetery of Saint-Pierre-lès-Nemours.
16. Journal *Le Matin*, August 17, 1922.

CHAPTER XXXVI

Modifications of the Daguerreotype Process

MEANWHILE the daguerreotype, at the height of public favor, did not appear to be without defects, even to its admirers. The image had a lamentable fragility, the slightest rubbing effaced it. The blacks represented by the polished metal were not really black; the light produced in them very annoying reflections at certain angles. The subjects, reproduced as in a mirror, were reversed as to position; a great defect because they often reproduced well-known monuments, such as the buildings of Paris. The time of exposure—at first ten to thirty minutes—made the taking of portraits impossible and, last but not least, the apparatus weighed no less than 50 kilograms (110¼ lbs. T.N.) (1)

From the very first, the respect due to something so new and prodigious forbade any change. The detailed manipulations prescribed by the Master formed a ritual which no photographer would have dared to infringe upon without fear of the direct disaster. But the physicists and chemists, naturally inquisitive, at first tried to explain how the mysterious photographic image came into being in the obscurity of the camera. Jean-Baptiste Dumas, Biot and Doctor Donné (1801-1878) propounded one or more theories of the daguerrean image. (2) Golfier-Besseyre and Aug. Vallet (1815-1868) investigated the same subject. (3) Later, Fizeau (1819-1896), Léon Foucault (1819-1868), Choiselat and Ratel, Claudet, Becquerel, to cite only the French scientists who proposed theories on which these scholars did not often agree. (4)

It was not long before the opticians who constructed the daguerrean equipment modified them; later, the operators, emboldened, simplified the methods. Add to these the amateurs eager for glory, and jealous, lacking something better, who tried to affix their names to a modification of the process and thus the invention, having become public property, was transformed by all these efforts. Since the beauty of the blacks depended on the polish of the plate, a long time was given scrupulously and minutely to this operation. Baron Séquier (1803-1876) simplified the operation of polishing. The iodine often deposited unequally on the plate; Brébisson (1798-1872) made the iodizing easier and more even. (5) The optician Soleil (6) (1798-1878), and later Delannoy pointed out improved methods for developing the image with mercury.

Soehnée, to strengthen the picture, varnished the plate, which J.-Bte Dumas had also done from the beginning. Pretsch and Choiselat described new methods of fixation. (7) During all this time, Cauche claimed the glory for having substituted pumice-stone for the rotten-stone then used for polishing. (8)

In March 1840, Fizeau (9) found a much better solution for strengthening the image and reinforcing the blacks. This was the gold toning bath for which he published the formula in the following August. After having subjected the daguerrean plate to the mercury vapours, having washed it, then immersed it in hyposulphite of soda or in salt water (in 1840 salt water was still used for fixation) (10); in short, after the plate had been treated according to the primitive method, Fizeau plunged it into a hot mixture of the two following solutions:

A. 1 gram of gold chloride in a half-liter of water (11)

B. 3 grams of hyposulphite of soda in a half-liter of water

Immediately the contrasts of the image were accentuated. A thin layer of gold darkened the silver of the plate, which represented the blacks, while on the other hand, the mercury which formed the whites took on a much more vivid brightness. This was the first great improvement of the process. These golden images, when properly toned and fixed, could be considered permanent. The plates treated in this manner, after eighty years, are today as beautiful as they were on the day they were made. In the following October, Walter made known that a combination of bromine and chlorine shared with iodine the property of fixing the mercury vapours. (12) Talbot wrote to Biot in January 1841, that the daguerrean plate exposed to the emanations of iodide of bromine acquired great sensitiveness. Claudet, before Talbot, experimented with the same object in view, but he used the chloride of iodine. His method was used and published in France by Lerebours and Gaudin. In January 1841 (14), Fizeau in France also increased the sensitiveness of the plate by submitting it after iodizing and for a very short time to the fumes of a solution of bromine, in water. Of these three methods so closely related, two were almost at once abandoned, and Fizeau's formula, being much the best, was the only one employed. The engraver Lemaître was the first one to make use of it. (15) The time of exposure was by this reduced to fifteen times shorter.

According to the historian Eder (16), the credit for having been the first to use bromine and chlorine for accelerators belongs to Kratochwila and to Natterer brothers at Vienna, who had published their formulas in January and in March 1841 respectively. In America, Goddard is said to have indicated the use of bromine in December 1839 (17); notwithstanding these claims, it is generally conceded that Claudet's process with iodine chloride toward the end of 1840 must be considered as anteceding the others.

In the ensuing years bromine accelerators were offered under more convenient forms and various names: "liqueur de Reiser, liqueur hongroise, bromure de chaux de Bingham, bromure d'iode de M. de Valicourt, chlorobromure de chaux du Baron Gros, procédé américain" (18) etc. We must add "perbromure de carbone" "a newly discovered substance" by the pharmacist Hamard which was to be used — if ever — as a gas. (19)

Apparatus. — The builders of apparatuses did not remain inactive. I have said that Susse and Giroux had the privilege of selling the apparatus recommended by the inventor, but the camera used by Daguerre was a complicated mechanism, bulky and heavy. Neither Susse nor Giroux were able to make the necessary improvements, because this was not in the line of their business. Baron Seguier (20) was the first to lighten the primitive instrument. Before the end of 1839, he described a camera one-third the size and weight of Daguerre's camera. The camera was separated from its stand and could be used perpendicularly and horizontally. Equipped with a bellows it became truly portable. It was also made in different sizes. The daguerrean plate measured 0.164m by 0.216m. Apparatuses were also made for demiplates, for $\frac{1}{3}$, $\frac{1}{4}$, $\frac{1}{6}$ and even for $\frac{1}{8}$ size of the plate, and which were respectively in millimeters: 164 x 108, 140 x 82, 108 x 82, 80 x 70 and 60 x 40. Chevalier (1804-1859), Soleil, Lerebours, Buron and Montmirel may be named among the first to construct and sell cameras since 1840. The smaller sizes had the advantages of being less costly, easier to carry and being equipped with more luminous short focus lenses.

The Société Française de Photographie has an example of a "photographe" (21) constructed by Chevalier in 1840, which may be taken as a typical camera of this period. The apparatus for a whole-size plate and its accessories are contained in a case, with handles, measuring 0.50m long, 0.28m wide and 0.21m high (20" x 11" x 8-½"), in which there are two basins or trays placed one in the other; a box containing ten prepared plates; the box for iodizing; the polishing board; the camera with its demountable lens; the mercury box; the ground-glass; the alcohol lamp; the drying fork; the black curtain.

The "expanding" chamber permits the two sides, hinged lengthwise in the middle, to fold into the interior of the box which is solidly constructed entirely of wood, without bellows. Its length is 42 cm. Focusing is done by means of a gear which enables one to advance or draw back the ground-glass and plate holder in the interior of the chamber. The box runs in grooves. Two screws permit the fixing of the camera on a board-like support, which can be moved up and down or sideways. The lens and its accessories are kept inside the camera after the operation is finished. The objective is composed of two achromatic lenses. The diaphragms, with different size openings, were placed in a slot in the lens barrel. In front of the whole apparatus a reflecting prism reversed the image in its proper orientation. In addition to the heavy box, one also had to carry a jointed tripod which was fastened to an oval plate by a screw and this supported the camera. The whole apparatus weighed 14 kilograms (almost 31 lbs.) and was called portable. The construction was made very carefully and was absolutely rigid, but—14 kilograms! How fortunate that the photographers were still of the heroic age. Chevalier sold this apparatus de luxe for 620 francs. (22)

In 1845, the panoramic apparatus of Martens (23) made its appearance which produced views 0.38m high x 12 cm. wide (17½" x 5"). A horizontal movement of the lens enabled him to cover the different points on the horizon and the plate presented a cylindrical curvature, with the image always in focus. Finally, a narrow vertical slit, following the rotary motion of the lens, permitted only the central part of the field to pass, which had no perceptible aberration, thus assuring perfect sharpness in all parts of the image. In the meantime, the curvature of the plate presented such difficulties that he was forced to construct panoramic apparatuses using plane plates, in which he succeeded a little later. (24) We have already shown the cost of Chevalier's photographic apparatus. In 1839 the inventor's daguerreotype apparatus sold for 400 francs. A French apparatus sent to Vienna, Austria, about November, cost 400 francs. (25) In 1841 the price of an apparatus for making full-size plates was 250 to 300 francs in Paris; for half-size plates, 170 to 200 francs; for quarter-size plates 100 to 130 francs; these cameras were furnished with a single achromatic lens. The plates cost from 1 franc to 4 francs, according to their sizes, to these different expenses must be added a hundred francs or so for accessories and, if one considers the value of money in 1840 with that of our time, it will readily be seen that daguerreotypy was a pastime for the use of the rich alone. However, the number of amateurs and professionals was so large that, in 1846, the annual sale was estimated to be two thousand apparatuses and half a million plates in Paris alone. (26)

Optics. — I have dealt in Chapter V with the optics of the camera in the early years of the nineteenth century. Achromatic lenses, which were corrected for aberration of their refrangibility by the use of proper lens glasses, had therefore been known for fifty years; but they were only used for spectacles, the camera was of little importance at that time. The spherical aberrations also were very troublesome for artists who used the camera.

We know that the image which passes through a bi-convex lens is projected in the shape of a spherical concave segment. Received on a plane surface, it shows sharply only in part; the center is sharp and the edges blurred; or, if the ground-glass is slightly moved towards the lens, the edges become distinct and the center blurred.

Wollaston, in 1812, remedied the fault somewhat by substituting for the bi-convex lens in the camera obscura, a meniscus lens, in which the curvatures were in the ratio of 2:1, and which he named periscopic.

The concave surface faced the exterior, and the convex surface the interior of the chamber; but, above all, the sharpness resulted from a reduced aperture of the diaphragm. The meniscus was 10 cm. in diameter, the diaphragm 5 cm.: thus a large part of the luminosity was lost. This was the earliest improvement of the optics of the camera obscura. Chevalier, in 1819, substituted a prism and, in 1823, a meniscus prism for Wollaston's lens. (27)

Daguerre had equipped his camera with an achromatic and periscopic lens and, although these had long been known, he still cited them as a valuable contribution to his association with Niepce. Evidently he also used a diaphragm with a reduced aperture.

As soon as the camera enabled photography to replace drawing by hand, it was evident that the quality of the lens was of prime importance, and it certainly was — in the words of Chevalier — "the soul of the apparatus". The opticians were therefore compelled to improve the lens and after correcting the defects or known aberrations as far as possible, they tried to render lenses more luminous and so reduce the time of exposure. A simple method was to shorten the focus; they made lenses of large diameter and very short focus, which made the taking of portraits possible. Cauche was the first to propose an achromatic prismatic objective which showed the image in its proper position. (28) But this was a delicate and costly instrument. Buron, Lerebours and Soleil furnished their daguerreotype apparatus with improved lenses, corrected for chromatic and spherical aberrations. (29) but the best solution was found by Chevalier.

Since 1834, he had constructed an objective for telescopes consisting of two achromatic lenses. He applied this fortunate invention to the camera and, after some preliminary attempts, he furnished his *photographe* of 1840 with an objective in which he combined achromatic glasses. Two lenses sufficed for portraiture; to make a landscape, it was necessary to replace the front lens with another special one. Thus the focus was variable. The front lens was 6 cm. in diameter, the other 8 cm. This arrangement shortened the focus without diminishing the field of the image. A diaphragm, which opened and closed with a button eliminated the residual aberration already in part corrected by the fixed diaphragm between the lenses. In this way the same apparatus could be used both for portraits and landscapes. The position of the image was reversed by a silver-backed prism; moreover, it was not distorted as it would be by a too-short focus lens, and the image retained its luminosity. (30) That instrument, presented in a competitive exposition held by the Société d'Encouragement in 1840, received the highest award. It consisted of three lenses, one for taking landscapes, and cost 270 francs for full size plates. (31) If one was content with only two lenses, for portraits, the price was 180 francs. (32)

Some opticians sought to remedy the curvature of the field by making the image on a concave spherical plate; others, on a plate partially cylindrical in form, and there were apparatuses thus constructed, such as that of Martens. (33) After Chevalier, Professors Ettingshausen and Petzval of Vienna calculated a lens combination which the optician Voigtländer constructed and put on the market. The objective, composed of four lenses, was presented by Arago to the Académie des Sciences, March 1, 1841. (34) It shortened the exposure at least a third. These German lenses, luminous and sufficiently corrected for portraiture, were very popular in which their foreign origin aided, for distance lends enchantment. They were costly: 450 francs (35); and this also contributed to their success. Our opticians protested a great deal because they believed their lenses to be just as good, and said that there was nothing extraordinary about the Voigtländer lenses except the price (36) but their recriminations were useless and they were obliged to designate their lenses: German System. (37) Then they sold; Chevalier relates the following (38): "Shortly after the invention of the daguerre-otype, M. Ettingshausen came to Paris (39) and I had the pleasure of having several talks with him about the attempts I had made in equipping the camera with my new telescopic lens. M. Ettingshausen was able to engage several workmen for making lenses in accordance with the points gathered during our meetings and by the examination of my objective. They did not copy the curvature of my lenses, because they did not know enough, nevertheless, they remained superior to those of Voigtländer. In short, they exploited my idea, but they exploited it very poorly." L'Abbé Moigno (40) and de Valicourt (41) confirm Chevalier's statements. However that may be, I have given a comparison of the prices of these lenses by Chevalier and those made by Voigtländer. A catalogue of Lerebours in 1842 quotes the lens (German system) for full-size plates at 200 francs.

In May 1844 (42), Claudet observed that the troubles of the daguerre-an images attributed to the poor polishing of the plates really arose in the lens. Experiments showed him that the focus of the photogenic action did not coincide with the visual focus. He determined the different circumstances under which this chemical focus is produced longer than the visual focus with achromatic lenses and shorter for the others, and pointed out how this error may be corrected. Lerebours, the optician and friend of Claudet, constructed in France lenses which were exempt of the chemical focus. (43)

One could mention among the lesser improvements in the optics of photography the attempt of Bisson (44) to harmonize *"the actions of the different light rays which do not require the same time of exposure"*. He placed a plane glass before his lens *"coloured green, as given by the solar spectrum"* and, surprising as this may be, obtained excellent results.

A great difficulty then, and one which still exists, is the determination of the time of exposure necessary for the formation of the image in the camera. The first I believe who tried to obtain this precise measurement with a photometer was the optician Soleil. (45) The exposure was in proportion to the time required to blacken a sensitive paper; a simple but unsatisfactory method, still, however, considered the best. Baron Séguier applied to the ground-glass similar tints to those of the image and for each of which the exposure was determined experimentally. Buron constructed also in 1843 a photometer designed by Donné, which aroused furious claims for the priority. (46) It does not seem that this instrument deserved so much honour. Claudet devised later, in 1848, the (47) photographometer and in 1851, the dynactinometer for measuring the time of exposure. But all these inventors solved the problem no more than those of today.

MODIFICATIONS OF THE DAGUERREOTYPE PROCESS
REFERENCES: CHAPTER XXXVI

1. *Description des nouveaux Daguerréotypes perfectionnés et portatifs* (Description of the new daguerreotype apparatus improved and portable) by Buron, Paris, 1841, p.5.
2. On Biot see: *Comptes rendus*, August 5, 1839; for Donné *idem*, September 16, 1839; for J.-B.Dumas, *Rapport sur le Daguerréotype* by Melloni, Paris 1840, p.63.
3. *Comptes rendus*, 1839, 2nd semester, pp.378, 379, 455; 1840, 2nd semester, p.568.
4. *Comptes rendus*, 1843, 1st semester, pp.759, 1436 — 2nd semester, pp.173, 260, 356, 480, 605, 1070; 1846, 2nd semester, pp.679, 800, 856; 1847, 2nd semester, pp.554, 594. — *Essai de Théorie daguerrienne et Résultats pratiques* (Essay on the daguerrean theory and its practical results.) by a professor of science, Paris, 1844.
5. *De quelques Modifications apportées au Daguerréotype* (Some modifications contributed to the daguerreotype process) by A. de Brébisson, Falaise 1841.
6. *Guide de l'Amateur de Photographie* by Soleil.
7. *Comptes rendus*, 1839, 2nd semester, p.512 — 1840, 1st semester, pp.252, 391, 423, 479, 488, 628, 766.
8. *Comptes rendus*, 1839, 2nd semester, p.595.
9. *Comptes rendus*, 1840, 1st semester, p.488 — 2nd semester, pp.237, 824, 906. Fizeau, 1819-1896, member of the Académie des Sciences in 1863. The first idea of toning for the purpose of strengthening the image is to be credited to Choiselat who used silver chloride in order to obtain this effect. Gaudin is also reported to have used copper chloride before Fizeau.
10. *Le Daguerréotype. Description nouvelle du Procédé* . . . . p.9. This pamphlet was written by Vincent Chevalier although without giving the name of the author. *Le Daguerréotype considéré sous un point de vue artistique, mécanique et pittoresque*, by an Amateur (see p.152, F.N.13) Paris, 1840, pp.11, 15.
11. A liter = 0.908 dry quarts or 1.0567 liquid quarts, in volume — 1 kilogram of water. (T.N.).
12. *Comptes rendus*, 1840, 2nd semester, p.568.
13. *Comptes rendus*, 1841, 1st semester, p.225.
14. *Comptes rendus*, 1841, 1st semester, pp.1059, 1187, 1189.
15. *Derniers Perfectionnements apportés au Daguerréotype* (Latest improvements added to the daguerreotype apparatus) by Gaudin and Lerebours, Paris 1841. *Détails pratiques sur l'Emploi du Brome* (Practical details on the use of bromine) by Fizeau, p.76.
16. Eder. *Geschichte der Photographie*, Halle 1905, p.217. This claim is not new. One finds it advanced by Reindl in 1842 but without much success. The dates quoted alone are contradictory. See *Mélanges photographiques* (Photographic Medley) by Charles Chevalier, Paris 1844.
17. *American Journal of Photography*, 1892, p.241.
18. Bromine was discovered in 1826 by Balard, pharmacist at Montpelier who called it "muride", later Gay-Lussac called it "brome" from bromos (stench), because it had a bad odour.
19. *Nouveaux Procédés photographiques par M.Hamard, pharmacien à Fresnay (Sarthe). Découverte d'une nouvelle Substance accélératrice.* 1847. (New photographic process by Hamard, pharmacist at Fresnay (Sarthe). Discovery of a new substance which will increase the sensitivity.)
20. *Comptes rendus*, 1839, 2nd semester, pp.560, 772.
21. At first, the apparatuses were called "daguerreotypes" and the photographs "images daguerriennes". The word photography was always used by Arago in 1839 in its present general meaning; later the apparatuses were called indiscriminately daguerreotypes or photographs. Some years later the images also took the name of daguerreotypes.

HISTORY OF THE DISCOVERY OF PHOTOGRAPHY
REFERENCES: CHAPTER XXXVI—Cont'd

22. *Nouvelles Instructions sur l' Usage du Daguerréotype*, by Ch.Chevalier, Paris, 1841, p.17.
23. *Comptes rendus*, 1845, 1st semester, pp.1799, 1835; 2nd semester, p.242.
24. *Description d'un Daguerréotype rectiligne* (Description of a rectilinear daguerreotype) by M.Pleuvion. *Extrait des Mémoires de la Société Nationale des Sciences, de l' Agriculture et des Arts de Lille*. Lille, 1851.
25. Eder, *Geschichte der Photographie.*
26. *Répertoire d'Optique moderne* by Abbé Moigno, 2nd part, Paris 1847, p.705.
27. Ch.Chevalier, *Notice sur l' Usage des Chambres obscures et des Chambres claires* (Note on the use of the camera obscura and the camera lucida) Paris 1829. *Etude sur la Vie et les Travaux scientifiques de Charles Chevalier* (Study on the life and scientific works of Charles Chevalier) by Arthur Chevalier, his son, Paris 1862.
28. *Comptes rendus*, 1839, 2nd semester, p.595.
29. *Description de nouveaux Daguerréotypes perfectionnés et portatifs* (see F.N.1) by Buron, Paris 1841. *Description et Usage du Daguerréotype à Portraits* (Description of the use of the daguerreotype process for portraits) by Buron, Paris 1842.
30. *Nouvelles Instructions pour l' Usage du Daguerréotype* by Ch.Chevalier, Paris 1841. *Comptes rendus,* 1841, 1st semester, p.447.
31. The focus was 35cm. of the apparatus for plates of 164 x 216mm. The focus of Daguerre's apparatus was 55cm.
32. *Nouveaux Renseignements sur l' Usage du Daguerréotype* (New information on the use of the daguerreotype) by Charles Chevalier, Paris 1846.
33. *Mélanges photographiques* (Photographic Medley) by Charles Chevalier, Paris 1844.
34. *Comptes rendus*, 1841, 1st semester, pp.402, 514—1850, 2nd semester, p.245.
35. *Traité de Photographie* by E. de Valicourt, Paris 1845.
36. *Manuel complet de Photographie* by E. de Valicourt, Paris 1862, vol.I, pp.8, 10.
37. *Derniers Perfectionnements apportés au Daguerréotype* by Gaudin and Lerebours, Paris 1841, p.6 and 1842, p.7.
38. *Mélanges photographiques* by Ch.Chevalier, Paris 1844.
39. In April 1839 according to Eder. See also: *Theorie und Geschichte des Photographischen Objectivs* by Moritz von Rohr, Berlin 1899.
40. *Répertoire d'Optique moderne*, 2nd part, by Abbé Moigno, Paris 1847, p.705.
41. *Photographie sur Métal, sur Papier et sur Verre* (Photography on metal, paper and glass) by E. de Valicourt, Paris 1862, p.1, XVI.
42. *Comptes rendus*, 1844, 1st semester, p.954.
43. *Comptes rendus*, 1846, 2nd semester, p.634.
44. *Comptes rendus*, 1844, 2nd semester, p.1039.
45. *Comptes rendus*, 1840, 1st semester, p.842. *Le Daguerréotype mis à la Portée de tout le Monde* (The daguerreotype placed at the doors of the whole world) by E.-T. and E.Montmirel, Paris 1842.
46. *Comptes rendus*, 1843, 2nd semester, p.686.-
47. *Comptes rendus*, 1851, 1st semester, p.130—Claudet, *Nouvelles Recherches sur la Différence entre les Foyers visuel et photogénique* (New researches on the difference between the visual and photogenic focus) Paris 1851.

CHAPTER XXXVII

Portraits

AS soon as Arago had announced Daguerre's discovery, the whole world wondered whether this new art could be applied to portraiture. It had always been customary for the wealthy to have their portraits made. In 1839, these were generally oil paintings; pastel drawings, so favoured in the eighteenth century, had gone out of style. But paintings were costly. Persons in easy circumstances patronized famous artists who could do excellent work. The fashion, or rather the desire, for portraits, however, had spread even to the lower middle class, and those of limited resources looked about for painters who would do the work at a low price even if they were of doubtful talent, who produced deplorable colouring without resemblance to the sitter. This lack of resemblance to the original — a matter so hard to attain by manual drawing — was of course familiar to the clients.

To lessen the cost, they were satisfied with portraits drawn by hand, and the artists, who wished to economize in time and still produce portraits resembling the subject as closely as possible, had for a long time taken advantage of mechanical methods. I do not pretend to give a history of portraiture here, which would require volumes, but I have enumerated in Chapter VII some of these methods. On page 40, we refer to an illustration drawn by Albert Dürer, in 1535, of an artist tracing with crayon on the canvas the outlines of his model as viewed through a sight-hole. Jean Dubreuil described in his work on perspective, written in the seventeenth century, a trellis which well-known painters employed. The whole world knows of the success of the portraits called "*à la Silhouette*", about 1760. These were nothing but outline designs of a profile in black projected on white paper. An improvement on this method was named the *physionotrace*, invented by Chrestien in 1785, in which the portrait, begun in the apparatus, was subsequently finished by hand.

The inventor sold the reduced specimens by the dozen and offered in addition a reproduction in a large size; very much like the photographers of today. But all this required certain resources only at the disposal of the wealthy. And now a process was announced, less costly, which reproduced the model, whatever it might be, faithfully and with certainty. Here was good news for everybody, especially for the less wealthy who had not been able to afford any kind of a portrait.

Desires are ever in advance of reality. Arago spoke of from five to six minutes exposure as necessary to obtain an image. In practice fifteen minutes of perfect immobility were required in the full sunlight. Arago's exposure was sufficient for white walls but not of human countenances. Well! Heroic patients remained motionless in the sunlight for fifteen to twenty minutes, and then could contemplate their portrait at the price of discomforts and of horrible grimaces which the daguerreotype faithfully registered. "One always got sunburned" says Gaudin. (1) "The first portrait of this sort to be obtained was exhibited by M.Susse, of the passage des Panoramas. The countenance was very black, the contracted features and the grin testified to the sufferings endured. Nevertheless, the eyes were half open: the patient had held still!" In order to eliminate this contraction of the features, the sitter was told to close the eyes. "It was no longer the heads of victims under torture but the heads of resigned blind people which the opticians exhibited in their show cases," (2) says Valicourt, who adds, "It was in this way that portraits were made at the beginning of the daguerreotype." And as a matter of fact, an edition of Daguerre's pamphlet dated October or November 1839 contains the following instructions by Susse Frères *for making the portrait*: (3) "In order to make the portrait, it is also necessary to have a strong light. One will only succeed properly by exposing the person to the sun in the open air with white draperies as a reflector." Thus, before the end of 1839, it was already customary to make portraits by daguerreotype. Therefore, the assertion of Harrison must be rejected as absolutely inaccurate (4) that the first daguerrean portrait was made by Draper, in New York, towards the end of 1839, and the statement of Sachse (5) that the first daguerrean portrait *executed in the world* was made by Robert Cornelius, of Philadelphia, in November 1839. Draper had to pose his model for a half hour in the open sunlight, the face whitened with flour and with closed eyes. What a beautiful image this must have presented! Alas! Neither to Draper nor to Robert Cornelius belongs the satisfaction of having been the first. Before Daguerre's apparatus could possibly have been sent to or arrived in America, many abominable horrors had already been made here.

King Louis Philippe was among those impatient people who too early demanded a copy of their features by daguerreotype. He posed in the garden of the Tuileries, on the terrace on the bank of the river and the result was disastrous. (6) The following song was undoubtedly composed for this great disappointment:

> Although with flattery ripe
> And truth its duty
> The daguerreotype
> Disfigures beauty, etc. . . .

Owing to favorable circumstances, however, success was assured. In November 1839, the painter Goupil, accompanying his teacher Horace Vernet on a trip to the Orient, used the daguerreotype and they both succeeded, between Smyrna and Malta, in obtaining with a fast exposure a view of the deck on board the *Ramsès*, showing "four persons standing, two of whom are clearly distinguishable". (7) The result is still more remarkable because the plates could not be developed until several months after they were taken.

After 1840, a great number of portrait artists established studios and advertised them to the public. Since clients had to remain without moving during the long time required (in 1840, from 4 to 20 minutes) (8), accessories were added in order to lessen their fatigue. The most important one we know was the headrest. Forest, a manufacturer, found an ingenious way to avoid portraits' being unsharp. He made his apparatus independent of the movements of the sitter. When the client fidgeted, the apparatus followed his movements and the inventor asserts that the image was sharp. (9) Since it was impossible to keep the eyes open when facing the sun, they interposed a blue glass between the sun and the subject, which softened the great force of the light. When it was observed that the light passing through the blue glass did not unduly prolong the exposure, studios were equipped with blue glass skylights. Some photographers maintained that blue light, being very actinic, made the exposures shorter than in white light. This opinion we still hear advanced from time to time.

The opticians Lerebours and Buron, followed by others, used very short focus lenses and reduced the dimensions of the picture. They also made portraits in sunlight in two or three minutes by the interposition of blue glass, the sitter being placed 50 cm. from the lens and, for a standing portrait, 2 meters further. (10) All portraits dating from 1840 are made in this manner. Brébisson also made groups thus (11), and it goes without saying that all these pictures were distorted.

But it was not until 1841 that portraits were made in great numbers, because of the shortening of the time of exposure. Chemistry and optics aided. In his memoir: *"Recherches sur les Rayonnements chimiques qui accompagnent le Lumière solaire et la Lumière électrique"* (Researches of the chemical rays which accompany sunlight and electric light), Edmond Becquerel pointed out that an image formed in the camera on iodized paper or plate with an insufficient exposure could be strengthened if exposed to the sun under a red or yellow glass. Baron Séguier, the opticians Buron and Lerebours, and the calculator Gaudin applied this property of "continuing rays" to the daguerrean image. The plate having been removed from the camera, was exposed under an orange or red glass and exposed to the sun for ten to fifteen minutes. The image, hardly visible, appeared little by little. It could be fixed and toned with gold without developing it with mercury. Whenever the exposure was too short, the plate was subjected to the mercury and to the ordinary manipulations. By this method Buron made portraits with exposures of a few seconds in the sun. (12) Bisson exhibited in June portraits made in ten seconds in the shade. (13) Gaudin did still better. He attained an exposure of 1/15th of a second. (14) But his performance met only with incredulity by many who made merry at his expense. (15)

At the end of 1840 Claudet, in London, found a means for increasing the sensitiveness of the plate by subjecting it, after iodizing, to the emanations of iodine chloride. Lerebours, at Paris, using Claudet's method, obtained also portraits in the shade in fifteen or twenty seconds. (16) Fizeau at the same time subjected the iodized plate to the vapours of a very strong solution of bromine in water and the exposure was reduced to thirty seconds. (17) Gaudet, in May 1841, photographed windblown clouds, and in October sent to the Académie des Sciences an instantaneous view of the Pont-Neuf showing moving carriages and pedestrians which he stated were obtained in 1/19th of a second. (18) It would be interesting to inspect these pictures in the archives of the Institut where they are at present. Unfortunately these archives are not easily accessible. Gaudin's daguerreotype was obtained by using iodine bromide. Gaudin's exposures usually took 1/10th of a second, if he is to be believed (19); we must add that his contemporaries did not believe him. In the meantime, the Société d'Encouragement pour l'Industrie nationale bestowed upon him in 1842 (20) a silver medal for just this photograph of moving clouds which I have mentioned above. At any rate, Gaudin's performance is no more incredible than that of the Austrian Natterer who, in 1841, with an exposure of one second, photographed a moving crowd in the Kaiser Josef Platz at Vienna. Eder believes this specimen to be the first instantaneous photograph in the world; it would be interesting to find the one by Gaudin and compare these two incunabula.

In the beginning of the year 1841, we invariably find the double lens of Chevalier and the four-lens objective of Voigtländer, by the use of which were obtained portraits "without exposing to the sun the face of the person to be photographed". All these methods tended to reduce the time of exposure considerably, moreover they rendered it not only possible but helped the daguerrean picture greatly. It is really from 1841 that the profession of the photographic portraitist dates. "The studios for taking portraits" says Lerebours, "expanded immensely; portraits by daguerreotype were made in all large cities and, what will undoubtedly surprise many, the only two establishments of this kind in the city of London often took in up to 1,500 francs in a single day." (21) Lerebours assures us that he himself made more than 1500 portraits in 1841. (22)

The first portraits were of small dimensions, owing to the short focus lens used. The picture was made on a quarter, a sixth, or even an eighth of a plate, this last being only 6 x 4 cm. When the time of exposure was shortened, the portraits were made on a third and even a half and finally on a whole plate. To complete this story, I reproduce the advertisement of a Parisian photographer in 1841:

PORTRAITS INSTANTANES
par tous les temps possibles
sous un pavillon entièrement en verre bleu
PRIX: 15 FR.

(Instantaneous portraits, in any weather. Inside a pavillion enclosed entirely in blue glass. PRICE: 15 francs.)

HISTORY OF THE DISCOVERY OF PHOTOGRAPHY
REFERENCES: CHAPTER XXXVII

1. *Traité pratique de Photographie* (Treatise on Photography) by M.A.Gaudin, Paris 1844, p.10.
2. *Photographie sur Metal, sur Papier et sur Verre* by E. de Valicourt, Paris 1862.
3. *Histoire et Description des Procédés du Daguerréotype et du Diorama rédigés par Daguerre et augmentés de Notes et d'Observations* (History and description of the daguerreotype processes, of Daguerre's diorama and additional notes and observations) by Lerebours and Susse Brothers. Paris 1839.
4. W.Jerome Harrison, *History of Photography*, London 1888.
5. *American Journal of Photography*, 1892, p.241.
6. *Le Passé, le Présent, l'Avenir de la Photographie* (Past, present and future of photography) by Alophe, Paris 1861.
7. *Le Daguerréotype considéré sous un Point de Vue artistique, mécanique et pittoresque* (The daguerreotype from an artistic, mechanical and picturesque point of view) by an amateur, Paris 1840, pp.21 and 31 — *Nouveau Manuel complémentaire pour l'Usage pratique du Daguerréotype* (New supplementary manual for practical use in daguerreotypy) by Richebourg, p.18. This pamphlet, bearing no date, was published in 1842.
8. Remarks of Lerebours in Daguerre's pamphlet quoted above, September and October 1839 — *Notions particulières pour faire les Portraits au Daguerréotypy* (Special instructions for making portraits) by Vincent Chevalier, Paris 1841.
9. *Comptes rendus*, 1840, 2nd semester, p.168.
10. *Description et Usage du Daguerréotype à Portraits* by Buron, Paris 1842.
11. *Description de nouveaux Daguerréotypes* by Buron — *De quelques modifications au Daguerréotype* by Brébisson — *Notions particulières pour faire les Portraits au Daguerréotype* (Special instructions for making portraits) by Vincent Chevalier — *Derniers Perfectionnements apportés au Daguerréotype* by Gaudin and Lerebours.
12. Buron, p.35.
13. *Comptes rendus*, 1841, 1st semester, p.1060.
14. *Comptes rendus*, 1841, 1st semester, p.1187.
15. *Journal des Artistes*, November 14, 1841.
16. *Comptes rendus*, 1841, 1st semester, p.1060.
17. *Comptes rendus*, 1841, 1st semester, p.1189.
18. *Comptes rendus*, 1841, 2nd semester, p.832.
19. *Derniers Perfectionnements apportés au Daguerréotype* by Gaudin and Lerebours, Paris, November 1841, p.43.
20. *Bulletin de la Société d'Encouragement*, 1842, p.124.
21. *Derniers Perfectionnements, etc.* by Gaudin and Lerebours, November 1841.
22. *Derniers Perfectionnements, etc.* by Gaudin and Lerebours, edition, May 1842.

CHAPTER XXXVIII

The Daguerrean Image at Its Zenith

AFTER the progress which I have enumerated, and other small improvements which were found in the practice of the art, the daguerreotype attained its perfection about 1845 and remained for several years the only process in use. Generally speaking, it is from those days that we have the finest examples. La Société d'Encouragement pour l'Industrie nationale had, since 1840, awarded large sums to compensate for the improvements of the process. I have already named some of those who received the medals distributed in 1842: Chevalier and Voigtländer for their lenses, Gaudin for his instantaneous pictures, Soleil, Buron and Desbordes for their apparatus, the brothers Breton for having been the first who obtained pictures on plates almost a meter in height. And we must not forget Montmirel who received a bronze medal for having invented a headrest. (1)

The first photographic exposition was held in 1844. Derussy, Sabatier-Blot, Bisson, Baron Gros, Thiesson and especially Thierry, of Lyons, received awards. Arago presented Thierry's pictures which were unique in their beauty to the Académie des Sciences. (2) Five years later, at the exposition of 1849, the list of awards contained some new names: Warren-Thompson, Vaillat, Plumier. It must be noted that at this time Vaillat was said to have taken 2000 portraits a year at an average price of 10 francs and Derussy 3000 portraits; and the reporter for the heliographic class at the exposition estimated that 100,000 portraits were made that year. (3)

It would have been, of course, a great advance if these delicate daguerrean pictures could have been in colours, but photography in colour, a momentary glimpse of Daguerre's, was still in the domain of fancy. Since this was not possible, one turned to colouring the daguerrean image. The first attempt — that of Chevalier in 1840 (4) — is very interesting. The image itself being extremely delicate to the touch, Chevalier used a glass which was carefully placed over the image to which he applied flat tints in transparent colours "corresponding as much as possible to those portions which they were supposed to represent". After this the daguerreotype was covered with the glass so that the colours were in register with the design and they were framed together. This

207

method gave very remarkable effects, says the author, and very much like those produced by coloured lithographs. Let us take his word for it.

In 1842, Lechi (5) dusted on the daguerreotype, after it had been made, very finely ground powders of appropriate colours and then immersed the plate in hot water. The colour was retained in inverse ratio to the impression, a large amount on the shadows and very little on the lights. Thus the skin showed very little colour. Other methods followed which were kept as studio secrets and which were very similar. In general, dried powdered colours were dusted with a fine brush on the daguerreotype after it had been washed in a gum solution, then dried. The manipulation was delicate and had to be repeated which often resulted in disaster. Other such methods of Leuze, de Barbier, de Roginel are somewhat more complicated. (6)

But it was not until much later when the daguerreotype was near its decline that the painter Ziegler (7) (1804-1856) in France, coloured them as fine as miniatures. Maucomble, another miniature painter, had the reputation as late as 1850 of being without a rival in the colouring of daguerrean images. We could also cite the Mayer brothers, later photographers to the Emperor. Coloured daguerreotypes were especially the fashion in England and in America. Some of them were exceedingly beautiful and it must be admitted that they greatly improved with time and showed a kind of iridescence. This often was rose-coloured which seemed to impart a charming freshness to the delicate flesh colour of the portraits.

Attempts were also made to vary the general cold shade of the daguerreotype, as toning with gold or other toning solutions, all more or less red. Bisson, in 1842, Gaudin (8), in 1843, gave formulas for sepia, red and also blue tones.

But the principal preoccupation of photographers was to cut down the time of exposure. Although this had been reduced to less than a fraction of a second, the pictures representing persons or moving objects — which we call instantaneous — were very rare and were presented to the Académie des Sciences as curiosities. I have cited several examples of portraiture. We must add Bisson's daguerreotypes of 1842, portraying a smiling infant, a moving procession, pedestrians and carriages crossing the Pont-Neuf (9); in 1845, pictures of animals by Thiesson; in this case, dogs were trained to remain motionless for a brief moment. The photographer Malacrida, directed by Dr. Jacquart, photographed, in 1848, the chimpanzee at the Museum of Natural History. (10) In

1851, the brothers Macaire, of Havre, obtained daguerrean views of moving boats, breaking waves, etc. This was as far as one got with the daguerreotype. (11)

Certain operators proved on the other hand to what extent a plate might be sensitive to obtain an image in a subdued light. Thus Donné, in February 1840, obtained pictures with the solar microscope illuminated by the light from an "oxy-hydrogen gas inflamed over limestone". (12) This was the earliest attempt to make photographic enlargements with artificial light. Then again Bianchi, in 1842, used artificial light and Pinaud also, in 1843, measured the sensitivity of a daguerrean plate with an electric spark. (13) The brothers Natterer, of Vienna, in 1841, made an image by the light of two oil lamps with an exposure of thirty-five minutes. (14)

Scientists also built great hopes on this new process of reproduction. They had read Arago's enthusiastic discourse in 1839, who was certain that one of these days a photographic map of the moon and, of course, of the heavens would be obtained; he also indicated two branches of science, photometry and micrography to which the daguerreotype could at once be applied. As a matter of fact, it was, I believe, micrography which afforded the first scientific application of photography. In October 1839, Donné presented to the Académie des Sciences a print of a microscopic design taken from an eye of a fly and, in February 1840, several images obtained by the use of a *daguerrean-microscope* which had been constructed by the optician Soleil and the design for which originated with Doyère. In the following month, Chevalier also showed micrographs which, the naturalist Turpin thought were not remarkable. (15)

Hubert (16), in June 1840, suggested an apparatus which would photographically register the readings of different meteorological instruments; but an English scientist, Jordan, had used this idea before him. Hossard, in 1843, photographically registered the variation of the thermometer. (17) Fizeau and Foucault pointed out in 1844 methods of measuring the intensity of light. (18) They also made a photograph of the sun on a daguerrean plate April 2, 1845, at the request of Arago. (19) In the same year the engineer Malacarne of Venice made photographs of the moon. (20) In the same year 1845, Serres employed the daguerreotype for anthropology, intending to install his work in a special museum. (21) I do not know whether this collection is still in existence at the Museum of Natural History. Faye, in 1849, devoted himself to the solution of different problems of solar observation by photography.

Fleury thought that the distance from the stars might also be measured in this manner. On July 28, 1851 (22), during a solar eclipse, Father Secchi photographed it on a daguerreotype. He was not the only one. Malacarne, of Venice, with others, and here Vaillat and Thompson, under the direction of Porro, made pictures of it. (23) All this, however, did not prevent Vogel from writing: "Berkowsky is the first who has attempted to introduce in astronomy the processes which permit the fixation of images in the camera obscura. This was done in 1851 at the observatory of Koenigsberg, by the use of the celebrated heliometer of Bessel during a total eclipse of the sun." (24) Draper, in America, however, without more certitude, is also supposed to have made the first photograph of the moon, and in 1840 also made enlargements of daguerreotypes by means of a device, which is difficult to imagine.

THE DAGUERREAN IMAGE AT ITS ZENITH
REFERENCES: CHAPTER XXXVIII

1. *Bulletin de la Société d' Encouragement*, 1842, p.124.
2. *Comptes rendus*, 1844, 2nd semester, pp.339, 418, 489, 715. *Daguerréotypie* by J.Thierry, Paris and Lyons, 1847.
3. The report was published in *La Lumière*, February 16 and 23, 1851.
4. *Nouvelles Instructions sur l' Usage du Daguerréotype* by Charles Chevalier, Paris 1841, p.58.
5. *Comptes rendus*, 1842, 2nd semester, p.752.
6. Described in the *Manuel complet de Photographie* by E. de Valicourt, Paris 1862, Vol.I, p.111 and in the *Répertoire encyclopédique de Photographie* by H. de La Blanchère, Paris 1863.
7. *La Lumière*, May 1851.
8. *Comptes rendus*, 1842, 1st semester, p.253. — 1843, 2nd semester, p.1072.
9. *Comptes rendus*, 1842, 2nd semester, p.345.
10. *Comptes rendus*, 1848, 2nd semester, p.427.
11. *Comptes rendus*, 1851, 2nd semester, p.402.
12. *Comptes rendus*, 1840, 1st semester, p.288.
13. *Comptes rendus*, 1842, 1st semester, p.173. — 2nd semester, p.761.
14. Eder, *Geschichte der Photographie*, p.217.
15. *Comptes rendus*, 1839, 2nd semester, p.485. — 1840, 1st semester, pp.339, 423, 583, 587, 667.
16. *Comptes rendus*, 1840, 1st semester, p.876. — 2nd semester, p.574.
17. *Comptes rendus*, 1843, 1st semester, p.395.
18. *Comptes rendus*, 1844, 1st semester, pp.746, 860.
19. *Astronomie populaire* by F.Arago, Paris 1855, Vol.II, Book XIV, chap.XXII.
20. *La Lumière*, April 1, 1854.
21. *Comptes rendus*, 1845, 2nd semester, p.242.
22. *Comptes rendus*, 1849, 1st semester, p.241. — 1850, 2nd semester, p.497 — 1851, 2nd semester, pp.128, 285.
23. *Bulletin de la Société Française*, 1858, p.95.
24. *La Photographie et la Chimie de la Lumière*, by Vogel. Paris 1876, p.130.

CHAPTER XXXIX

Photography on Paper

THE word *photography* is found, at least so I believe, for the first time in Arago's report to the Chamber of Deputies on July 3, 1839, and there was used in the general sense in which we employ it today. But, shortly after, this same word designated only photography on paper, in contrast to the daguerrean method on metal plates. (1) When the daguerreotype disappeared, prints on paper only remained and the sense of the word was extended to designate all the processes generally.

Before the daguerreotype, metal was rarely used as a support for the image. The daguerrean image was abnormal. Wedgwood before 1800 made prints on paper. Niepce, before he found pewter plates, began in 1816 with images on paper. Talbot also thought only of paper. The metal plate was only a means, a transitory step in the onward march of photography. Daguerre had given to his process unique qualities and he profited besides by the surprise caused by the extraordinary discovery. "Among the facts" says Jean-Baptiste Dumas (2), "which make up the happenings to which silver has given birth, not the least extraordinary, certainly, is the very remarkable and unexpected role played by silver iodide." "Many improvements" said Melloni (3), "have worked together to contribute to the great ease and speed of the process, exciting universal enthusiasm." Against this enthusiasm, paper had a long struggle. "One must not expect from paper the perfection of a daguerreotype" says Biot. (4) It must be admitted that the processes of Talbot and Bayard, which were the only ones known at the time of daguerreotype, had great defects. Bayard's process required so long an exposure that it was practically impossible. Working with the uncertain formulas given by Talbot in 1839 and 1840 (5), success was almost an accident. Herschel qualified these pictures as child's play. They seemed very coarse in comparison with the delicate finesse of the daguerreotype. The grain of the negative paper when added to that of the positive paper aggravated this coarseness. Aside from this, it was considered for a long time a shortcoming to be obliged to print the image under a negative.

In the meantime operators—who were very scarce—tried their hands at it and among the very first we must mention the Germans, Von Kobel and Steinheil, who in April 1839 exhibited at the Bavarian Academy in

Munich images on paper which they had obtained by Talbot's process. Many experimenters continued trying to find new sensitive papers, other than that used by Talbot, and no doubt better ones, but none succeeded. I have already mentioned Fyfe, Desmarets and Lassaigne, in 1839, and to these must be added Mungo Ponton and in the years that followed, Hunt and Herschel. Hunt found the *ferro-cyanotype* papers sensitized with silver nitrate in potassium ferrocyanide; those with bromide and silver nitrate, which were developed with mercury, and the *chromatype* papers sensitized with sulphate of copper and potassium bromide not sufficiently for the camera. Herschel contributed the *chrysotype* paper, sensitized with iron ammonium citrate developed in a gold solution, and paper with ferrotartaric acid in which the image developed under steam. (6) All these methods have nothing but a retrospective interest. Only Mungo Ponton's process had important results, because the pigment processes utilized bichromate later. (7)

Ponton immersed the paper in a solution of potassium bichromate and when dry, the paper became sensitive to the light, not for use in the camera however, but for some kind of prints of transparent gravures and some photographic negatives. After the bichromate had been removed by thorough washing, the greyish-brown image alone remained on the paper. If the subject was a gravure, the result was a negative. Edmond Becquerel (8), in March 1840, continued Ponton's researches and perfected them. The paper was printed and the image, being only faintly visible before the washing, Becquerel immersed it in an alcoholic solution of iodine, washed it and let it dry. The white parts of the paper turned blue and the yellow parts remained more or less clear. The blue colour resulted from the formation of iodized starch, the only kind of paper which could be used being sized paper. Becquerel's experiments were continued later by his pupil Poitevin and resulted in the discovery of the carbon process and of photocollography. Raifé also is the author of a process on paper (1840 and 1841) which was not heard of later. (9) Berthot in 1841 thought out a paper coloured with sulphur of lead and which the light bleached in the camera under the influence of hydrochloric acid. (10) The images were positives. Herschel in 1843 sent to Arago a beautiful paper print "prepared with iron, lead and mercury". (11) Gaudin, in 1845, sensitized papers with hydrochloric acid and silver nitrate, developed with iron sulphate and fixed with ammonia. (12)

The only process used in France during 1841 was that which Talbot discovered in December 1840 and which was published in June 1841.

TALBOT'S FORMULA

First operation:

SOLUTION A $\begin{cases} \text{Silver nitrate} & \text{100 grains} \quad (6 \text{ gr. } 48) \\ \text{Water} & \text{6 ounces} \quad (168 \text{ gr.}) \end{cases}$

SOLUTION B $\begin{cases} \text{Potassium iodide} & \text{100 grains} \quad (6 \text{ gr. } 48) \\ \text{Water} & \text{1 pint} \quad (0 \text{ lit. } 568) \end{cases}$

Coat the paper with SOLUTION A, dry slowly; immerse the paper in SOLUTION B, wash and dry. The paper can be preserved for a long time.

Second operation:

BATH C $\begin{cases} \text{in} \\ \text{equal} \\ \text{parts} \end{cases}$ $\text{D} \begin{cases} \text{Silver nitrate} & \text{100 grains} \quad (6 \text{ gr. } 48) \\ \text{Water} & \text{2 ounces} \quad (56 \text{ gr.}) \\ \text{Acetic acid} & \frac{1}{6} \text{ volume} \end{cases}$ $\text{E} \begin{cases} \text{Saturated solution of gallic acid} \\ \text{precipitated in cold water.} \end{cases}$

When using, immerse the paper in BATH C and print it while moist.

DEVELOPMENT AND FIXATION

After exposure, immerse the paper in Bath C. The image will become visible in two minutes if it is slightly heated. Then wash and fix in a solution of potassium bromide.

The print was negative; however, the inventor pointed out at the end of his report the means for obtaining direct positives. This is the Calotype Process. (13) I do not know of any prints obtained by the methods enumerated above; but Calotypes are still in existence. It is not necessary to add that these images are today extremely rare.

In 1844, Tanner, a pupil of Talbot, taught the Calotype Process to some photographers at Lille, one of whom was the printer Blanquart-Evrard (1802-1872). But in 1844, as in 1841, the images were defective, neither fine nor transparent in the middle tones, and the results were always uncertain. Blanquart, after having improved the Calotype, presented it in 1846 as a new process without mentioning Talbot's name, but this was, he said, only an "oversight". (14)

BLANQUART-EVRARD'S FORMULAS:

Immerse a piece of paper for one minute in the following solution:

Silver nitrate   1 part
Distilled water   30 parts

dry slowly and then immerse it for two minutes in the following solution:

Potassium iodide	25 parts
Potassium bromide	1 part
Distilled water	560 parts

Wash it in distilled water; dry it. The paper can be kept for several months.

Before use, flow a glass held horizontally with a small quantity of the following mixture:

Silver nitrate	6 parts
Acetic acid (glacial)	11 parts
Distilled water	64 parts

Place the side of the paper which has received the first coating of nitrate on the glass and cover it with several sheets of wet paper in order to keep it moist. Place a second glass on top of it and expose it in the camera. The exposure will require several seconds in good light in open air. The image is not visible.

DEVELOPMENT AND FIXATION:

Immerse the paper in a saturated solution of gallic acid in water. The image will become visible almost immediately. Wash it and immerse it for fifteen minutes in a solution (1/40) of potassium bromide. The print is negative. After drying, it is rendered transparent by placing it on a hot waxed plate.

POSITIVE PRINTING PAPER: (15)

Immerse the paper for two minutes in the following solution:

Saturated solution of sea salt	3 parts
Distilled water	10 parts

Dry between blotters and immerse it for several minutes in the following bath:

Silver nitrate	1 part
Distilled water	5 parts

After drying, it is ready for use. Expose the positive paper under the negative and cover them with thick glass. At the end of twenty minutes the visible image will attain the desired intensity. Wash and immerse in the following bath:

Hyposulphite of soda	12 parts
Water	100 parts

Wash and dry.

Such was Blanquart-Evrard's process, from which are derived all those which followed and which mark the beginning of photography on paper. How little it was utilized is best shown by the fact that no one recognized Talbot's process, so little modified by Blanquart. The earliest prints of Blanquart, still extant, are very fine and his salted paper base retains, after seventy-five years, images as perfect as on the date they were made. However, it is probable that he would have joined his predecessors, who worked on paper, in oblivion if negatives on glass had not been discovered at this time.

PHOTOGRAPHY ON PAPER
REFERENCES: CHAPTER XXXIX

1. Arago used the word *copie photographique* (photographic copy). *Le Magasin Pittoresque*, in November 1839 announced Daguerre's discovery under the title: *La Photographie ou le Daguerréotype*. In 1851 Ziégler stated: (*La Lumière*, April 20, 1851) "We have not chosen the word *Photographie*; it has been in use for a long time; it signifies in France, in Germany and in Belgium, *Daguerréotype sur papier* (Daguerreotypy on paper).
2. Lecture course at the Faculty of Sciences.
3. *Rapport sur le Daguerréotype lu à l'Académie Royale des Sciences de Naples* (Report on daguerreotypy read at the Royal Academy of Sciences of Naples) by M. Melloni, Paris 1840.
4. *Comptes rendus*, 1840, 1st semester, p.483.
5. *Comptes rendus*, 1839, 1st semester, pp.170, 207, 302, 341, 409, 838 — 1840, 1st semester, pp.247, 483 — 2nd semester, p.574.
6. *Mélanges photographiques* by Ch. Chevalier, Paris 1844 — *Recueil de Mémoires et de Procédés nouveaux concernant la Photographie* (Collection of memoirs and of new methods concerning Photography) by Ch. Chevalier, Paris, Dec. 1847.
7. Chromium was discovered by Vauquelin, in 1798, who also discovered the action of light on chromic acid. *Annales de chimie*, Vol. XXV and LXX.
8. *Comptes rendus*, 1840, 1st semester, p.469.
9. *Comptes rendus*, 1840, 1st semester, p.843 — 1841, 1st semester, p.122.
10. *Comptes rendus*, 1841, 2nd semester, p.92.
11. *Comptes rendus*, 1843, 1st semester, p.210.
12. *Comptes rendus*, 1845, 1st semester, p.857.
13. *Comptes rendus*, 1841, 1st semester, pp.182, 492, 1055 — 1844, 2nd semester, p.489.
14. *La Photographie, ses Origines, ses Progrès, ses Transformations* (Photography, its origin, progress, and its changes) by Blanquart-Evrard, Lille, 1870. *Comptes rendus*, 1846, 2nd semester, pp.639, 1083 — 1847, 1st semester, pp. 46, 117, 448, 653; 2nd semester, p.812.
15. *Procédés employés pour obtenir les Epreuves de Photographie sur Papier* (Process employed for obtaining photographic negatives on paper) by Blanquart-Evrard. Paris 1847.

CHAPTER XL

Photographs on Glass

NIEPCE de Saint-Victor (1805-1870), born at Saint-Cyr, near Chalon-sur-Saône, was a cousin of Nicéphore Niepce whom he called
"my uncle". The place he occupied in the Niepce genealogy can be seen
from Chapter XII. He was lieutenant of Cavalry at Paris, when he
conceived in 1846 (1) making negatives on glass. Unfamiliar with photography, his progress was slow. Having left the school at Saumur as
non-commissioned officer in 1827, he did not become a lieutenant until
1841. His experiments in colouring materials gained for him the advantage of being called to Paris, in 1845, for his service in the municipal
guard. From this time on, it was chemistry, and not war services, which
procured his advancement. Captain in 1848, Chevalier of the Légion
d'honneur in 1849, Major in 1854, the Emperor Napoléon III appointed
him, on the recommendation of the Académie des Sciences (2), Com-
mander of the Louvre Palace, a quiet office where he could devote himself entirely to his scientific work.

The wonderful discovery of his relative, having unjustly been forgotten, awoke in him the desire to revive Nicéphore Niepce's processes,
to improve them, and to make heliography practical and useful. It was,
therefore, a photographic engraving process which he sought and which
in fact he found later. On the way, however, he was led to the consideration of printing negatives on glass and from this he solved the problem
of photography on paper.

His first communications to the Académie des Sciences date from
October 25, 1847. (3) On that day, he described in a memoir the effects
of iodine on the blacks in engraving and of designs and the means of
reproducing them without altering them. In the second memoir which,
like the first, seems to have been inspired by Becquerel's work on iodized
starch, we find his process for obtaining negative images on glass. Niepce
de Saint-Victor used at first starch and iodide, later gelatine, which he
finally abandoned for albumen. (4)

NIEPCE DE SAINT-VICTOR'S FORMULAS

Beat the white of two or three eggs and add 12 or 15 drops of water
saturated with potassium iodide. Let it stand; pour it off, this decanted
liquid can be kept for forty-eight hours. Pour the albumen solution to

the height of 2mm. into a flat tray and then place the glass plate in such a fashion that the albumen will adhere only to the face. Dry it in a cool place then pass the plate for ten seconds into the following bath:

Silver nitrate	6 grams
Acetic acid (glacial)	12 "
Distilled water	60 "

Then wash it in distilled water. Expose it in the camera. Develop it with gallic acid just as in Blanquart-Evrard's method on paper. Fix in the same manner.

The negative on glass had one great defect, it needed a much longer exposure than the daguerrean plate and, of course, could not be used for portraiture. Niepce de Saint-Victor increased the sensitivity of his plates by mixing with the white of eggs two or three grams of honey and by increasing the amount of potassium iodide. (5) He also increased the rapidity of the daguerrean plate: two or three seconds for a landscape and five to eight seconds for a portrait. Beyond this, the daguerreotype was out-distanced, because the positive print on paper from the negative possessed qualities which made comparison entirely impossible. The paper print cost 3 cents, a plate 80 cents. The image on paper, a real black and white image, was soft, easy to carry and ideal for the tourist and collector. It was soon found that the negative, from which many prints could be made, could be favourably compared with the engraver's plate.

All the improvements and researches made from this time on, which had hitherto been wholly given to the daguerreotype, were now used only for glass and paper. Of course, at the same time as negatives on glass, there were also made glass positives which served as transparencies. In August 1849 (6) Blanquart-Evrard simplified the method for making negatives on glass, which consisted in flowing the albumen, to which a few drops of potassium bromide had been added, and then flowing it with a solution of silver nitrate containing a few drops of acetic acid. These glass negatives, he said, became "permanent glass matrices and would furnish an unlimited number of prints". In practice, however, the number of prints was limited by the considerable time required for daylight printing on silver chloride paper. In 1850, almost at the same time as Niepce de Saint-Victor (7), he proposed the use of a dry paper negative and of a dry albumenized paper positive. For the preparation of the latter, he added sodium chloride to the white of eggs and then floated it on silver nitrate. These dry papers offered a considerable advantage, because they could be used for a long time after their preparation and therefore could be sold, ready for use, which was a great convenience for amateurs.

If the exposure in the camera was too long, Niepce de Saint-Victor, and later Humbert de Molard (8), reduced it by adding to albumen a slight proportion of sugar, honey, molasses, whey or other mucilaginous substances. The exposures were thus reduced by two seconds. Legray, after Blanquart-Evrard, used potassium fluoride and obtained instantaneous negatives but the fluoride had more disadvantages than advantages. (9) Poitevin recommended gelatine on glass after Niepce had abandoned it. Bousiges, a little behind his time, invented a method of obtaining positives on paper direct in the camera and Chevalier contested this glory which had already passed into oblivion. (10)

In 1851 methods for making positives and negatives went on side by side. Humbert de Molard concluded his researches on accelerating substances. (11) Talbot must be cited among the numerous experimenters applying their efforts to the curtailment of the time of exposure. He prepared a negative paper which was so rapid that drawn characters "on a disc revolving at great speed during the flash of an electric spark" could be registered. (12) Legray describes waxed negative paper which was used dry. The paper was immersed in wax until it was thoroughly impregnated, dried and sensitized in a solution as follows:

Rice water	1.000
Lactose	40
Potassium iodide	15
Potassium cyanide	0,80
Potassium fluoride	0,50

dried again and immersed in:

Distilled water	300
Silver nitrate	20
Acetic acid (glacial)	24
Bone black	5

The paper will keep for fifteen days and the image will be as full of fine detail as on glass. (13) Bayard introduced a positive paper which could be printed on in one second in the sun, and even in the weak light of a Carcel lamp in less than an hour while dry. (14) At the same time as Talbot, Blanquart-Evrard published a formula for a positive albumen paper sensitized with silver citrate and gallic acid with a twenty seconds printing time in daylight; the image was developed in a few minutes.

It was fixed with hyposulphite of soda and the tone could be modified, making it stronger or weaker, so as to render "all prints saleable". (15) We would say "intensify" or "reduce". It was now finally a commercial process. This is demonstrated by the fact that Blanquart-Evrard established at Lille, in September 1851, a photographic printing establishment of which I shall speak in the following chapter.

But it was the Englishman Scott Archer who contributed the happiest discovery by substituting collodion for albumen. Gustave Legray, painter and photographer had, it is true, spoken of collodion. "I am working at this moment" said he in 1850 (16) "on a method on glass by using methyl-hydrofluoric ether, potassium and sodium fluoride dissolved in alcohol at 40°, mixed with sulphuric ether and saturated by collodion. I then allow this to react on aceto-nitrate of silver and I obtain a picture in the camera in twenty seconds in the shade. I develop the image with a strong solution of iron sulphate and fix with hyposulphite." He speaks of it again in 1851, but merely as sizing for paper, until Scott Archer published at the beginning of 1851 a formula which rapidly became current practice. His countryman Fry was the first to use this and so produced beautiful portraits; Brébisson brought Archer's method to France. (17)

FORMULA FOR COLLODION:

Collodion	Very dry guncotton (18)	1 gram
	Sulphuric ether	90 grams
	Ordinary alcohol at 33°	60 grams

Prepare a mixture of:

Collodion	50 grams
Alcoholic solution of silver iodide	15 grams
Alcoholic solution of iodide of iron	6 grams

Flow this mixture on the glass. It will take at once. Immerse in:

Distilled water	60 grams
Silver nitrate	4 grams

and while wet expose in the camera. The exposure is short, two or three seconds; much shorter than for the daguerrean plate. The development and fixation do not differ from the methods formerly employed. The resulting negative possesses qualities of fineness and beauty which no other process has equalled thus far. Of course the collodion which has been in use for so long a time was rapidly improved but this is outside the scope of this work.

Le Moyne also found an ingenious process. Having flowed the albumen on a glass plate, he immersed the plate in a tincture of iodine to which he added one-tenth nitric acid and sensitized with a solution of 10 percent silver nitrate, he then washed it in potassium fluoride, immersed the plate in another 20 percent bath of silver nitrate and exposed it in the camera. This image was developed no longer with gallic acid but with concentrated sulphate of iron, heated to 90°C. Finally, the fixation was made in a bath of cyanide of potassium and hyposulphite of soda. (19) The pictures then presented *"the appearance of opaque images, yellowish white surrounded by a diaphanous medium"*, and showed positive or negative according to the background of the object being dark or light. In order to make a positive, the albumenized side was coated with black varnish. Such positives usually framed with a background of black velour were called *amphitypes* (20) and this simple process was adopted by many professionals in the years which followed, but collodion replaced the albumen process. Talbot and other inventors claimed the credit for this double image process. (21)

And thus glass and paper sent the silvered plate of Daguerre into oblivion. The first portraits on paper which were seen in Paris seem quite defective, but they were rapidly improved and their low price made them popular. At the Exhibition of Industrial Products in 1844 only daguerreotypes were exhibited. In 1848 they still appeared in numbers but mixed with paper prints. (22) At London in 1851 they no longer were so numerous; at Paris in 1855, swamped in the mass of other processes, the daguerrean images no longer attracted. (23) They were regarded as rarities, as souvenirs, as something out of fashion.

Perhaps at the end of this chapter we ought to recall the negative images on glass of the sun and moon, made by Niepce de Saint-Victor in June 1850, owing to their interesting quality. (24)

1. *Recherches photographiques*, . . . (Photographic researches) by Niepce de Saint-Victor *suivies de Considérations* (followed by comments) by M.E. Chevreul, member of the Institut, *avec une Préface biographique et des Notes* (with a biographical preface and notes) by Ernest Lacan, Paris 1855. At the World Exhibition in 1855, Niepce de Saint-Victor exhibited a negative on glass made in 1846; *La Lumière*, October 20, 1855.
2. Meeting of March 28, 1853.
3. *Comptes rendus*, 1847, 2nd semester, pp.579, 785.
4. M.Clerc writes: "Becquerel used the chemical reaction of iodine on starch and Niepce-de-Saint-Victor used starch as a vehicle for the iodide".
5. *Comptes rendus*, 1848, 1st semester, p.637 — 1850, 1st semester, p.709 — 1850, 2nd semester, p.245.
6. *Comptes rendus*, 1849, 2nd semester, p.215.
7. *Comptes rendus*, 1850, 1st semester, pp.663, 709 — *Traité de Photographie sur Papier* (Treatise on Photography on Paper) by Blanquart-Evrard (of Lille) *avec une Introduction* by George Ville, Paris, June 1851.
8. *Comptes rendus*, 1850, 2nd semester, pp.208, 245.
9. *Comptes rendus*, 1850, 1st semester, p.779 — 2nd semester, pp.5, 245.
10. *Comptes rendus*, 1850, 1st semester, p.647 — 2nd semester, pp.71, 630, 726, 752.
11. *Comptes rendus*, 1851, 1st semester, p.468.
12. *Comptes rendus*, 1851, 1st semester, p.911.
13. *Comptes rendus*, 1851, 2nd semester, p.643.
14. *Comptes rendus*, 1851, 1st semester, p.552.
15. *Comptes rendus*, 1851, 1st semester, pp.535, 639 — *Traité de Photographie sur Papier* by Blanquart-Evrard (Lille) and Introduction by George Ville, Paris, June 1851, p.186.
16. *Traité pratique de Photographie sur Papier et sur Verre* (Practical treatise concerning photography on paper and glass) by Gustave Le Gray, painter and photographer, Paris, June 1850 and *Nouveau Traité théorique et pratique de Photographie sur Papier et sur Verre contenant les Publications antérieures et une nouvelle Méthode pour opérer sur un Papier sec restant sensible huit à dix Jours* (New theoretical and practical treatise concerning photography on paper and glass including previous publications and a new method for making them on dry paper, which is durable from eight to ten days) by Gustave Le Gray, painter and photographer, Paris, July 1851.
17. *Nouvelle Méthode photographique sur Collodion*, by Alphonse de Brébisson, Paris, May 1852.
18. Guncotton was invented in 1846.
19. *Comptes rendus*, 1851, 2nd semester, p.305 — *Photographie sur Verre, Mémoire concernant l'Obtention à la Chambre noire d'Epreuves positives sur Verre de nature à servir également de Clichés pour les Reproductions sur Papier* (Photography on glass with notes concerning the making of positives on glass in the camera and in a manner which will also serve as negatives for reproduction on paper) by J.-R.Le Moyne, engineer of bridges and roads, Limoges, September 1851.
20. This word was suggested by Talbot.
21. *Comptes rendus*, 1851, 2nd semester, p.623 — *A Guide to Photography*, by Thornthwaite, London, May 1852 — *La Lumière*, January 30, 1852, reports the claim of Thomas Woods — *Traité de l'Impression photographique sans Sels d'Argent* (Treatise on photographic images without silver salts) by A. Poitevin, Paris 1862, p.33.
22. *La Lumière*, March 2, 1851.
23. Ernest Lacan, *La Lumière*, September 15, 1855.
24. *Comptes rendus*, 1850, 1st semester, p.709 — *Recherches photographiques*.

CHAPTER XLI

Photomechanical Processes

THE object of the photomechanical processes is to transform photographs into plates suitable for printing pictures by the ordinary means of the printing press. These pictures do not differ from the prints obtained from etchings, typographical printing plates or those printed from stones, etc. From this it is obvious that the invention of a photomechanical process had to overcome two difficulties: to find the proper technical method which will give a printing plate and to produce impressions at a commercial price which could compete with the process then in use. The first part of the problem was easily solved, as will be seen, but photomechanical processes did not enter the field of the printing industry until long after 1851, which is the time limit of this history. It is, therefore, only the beginning of printing from photographic plates with which I deal here.

When Daguerre began to show his exquisitely delineated images on this metal plate, in which there seemed nothing lacking but etching with acid, artists and scientists naturally turned to the engraving processes. The idea that one could obtain proofs on paper from a photographic plate already so nearly finished was at once accepted, all the more readily since Niepce had chosen a metal base precisely with this object in view. Jean-Baptiste Dumas, in 1839 (1), states that he at once conceived the hope that engraving would become a part of Daguerre's process; because the whites of the design were formed from a very fine mercury powder, the acid attacking the blacks, or where the metal is bared before the mercury could be dissolved. And lithography, because, transferred on a sheet of paper covered with lithographic ink, the image was formed by mercury powder, the paper carrying this design would in its turn be transferred to stone wherever the mercury had formed a resist and the ink would only take on the blacks.

As a fact, these were the first two methods employed. Donné, who at the same time as Dumas, perhaps before him, had explained the formation of the daguerrean image, Donné showed at the Académie des Sciences, on September 23, 1839, an engraved daguerrean plate and proofs on paper obtained from this plate. A month later he presented new proofs, twenty impressions of a Head of Antinous (2) and, on June 15th following, gave a lecture on his method of operation. He merely flowed on the daguerreotype a mixture of 3 parts of nitric acid and 4 parts of water, exact proportions, and allowed it to etch 3 or 4 minutes. The plate was ready for printing but silver is a metal too soft to resist the wear from many impressions. Only forty impressions could be printed.

I think Donné's attempt was the first in order of time. That of Dr. Berres of Vienna dates from April 1840, that of Dr. Krasner from November 1840, that of W. B. Grove of London from August 1841. (3) All these claim priority, and we must add Saxton of Philadelphia who, two years after Donné, also claimed to be the first. (4) Donné's intention was to experiment only, not to establish an industry. It was left to those of the craft to perfect the work that had been begun, but they paid little attention to this matter and the process was abandoned.

Fizeau, a little later, took up again the attempt to engrave daguerreotypes and perfected the method. Arago, in March 1841, already described his results as "admirable". (5) A daguerreotype, of course, was etched first, while hot, with a mixture of nitric, nitrous and hydrochloric acids; or with nitric acid, potassium nitrite and sea salt. One could also use a solution of bichloride of copper, but with less chance of success. The acid attacked the blacks of the image and left the whites protected by the mercury unaffected; but this action was soon arrested by the formation of silver chloride. It was then washed in a solution of ammonia before etching it again. The etching was now completed, but if the depth was not sufficient, the image was weak. Fizeau then coated his plate with linseed oil and, wiping it off, as intaglio printers do, left the oil in the interstices; later, using the galvanotype process, which had just been discovered (6), he gold-plated his plate. Only the raised parts took on the gold, because the interstices were filled with oil.

When the oil was removed from the gold-plated galvanotype by washing it in potash, it was dusted with a resin, in the manner which etchers employ. It then looked like an aquatint plate, which translates the middle tones, without the defects of the etched daguerreotype, and then could be etched several times again with nitric acid, until sufficiently deep, because the acid reacted only in the hollows where only the silver remained. These gold or silver-plated galvanotypes, however, became greatly worn on long runs. Fizeau copper-plated these plates by a galvanoplastic process. When the copper wore down, the residue was removed with a weak acid which did not touch the silver and, after depositing on it a new copper shell, the printing continued.

The latest improvements date from 1844. Fizeau had now associated himself with the engravers Hurlian and Lemaître. I do not know what part they took in the invention (7), but in 1841 Fizeau was the only one who had obtained perfect results, proofs of which are still extant. The publication *Excursions daguerriennes* by Lerebours of 1841 contains a photograph of the City Hall of Paris, engraved by Fizeau's process. This is as beautiful as the steel engravings on the other page.

Grove, Dr.Berres and Dr.Heller, of Vienna, in an ingenious process in 1842, like Fizeau, employed galvanoplasty. Berres, who seems to have been the most successful, exploited his process commercially in 1843, which he named *phototypy*, which name was later given to another process. (8) Choiselat and Ratel, like Fizeau etched the plates with bichloride of copper (9); they produced their first plate before 1842. Notwithstanding all the claims of these inventors, their work never succeeded in practice.

In 1842, the Société d'Encouragement pour l'Industrie nationale rewarded Donné and Berres, and in 1843 Choiselat and Ratel, and, having offered a competition for "*a method of multiplying the images obtained by the action of light to the number of at least two hundred*", decided in 1848 that the object of the competition had not been attained by anyone. (10) Nevertheless, the society awarded medals to Niepce de Saint-Victor, Fizeau and Poitevin. (11)

It was the competition which the Duc de Luynes promoted through the Société Française de Photographie in 1855 which finally, after several years, brought success. In 1853 Niepce de Saint-Victor published his heliogravure process which, after some improvements, was generally used; still later Poitevin (1819-1882) contributed a new and fruitful solution to the problem of photomechanical reproduction with bichromated gelatine.

It is interesting to recall the experiments of Poitevin prior to 1851. This inventor observed (1842) that when the daguerrean plate was immersed in a galvanoplastic bath, the copper deposited only on the whites, formed by mercury amalgam, to the exclusion of the bare silver. He deposited copper on the daguerreotype and placed the copper shell on a sheet of gelatine, to which he fixed it. Thus he obtained beautiful negative images from which positive prints could be made in the printing frame on sensitive paper, (1847). (12) This ingenious method of reproducing the daguerrean image led him to the discovery that the gelatine swelled in those parts where the copper had not deposited, and thus the design is reproduced in intaglio and in relief. He was even able to obtain moulds in sulphur and make "very satisfactory" gravure prints.

His work with negatives on glass coated with gelatine (1849) confirmed his observation that wet gelatine did not swell in the blacks and formed an intaglio image; he turned to galvanoplastic copper plates suitable for the printing press. But he did not take up this work seriously until 1854. In his other experiments (February 1848), the daguerrean plate with its copper deposit was washed with gum water and wiped dry; then it was inked with a roller, the ink taking on the copper but not on the silver. Poitevin concluded from this that the image could also be reproduced on the lithographic stone.

Thus the various gravure processes before 1851 presented only meagre results, but still they were superior to those obtained by photolithography. Donné, while trying to engrave the daguerreotype, also used lithography with the aid of the printer Dupont but this ended in disappointment. (13) Zurcher, a workman employed by the brothers Dupont made in 1842 "in a satisfactory manner" direct transfers of gravures and drawings on stone by the action of light. (14) He also made images in the camera but always without reproducing the middle tones, the eternal objection to all these processes, and claimed only a partial success and "imperfect results". Blanquart-Evrard published in 1869 two reproductions by Zurcher. In the previous year Rondoni, a lithographer in Rome, had reproduced on a lithographic stone "the image of the Orion nebula by the daguerrean process". (15) It cannot be said that photography alone gave birth to this picture. And that is all. There is no other attempt before those of Barreswil, Davanne, Lemercier and Lerebours in 1852 and that of Poitevin in 1855.

But owing to the absence of a perfect transfer, many artists contented themselves with this partial method which simply put "the image in its place" and saved them drawing those lines by hand. Similar is the process of Boscawen-Ibbetson in 1840 (16); that of Dumontier in 1842 (17); that of Brébisson and later Edward in 1848. (18) Others simply copied the daguerrean image with a tool or pencil and it is by this method that photography entered into the illustration of books.

In the early months of 1840, the optician Lerebours sent several operators to Italy equipped with the daguerrean apparatus, who brought back from there a great number of photographs. Other travellers visited Spain, the Orient, etc. Lerebours collected, he stated, more than twelve hundred negatives; the best of them were reproduced here by engravers, and in 1841 Lerebours published an album of sixty views "the most remarkable monuments of the globe" under the title *Excursions daguerriennes* at a price of 100 francs. The work appeared at first in fifteen parts, of four views each, with explanatory text by different writers. Encouraged by the success, Lerebours in July 1842, commenced another series of *Excursions daguerriennes* in order to "correct an omission". As a matter of fact, he had forgotten Paris and France in this review of remarkable things on the globe. This time several processes of reproduction were used. There are found here mixed with steel engravings by Hurliman, Martens, Riffaut, etc., lithographs by Ciceri, Arnout, Mignan and a gravure by Daubigny. There is also included a photomechanical reproduction of a daguerreotype by Fizeau's process; it is a view of the City Hall in Paris. Another series contains a bas-relief of Notre Dame of Paris by the same process.

This was really not the first entry of photography in printing if we count as photography the album of plants, ferns, flowers, etc., by Ibbetson in 1840, *"the first book printed by the sun"* according to the author. (19) Everything in this album, including the title, was printed by contact on sensitive paper by the aid of stencils, forming negatives. In 1844, Talbot undertook a publication of photographs with text entitled *The Pencil of Nature*, of which five issues appeared; the photographs were on calotype paper. The following year he printed twenty-three views of Scotland without text. The edition was necessarily extremely limited.

The first publication which deserves this name as important to printing seems to be the *Promenades poétiques et daguerriennes* (20) by L.A. Martin in 1850, illustrated by photographs on paper inserted in the work. The year 1851 saw the creation of two photographic printing establishments, probably the only ones that ever existed; one at Paris, directed by M. de Lachevardière; the other one at Lille founded by Blanquart-Evrard. These concerns printed photographs on sensitized paper by the ordinary method, and issued albums in which the pictures were bound with the text. The first printed book by Blanquart-Evrard is the *Album photographique de l'Artiste et de l'Amateur* (The artist's and amateur's photographic album) in 1851; then came the voyage made by Maxime Ducamp in 1849, and the series: *Souvenirs photographiques, l'Art religieux au XIIIe siècle, Monuments de Paris, Souvenirs de Versailles, Souvenirs des Pyrénées, les Bords du Rhin, Variétés photographiques, Etudes et Paysages, etc.* (Photographic souvenirs, religious art in the thirteenth century, monuments of Paris, souvenirs of Versailles, souvenirs of the Pyrenees, the banks of the Rhine, photographic varieties, studies and landscapes, etc.)

The printing establishment of Lachevardière was less active after its first publication, *Paris Photographié* by Renard, which was not sold until January 1853 by Goupil and Vibert. These establishments had only a short life, and in 1855 they had disappeared. It is necessary to mention here that among these incunabula of photography which later will be zealously sought by collectors, were: The monuments of Italy by Piot, a photographic album in twenty parts, published in August 1851 (21); and, although dated after 1851, also two other remarkable works; one, *Photographie zoologique ou Représentation des Animaux rares des Collections d'Histoire naturelle, publiée par L. Rousseau et A. Devéria, Procédés des plus habiles Photographes* (Zoological photography, or the representation of rare animals in the collection of natural history, published by L. Rousseau and A. Devéria, taken by expert photographers). (22) These pictures, obtained from negatives by Bisson, were engraved by Riffaut who used Niepce de Saint-Victor's heliogravure process. The first part appeared on September 5, 1853. According to Lacan, the earliest engraved plate was that of lizards appearing in the second part. (23)

The other work was *Vues de Jersey*, verse by Victor Hugo, prose by Charles and François Hugo and August Vacquerie, illustrated by photographs of Charles and François Hugo. Lacan, who saw the latter, found them superb. (24)

HISTORY OF THE DISCOVERY OF PHOTOGRAPHY
REFERENCES: CHAPTER XLI

1. *Cours professé à la Faculté des Sciences* (Course given at the Faculty of Sciences.)
2. *Comptes rendus*, 1839, 2nd semester, pp.411, 485 — 1840, 1st. semester, pp. 583, 933.
3. *Echo du Monde savant*, June 20, 1840; *Proceedings of the Electrical Society*, August 17, 1841; *Handbuch der Galvanoplastik*, Dr.Chr.H.Schmidt, Leipzig, 1847, p.205.
4. *American Journal of Photography*, January 1892 — *Early Daguerreotype Days* . . . . by Julius F.Sachse, p.241.
5. *Comptes rendus*, 1841, 1st semester, pp.401, 509, 957; 1844, 2nd semester, p.119.
6. Galvanotypy was discovered almost at the same time (1838) by Thomas Spencer in England and by Jacoby in Russia.
7. *Bulletin de la Société Française de Photographie*, 1855, p.185 — 1857, p.252.
8. *Comptes rendus*, 1841, 2nd semester, p.1071 — 1843, 1st semester, p.1130 — 1844, 2nd semester, p.518.
9. *Comptes rendus*, 1844, 2nd semester, p.388.
10. *Bulletin de la Société d'Encouragement*, 1842, p.124; 1844, p.297; 1848, p.195.
11. Named *Lepoitevin* in the report.
12. *Comptes rendus*, 1849, 1st semester, p.153; 2nd semester, p.13 — *Traité de l'Impression photographique sans Sels d'Argent contenant l'Histoire, la Théorie et la Pratique des Méthodes et Procédés de l'Impression au Charbon, de l'Helioplastie, de la Photolithographie, de la Gravure photo-chimique, etc., etc.* (Report on printing photographic images without silver salts; containing the history, theory and practice of the methods and manipulation for printing on carbon, helioplasty, photolithography and photo-chemical gravure, etc., etc.) by Alphonse Poitevin with introduction by Ernest Lacan, Paris 1862.
13. *Comptes rendus*, 1840, 1st semester, p.933 — *Rapport sur le Daguerréotype* by Macédoine Melloni, Paris 1840, p.110.
14. *La Lumière*, December 2, 1854 — *La Photographie* by Blanquart-Evrard of Lille, 1869; 2nd edition enlarged, 1870.
15. *Comptes rendus*, 1841, 2nd semester, p.449 — *Echo du Monde savant*, April 28, 1842.
16. *Comptes rendus*, 1840, 2nd semester, p.292 — *Echo du Monde savant*, September 23, 1840.
17. *Comptes rendus*, 1842, 1st semester, p.246.
18. *Glanes photographiques* (Photographic gleanings) by Alphonse de Brébisson, January 1848, p.2.
19. *Athenaeum*, January 1853. Exhibition of photographs at the Society of Arts of London.
20. *La Lumière*, March 15, 1852.
21. *La Lumière*, August 17, 1851; January 29, 1853 — *La Photographie* by Blanquart-Evrard, Lille 1869, 2nd edition, 1870.
22. *Comptes rendus*, March 14, June 5, September 5, December 19, 1853; August 14, 1854.
23. *Recherches photographiques* by Niepce de Saint-Victor, Paris 1855, préface, p.XIX.
24. *La Lumière*, August 6 and October 8, 1853.

CHAPTER XLII

Colour Photography

SCHEELE in 1777 exposed paper impregnated with silver chloride to the solar rays under a glass prism and observed that the chloride blackened equally under the different coloured rays and that it blackened more rapidly under the violet rays. Senebier, in 1782, made the same experiments and calculated the time necessary for the chloride of silver to blacken under each of the colours of the spectrum. He also saw that the shade of silver chloride at one extremity of the spectrum differed from that at the other. Ritter, in 1801, observed that the rays beyond the spectrum (ultra violet) and therefore invisible, coloured silver iodide. Wollaston (1802), after Herschel (1800), found rays equally invisible at the other extremity of the spectrum, but that these did not affect the silver salts. Seebeck (1810) (1) determined that paper coated with silver chloride exposed for twenty minutes to the solar spectrum coloured reddish-brown under the violet and ultra-violet rays, and blue under the blue rays; the green rays coloured the paper light blue; the red rays coloured it a hydrangean rose; the yellow rays gave no particular colouration. We have seen that Daguerre attempted to print colours by means of phosphorescent substances and he declared that the problem could not be solved.

After photography was made public, Herschel (Sir William T.N.) having discovered the infra-red rays, Herschel (Sir John T.N.) recognized in 1839 "that a sheet of sensitized paper exposed to the strong concentrated light of the spectrum" records itself rapidly in different colours: red under the red rays, dark green under the green, dark blue under the blue. The yellow rays had no particular reaction. He also remarked that after the sensitized paper had been blackened by light and is then exposed to red light, it will turn red. Hunt, in 1840, exposed sensitized paper under glasses of different colours and he noted the variety of colourations obtained.

Edmond Becquerel used these previous experiments for his continuating red rays with which he put the finishing touches to the daguerrean images as related in Chapter XXXVII. Continuing with his attempts, he noted that a sensitized paper which had been exposed to the light did not act in the same manner under the spectrum as a paper

which had been kept in darkness, and that it took on different colourations according to the rays which produced them.

This led him to the discovery of photography in colours, and in 1848
(2) he communicated to the Académie des Sciences "that the solar spectrum could reproduce its image in colours corresponding to its own on a
silver plate" if one operated as follows: a sheet of highly polished silver
hung at the positive pole of a battery is immersed in weak hydrochloric
acid (125:1000), and a sheet of platinum hung at the negative pole and
moved back and forth in front of the plate for one or two minutes.
When the plate, having taken on different colours, looked like lilac, it
was removed, washed and dried. The plate having been placed in a drying stove at a temperature of 100°C., will in a few minutes take on the
colour of reddish wood. When exposed under the spectrum, it takes on
the colours of the spectrum and white in white light. The infra-red rays
are shown by a colouration (strong amaranth); the ultra-violet by a
"slate grey". Becquerel later devoted himself to making a sheet of silver
electro-positive by plunging it in sulphate of copper and sodium chloride,
using a battery. He also reproduced the solar spectrum and coloured
prints by contact. These colours were fugitive; they disappeared in daylight. Becquerel was never able to fix them.

Niepce de Saint-Victor in 1851 (3) repeated Becquerel's experiments.
He pointed out a number of chlorides which on the silvered plate would
reproduce one colour more than another. He thus reproduced by contact under transparencies: red, by strontium chloride; yellow, with
sodium or potassium chloride; blue, with bichloride of copper and ammonia; green, with nickel chloride; etc. Certain substances finally reproduced all the colours, including white. Immersing a silvered plate in a
bath composed of six parts of water to one part of copper chloride and
one of iron chloride, then drying it and heating the plate over a flame
until it became a cherry red, he obtained in the camera (1852) photographs of objects in colours, among others of a doll, dressed in bright
coloured cloth, which excited general admiration. (4) None of these
images could be permanently fixed. (5)

One of the legends which persists claims that the photograph of the
spectrum made by Becquerel and enclosed in a pasteboard box is preserved at the Conservatoire des Arts et Métiers and retains all of its
freshness. (6) I have not seen this image, but those of Niepce de Saint-
Victor, which I have seen, are entirely faded, especially the colours. One
can notice with difficulty the outlines of the image in reddish violet.

Later operators have used Becquerel's process and improved on it, hoping to fix the image. These are Poitevin in 1866, Chardon in 1887, Veresz in 1890, Pons in 1893, Saint-Florent in 1895. (7) All their photographs, although they have been preserved in the dark and with care, have perished. They present the bleached aspect of those of Niepce de Saint-Victor, although more recent. The images of Chardon retain some of the outlines of the design and some of the colour in the reds. Exception must be made for the images of Pons which look like aquarelles and might readily be taken for such. There are only four of them left and they are less discoloured although they were made under difficult circumstances. Half of each picture was covered with a paper, the other half being exposed to the sun for several hours. No difference can be noticed between the two parts. Pons died in May 1894 and never made the details of his manipulation public. (8)

This represents the first photographic colour process and is forgotten today.

1. Eder, *Geschichte der Photographie*, Halle, 1905, p.117.
2. *Comptes rendus*, 1848, 1st semester, p.181; 2nd semester, p.483; 1849, 1st semester, p.200; 1851, 1st semester, p.862 — *Annales de Physique et de Chimie*, 3rd series, Vol.XXII, p.451, Vol.XXV, p.447 — *Bulletin de la Société Française de Photographie*, 1858, pp.6, 17 — *La Lumière, ses Causes, ses Effets* by Edmond Becquerel, Paris 1868, Vol.II, Chapt.IV, p.209.
3. *Comptes rendus*, 1851, 1st semester, pp.834, 862, February 9 and November 6, 1852.
4. *La Lumière*, July 31, 1852. *Recherches photographiques* by Niepce de Saint-Victor, Paris, 1855, p.132.
5. *Bulletin de la Société Française de Photographie*, 1862, p.111; 1866, p.253.
6. M.Clerc writes: "The leather box in which the spectrum was exhibited, when opened in 1928, was found to be empty."
7. *Bulletin de la Société Française de Photographie*, for Poitevin, see: 1866, pp.13 and 318; for Chardon, 1889, p.61 and 1902, p.244; for Veresz, 1898, p.527 and 1902, p.244; for Pons, 1894, p.381; for Saint-Florent, 1896, pp.239, 252, 287.
8. All these pictures mentioned are now in the collection of the Société Française de Photographie.

CHAPTER XLIII

Projection and Enlargements

THE art of projection is ancient. In *Perspectiva* (1267), by Roger Bacon (1), may be found: "Mirrors can also be placed in such a manner one can perceive whatever goes on in the house or on the street. The spectator will actually see these things; but if one approaches the place where one believes they are, one will find the place empty. Because the mirrors are in a closed place, facing the real object, and the position in which the apparition is seen in the air, that is where the visual and the reflected rays meet in direct line with the mirrors. Thus, when the spectators approach closely to the vision, thinking that they will find there the objects, they will find there nothing but only their apparition."

Some see in this passage a description of the camera obscura, others a system of projection. Athanasius Kircher (2) states that a design in black ochre could be projected into a room by means of concave mirrors and daylight; that Roger Bacon had already projected his shadow in this manner and, on account of this, had been accused of necromancy. It is asserted that Porta in the sixteenth century projected into a dark room images painted on plates of glass or stencils cut in cardboard by means of a lens and daylight. These views were animated and the figures gesticulated if manipulated like marionettes. Having read the passages in which Porta (3) describes the spectacles given in the camera obscura, I am not convinced of the truth of this assertion. But Kircher in his *Ars Magna* (4) (1646) gives for the first time a clear and detailed description of projections made in this manner in the camera obscura by the aid of sunlight. The substitution of an artificial light for daylight, leading to the invention of the projection lantern, is due to a Danish mathematician, Walgenstein, who demonstrated an apparatus of this sort in Rome about 1660 (5), and at Lyons in 1665. (6) Minute details of his arrangement and the reasons for the phenomena which he produced are described by Milliet Dechales (1690), and by Zahn (1685). (7)

Figures 76 and 77 in M. Potonniée's *Histoire* sufficiently explain all that may be necessary. They represent the magic lanterns which underwent very few changes until the seventeenth century. It will be noted that the lanterns which were used at that time, and of which the illustrations reproduced give an idea, could not have given much light,

235

but this is only relative. They satisfied; Kircher states that if a concave steel mirror was placed behind this lantern, the illumination was "surprising".

One hundred years later, the magic lantern was taken up again, "an apparatus almost ridiculous on account of its too great celebrity" says Abbé Nollet. However, the learned physicist did not disdain to perfect it by placing between the source of the light and the "porte-objets" — which we call "slide-carrier"—a bi-convex lens larger than the glass plates on which were painted the images. This is the present-day condenser.

We must keep in mind that, in the eighteenth century, just as in the seventeenth, the magic lantern was used exclusively by charlatans for the purpose of amusement and, whenever possible, to deceive the crowd. Animated scenes accompanied by articulated silhouettes, were commonly used. "During a voyage to Holland in 1736", again quoting Abbé Nollet (8), "M.Muschenbrock showed me other clever views in which the figures moved as if they were animated. One, a windmill, another one a lady who bows in passing, another a machine in motion and a gentleman removing his hat. This was done by means of two glasses, one of which was fixed and the other carrying the movable part, which was put in motion by means of a string." But when the magic lantern was combined with the action of mirrors, effects were produced which were less innocent. Credulous people, and the Lord knows there are always plenty of them, readily accepted these luminous apparitions as evocations direct from Hades, a splendid pretext for extracting their money. The physicist Robertson (9) gave in Paris (1798) with great success representations where he called up ghosts and put them in motion. The more the public was warned and its credulity mocked, the more the spectators left convinced that they had seen an exhibition of magic.

However, attention must be called to the fact that the designers of the eighteenth century utilized the projection by megascope for the automatic enlargement or reduction of drawings, and the scientists of the same period employed the solar microscope in the study of natural sciences. Thus projections were used in science. The solar microscope, invented by Lieberkuyn in 1743 (10), is only a camera obscura in which the solar rays are directed on the screen by means of mirrors or heliostats. The light passes through the transparent microscopic object which is to be examined and which is placed between two slides held in grooves. A set of lenses composed of powerful achromatic magnifying glasses projects on the screen the image of the object considerably enlarged.

The megascope devised by Charles in 1786 is nothing but a camera obscura. An object of which one wanted to project the image, a statuette, design, etc., was placed in front of the camera on a moveable support and focused. Mirrors concentrated as much light as possible on it. The image of the object is then projected by the lens on to the screen, in the desired size, and the artist who is seated in the interior of the dark room, as in the use of a solar microscope, follows the outlines of the enlargement. However, the projections employed today in the examination of scientific facts, seem to me to date only from 1838. The honour belongs to Abbé Moigno (1804-1884) who, with the aid of a lantern, constructed by the optician Soleil, explained and showed to his audiences a series of optical phenomena. We have seen how Humphry Davy (1802) reproduced on paper, coated with silver salts, images projected by the solar microscope, but at a very small distance from the lens, and without being able to fix them. In October 1839, Bayard described an arrangement which permitted the photographing of the image, magnified by the solar microscope. It was Donné who, in the following February, contributed "the first photogenic images of natural objects received through the solar microscope and projected on daguerrean plates by means of oxy-hydrogen gas inflamed over limestone." (11) This, I believe, is the first example of enlarged photographs by a projection lantern, although Lefebvre and Percheron claimed to have made this experiment before 1839. Malacarne, a Venetian engineer, made photographic enlargements in 1845. Fabre, at Romans, was supposed to have made them before 1840. (12) But it does not seem that anyone thought of making photographic projections for the purpose of either amusing or instructing an audience before Moigno and Duboscq about 1851. (13) At any rate, this cannot have been possible until after Niepce de Saint-Victor published the formula for images on glass.

Jules Duboscq, an optician at No.21 rue de l'Odéon, Paris, received a gold medal at London in 1851, and the Société d'Encouragement pour l'Industrie nationale (14) recognized a little later his initiative in the following terms: "He has now made a happy revolution in the public teaching of science. England and France have recognized the great advantage which he has contributed by substituting enlarged presentations of figures and natural phenomena obtained by the magic lantern process for figures drawn on a blackboard. M. Duboscq (15) is the first who led the way in this. He is the first who recognized the absolute

necessity of substituting perfect images obtained photographically on
transparent glass for the coarse and crude paintings used solely up to
this time." Shortly after, Duboscq applied the electric light to the projection lantern, which was used from that time on "in the public lectures
on physical and natural science not only in France but also abroad". (16)

PROJECTION AND ENLARGEMENTS
REFERENCES: CHAPTER XLIII

1. *Rogeri Bacconis . . . Perspectiva . . . nunc primum in Lucem edita Opera et Studio Johannis Combachii . . .* Frankfurt, 1614.
2. *Ars magna,* p.793.
3. Joh.Baptista Porta . . . *Magiae Naturalis Libri XX,* Naples 1588, book 17, chapt.VI. See above chapt.III.
4. Athanasii Kircheri . . . e Soc. Iesu Presbyteri . . . *Ars magna Lucis et Umbrae in decem Libros digesta . . .* Rome MDCXLVI.
5. Athanasii Kircheri . . . *Ars magna Lucis et Umbrae . . . Editio altera priori multo auctior.* Amsterdam, 1671, p.767.
6. R.P.Cl.Fr.Milliet Dechales . . . *Cursus sue Mundus Mathematicus,* Lyons, MDCLXXXX, vol.III, pp.680, 696.
7. *Oculus artificialis teledioptricus sive Telescopium . . .* authore R.P.F.Joanne Zahn . . . Herbipoli MDCLXXXV.
8. *Leçons de Physique expérimentale,* Paris 1759, vol.V, p.572.
9. *Mémoires récréatifs, scientifiques et anecdotiques du Physicien Aeronaute* (Recreational, scientific memoirs and anecdotes of an aeronautical physicist) by E.-G.Robertson, Paris 1831.
10. *Leçons de Physique expérimentale* by Abbé Nollet, Paris 1765, vol.V, p.572.
11. *Comptes rendus,* 1839, 2nd semester, p.554; 1840, 1st semester, pp.288, 478. Oxyhydrogen light was discovered by Drummond in 1804.
12. *La Lumière,* February 25, 1854, February 7, 1852.
13. *L'Art des Projections* (Art of Projection) by Abbé Moigno, Paris 1872, preface.
14. *Bulletin de la Société d'Encouragement,* 1855.
15. Jules-Louis Duboscq was born at Vilaine (S.-et-O.) on March 5, 1817, was a pupil and son-in-law of the optician Soleil, for whom he began to work in 1830, and whom he succeeded in 1849. He received a municipal medal at the World Exposition in London in 1851, a medal of the first class in New York in 1853, another at the exposition of Paris, 1855, was made Chevalier de la Légion d'honneur in 1863, officer in 1885. He is credited with having made the first photographic projection apparatus, with the construction of the stereoscope, the application of electric light to projections, and the first moving pictures.
16. *Bulletin de la Société d'Encouragement,* 1855, p.455; 1856, pp.135, 183.

CHAPTER XLIV

Stereoscopy

THE origin of stereoscopy has been attributed to the English physicist Wheatstone (1802-1875) who, after others, having defined the theory in 1832, was the first (1) to devise an apparatus in which objects appeared in relief to our eyes, although drawn on a plane surface. He constructed his stereoscope with mirrors and exhibited on June 12, 1838 before the Royal Society of London, geometrical figures drawn on paper which appeared in space in three dimensions. (2)

Wheatstone's stereoscope was composed of two vertical boards, upon which one placed the two binocular images of the object to be reproduced. A board supports them, at the center of which was a rod with a screw supporting a set of eye-pieces. Some distance in front were two mirrors joining at a right angle and reflecting the two images. If one looked through the two eye-pieces, the object appeared in relief.

This invention did not attract any great attention, and it seemed that it could not be applied to any great extent, on account of the difficulty of procuring binocular images of an exact perspective by manual drawing. It had almost been forgotten when Sir David Brewster (1781-1868) invented in 1844 his refractive stereoscope wherein the images are viewed direct. He substituted refractive prisms in place of the mirrors by placing in the eye-piece two halves of a lens, the left half being placed before the right eye and the right half before the left eye. The two "dissimilar" designs, placed at a suitable distance, were seen superimposed and in relief. These images, however, have undergone great changes since 1838. Instead of hand drawn designs, almost impossible to obtain showing respective views of the right eye and of the left eye, they substituted photographic designs, easily made by moving the lens of the camera laterally for a distance equalling that which ordinarily separates the eyes (65mm. about 2½ inches).

Brewster had a model stereoscope made by the optician London, of Dundee. He exhibited a binocular portrait of Dr. Adamson which he had taken at the Exposition. (3) Notwithstanding the evident success of this experiment, the learned physicist could not find any optician in England who would undertake to manufacture stereoscopes for sale to the public. It was not until the Spring of 1850 that Brewster, while visiting Paris, was taken by Abbé Moigno (4) to call on the optician Jules Duboscq, son-in-law and successor to Soleil, whose workshop was, so Moigno says, "the center and starting point of optical progress".

Duboscq possessed a rare intelligence; he foresaw the future of stereo-scopic photography and undertook without hesitation the construction of Brewster's stereoscope. He did more—he modified it in a fortunate manner. Brewster's two images were on paper or metal; Duboscq put them on glass and, by pointing the apparatus upward, he viewed them as transparencies. This, of course, incomparably increased their luminosity. (5) The World Exposition at London in 1851 offered a unique occasion for the presentation of the new stereoscope. Duboscq exhibited there a collection of binocular images "representing living persons, statues, bouquets of flowers, objects of natural history, etc.", and a great variety of apparatus. The Queen of England ordered one of these for her own use and more than a thousand stereoscopes were sold in that year in England. (6)

Thus stereoscopic photography was born, and at once grew prodigiously; but this is outside of our subject. Meanwhile Wheatstone, in the preceding years, had attempted "to apply his stereoscope to unite the dissimilar designs of statuettes taken by daguerreotypy and talbotype". (7) These were supplied by Fizeau and Claudet. (8) Wheatstone opposed Brewster, stating that he had produced everything that Brewster had but earlier, and that he was the first to define and make practical in stereoscopy, even with prisms, all of which is true. These claims, inevitably accompanying success, induced Brewster to write the history of binocular vision and of stereoscopy. He soon discovered that this matter was ancient. The perception by our brain of a united image by our two eyes had always perplexed those scientists who searched for an explanation of this phenomenon. In the fourth century B.C., Euclid, and five hundred years after Euclid, Galen (131-200) had already dealt on this subject. The Middle Ages in their dense ignorance revealed nothing of this, but Leonardo da Vinci in the fifteenth century, and particularly Porta (9) in the sixteenth, gave perfect explanations of the sensation of relief by binocular vision. Subsequently François Aguilon (1613), Gassendi (1658), Harris (1775) and, in the nineteenth century, Du Haldat, Elliot, Wheatstone and others took up and perfected the same theories. All this had only one object, the study and explanation of the mechanism of vision. Wheatstone and Elliot alone had tried to present hand drawn images in relief by suitable apparatus.

Porta, however, in 1593 clearly described the separate images seen by our eyes and the combined image which results from them and Brewster restated not only the principle but described also the stereoscopic image itself. He asked himself why Porta, having endeavoured to construct from the same subject an image seen by the left eye and another one by the right eye, had not then united both images by means of the eye or of an instrument. However, such a result was not known when in 1859 the brothers Brown (10) observed at the Wicar Museum, at Lille, two images of such a peculiar aspect that they were immediately thought to be stereoscopic pictures. These are two brown drawings in distemper attributed to the Florentine artist Jacopo Chimenti (1554-1640) a contemporary of Porta. Both pictures are the same size: 295mm x 205mm; both represent the same person sitting on a low stool, drawing and holding a compass in the left hand. They have recently been mounted separately on bristol board, in order that they can be exhibited.

Making the optical axes meet, the brothers Brown viewed the united images in relief. The same experiment, attempted by the use of reduced photographic reproductions placed in the stereoscope, miscarried when Bingham repeated it in 1860 (11) but was successfully repeated by the Photographic Society of Douai in 1903. The differences that distinguish these two images when superimposed, for the perspective of the artist was faulty in making the binocular pictures, the relief sometimes visible and sometimes not, led some to the conclusion that these were stereoscopic pictures, while others believed that the artist had no thought of stereoscopy. When reproduced in natural size, I have found (12) evidence of relief, but only partially, in the stereoscope with mirrors, and dubious with reduced photographs. It is certain that men of the sixteenth century, having no mechanical means of reducing designs, have studied them in their natural dimensions and, what is more certain, they did not see them in a stereoscope, but attained the convergence of the optical axes by an effort of vision, as is done by many stereoscopists today. In using this elementary process, as did the contemporaries of Chimenti, the relief is easily seen. It disappeared if the right hand design was substituted for the left. Obviously, only the manuscripts of the sixteenth century, not available to us, could inform us of the artist's intentions in sketching these people. But their careful examination disclosed the fact that it was not a question—as has been asserted—of the simple reproduction of a single relief image, and that at the Museum of Lille, where they have always been, are preserved two unique proofs.

STEREOSCOPY

The taking of photographic views intended for viewing in the stereo-scope necessitated a special material. Some time passed before the single lens camera which took the two photographs in succession was replaced by a binocular camera. Brewster, however, had conceived a binocular camera as early as 1849. Quinet, some years later, reinvented Brewster's invention and vigorously defended the priority of his discovery with success.

It is impossible to relate the beginnings of stereoscopic photography without mentioning two apparatuses constructed by Duboscq in 1851 or 1852 at the latest. The first is a stereoscope with rectangular prisms having vertical axes through which one could view stereoscopic images of very large dimensions. Ordinary stereoscopic views on glass were pro-jected on a screen and viewed in relief by an entire audience, who had been previously furnished with these stereoscopes. This is the earliest attempt of this kind. The second is a stereoscopic lorgnon designed for books on natural science, illustrated with stereoscopic photographs. It was published in Germany, in 1857, under the title: *Geologische Bilder* (Geological Illustrations) a book illustrated by stereoscopic figures, and one of Duboscq's lorgnons was sold with each copy to be used in the study of the plates. (13) This valuable method of instruction has been lost. Should we not mention the use of the stereoscope made by Foucault and Jules Regnault who "verified the recomposition of white light by the simultaneous perception of two complementary colours given by polarized light"? (14)

HISTORY OF THE DISCOVERY OF PHOTOGRAPHY
REFERENCES: CHAPTER XLIV

1. For the history of the stereoscope see: *The Stereoscope, its History, Theory and Construction* . . . by Sir David Brewster . . . London 1856.— *Monographie du Stereoscope et des Epreuves stéréoscopiques* (Monograph on the stereoscope and the stereoscopic negatives) by H. de La Blanchère, Paris 1860.
2. *Phil. Transactions*, 1838, p.371.
3. *North British Review*, May 1852, p.176.
4. *Stéréoscope, ses Effets merveilleux, Pseudoscope, ses Effets étranges* (Stereoscope, its wonderful effects. Pseudoscope, its strange effects) by Abbé Moigno Paris 1852, p.14. Abbé Moigno says it was in the fall, but Brewster insists that it was in the spring.
5. *Catalogue des Appareils employés pour la Photographie sur Plaqué, sur Verre et sur Papier construits dans les Ateliers de M.J.Duboscq* (Catalogue of apparatus used for photography on metal, glass and paper constructed in the workshop of J.Duboscq) Paris 1862. The apparatus was patented on February 16, 1852.
6. *La Lumière*, November 1851, Brewster, Moigno, Duboscq, works quoted.
7. *Mémoire sur les Modifications et les Perfectionnements apportés au Stéréoscope* (Note on the changes and improvements contributed to the stereoscope) by Sir David Brewster, Paris 1858.
8. *Du Stéréoscope et de ses Applications à la Photographie* (On the stereoscope and its applications to photography) by A.Claudet, Paris, November 1853.
9. *De Refractione optices Parte Libri novem* (On optical refraction, in vol.IX) Naples, 1593, vol.IV, p.91; vol.VI, p.155.
10. *The Journal of the Photographic Society*, London, May 15, 1860, David Brewster.
11. *Bulletin de la Société Française de Photographie*, 1860, p.203 — *Gazette du Photographe amateur*, December 1896 — *Bulletin des Sociétés photographiques du Nord de la France*, December 1903 — *Photo-Revue*, January 24, February 28, March 13, 1904.
12. *Bulletin de la Société Française de Photographie*, July 1922.
13. *Bulletin de la Société d'Encouragement*, 1857, p.707.
14. *La Lumière*, November 30, 1851.

CHAPTER XLV

Photographic Motion Pictures

THE invention of animated photographs and the first apparatus for the purpose of producing them is so belligerently claimed by the entire world, and the marvelous discovery has so many birthplaces—obviously false with the exception of one—that its history cannot be written in one chapter. It would require a volume. I can only describe its beginnings briefly. Just as stereoscopy and as photography itself, so animated photography has used phenomena known for many centuries, but of which men did not know how to avail themselves. The camera obscura had been used for hundreds of years, and it was well known that the two eyes formed a single image, however, without thinking of photography and stereoscopy. This equally applies to persistence of vision, surmised already in the works of Lucretius .(1) (2) It was necessary that the human brain develop and become enriched by many new ideas in order to arrive at these deductions from the known facts which seem so simple to us. At first these led to photography, then to stereoscopy, and later, by natural progression, to animated photography, which we call cinematography. The honour for having made more of these marvelous deductions than all those in the years which preceded belongs to the men of the nineteenth century. The honour of counting, among those men of genius, the inventors of photography and cinematography belongs to France.

The images that exterior objects paint at the back of the eye remain there for a very short time. This physical phenomenon is supposed to have been described by Lucretius but only obscurely, because Lucretius talks of pictures which succeeded each other in dreams; this, however, is of no importance. It is probable that men knew a long time ago that they could trace fire-figures in the air by rapidly waving a burning torch. Some keen observer had been able to conclude that the image of the red torch persisted for a certain time, inasmuch as we see the general effect of the series of successive positions. Notwithstanding the fact that, since antiquity, many investigators have dealt with this subject, the science of moving figures made no progress until the nineteenth century. This experiment is found again in Brisson's dictionary. (3) (1781) "When embers are turned rapidly" said Brisson, "one sees a continuous circle of fire because this movement is made in too short a time for the mind to be able to grasp it. In short, the impression which the object makes on the eye while it is within a narrow compass of its circle, lasts a very short time only which the object needs to make the circuit, and for that reason the object is seen in all points of the circle at the same time." Experimental demonstrations of this fact were made at that period. Abbé Nollet (4) cites a polyhedron which turned on its axis and a circle which turned on one of its diameters, and which gave the impression of spheres. But his explanation does not seem to be as good as that of Brisson. All these effects, he says, depend on the following cause: "A moving object registers itself successively on different spots at the back of the eye; after this image passes rapidly from one to the other, the impression made on the first spot remains only until it commences to be felt on the second, on the third, etc."

In the years which followed, playthings were made inspired directly by this physical experiment. Such were the dazzling spinning top and Doctor Paris's (1825) thaumatrope. The former consisted of a top turning on a pivot on which were mounted two metal plates wound around with wire similar to the way one places them around a vase. The impression of this rotation to the apparatus gave to these symmetrically arranged wires the appearance of a brilliant metal vase. The thaumatrope, which came later, was still more simple; a pasteboard disc had a birdcage drawn on one side and a bird on the other. When the disc was rotated by briskly twisting and untwisting the wires, one saw both sides of the disc at the same time, thus obtaining an illusion of seeing the bird inside the cage. These are, in the form of amusements, the two experiments described by Nollet.

However, it must be noted that the thaumatrope showed at the same time and at the same point of space two objects distant from each other, while the polyhedron turning on its axis showed the same object at the same time at different points. But it was known in the eighteenth century that motion could change the form of objects as perceived by the eye. Nollet expressly stated this and this is not the only optical illusion which had been observed at that time. Brisson's dictionary enumerates seven of these under the title: "Laws of Vision in respect to Movements of visible Objects."

These investigations were continued in the nineteenth century and the most interesting observation concerning our subject is that of Roget (5), in 1825, who pointed out the distortion of rays in a moving wheel

246

seen through a series of vertical slits, in the nature of spaces in a fence. Plateau (1801-1883) professor at Brussels, seems to have been inspired by Roget in the experiment which he made in 1828. (6) Two geared wheels, absolutely alike, turning one behind the other, at uniform speed but in opposite directions, gave the illusion of a single wheel at rest. Faraday (1791-1867), two years later, repeated this experiment, known as Faraday's Wheel; but he pointed out that it could be done with a single disc and a mirror which reflected it and which acted as a second disc, a modification which largely contributed to the idea of the phenakisticope.

Plateau in 1831 "in order to preserve his rights to the results obtained by him" (7) published these new observations: "If we suppose two brilliant lines, straight or curved, turning at great speed in parallel planes and if the speeds of the two lines are synchronized, the eye viewing the system will distinguish, in a sort of stare which embraces the movement of both lines, the *stationary image of a third line* which will be darker than the background against which it appears. When the two lines are straight, each containing its rotation center, when their speed is equal and they move in opposite directions, and when the centers of movement are not superposed, the eye sees with surprise, on the kind of a cloudy and whitish surface produced by the lines, *a stationary dark grey line*, which is a perfect image of a hyperbola, passing through both centers of rotation. Now, if we suppose that the proportion of the speeds be altered just a little, the moving lines, after the intervals of time necessary to replace them in their original positions would not again resume these exact positions, so that, during each of these intervals, a different kind of a curve would be seen. But if the proportion of the respective speeds were altered only a very little, the difference between the two successive apparitions becomes inappreciable and we believe that the *image changes little by little in shape*, while passing through all the forms which may result from the variation from the initial positions . . . . When the two centers of movement are not superposed and the relation of the two speeds is altered only a little, the apparition does not change form, but will only show *turning slowly* around the center . . . ."

From these experiments came the phenakisticope. (8) This apparatus consisted "in a pasteboard disc pierced around its circumference by a certain number of small holes and bearing figures drawn on its interior surface. When this disc is turned around its center, opposite a mirror, and one eye is applied to the openings, the figures viewed by reflection in the glass, instead of blending in their regular rotation as viewed on the turning disc in any other manner, seem, on the contrary, to cease participating in the rotation of the circle, become animate and execute their usual motions . . . . In fact, *when several objects differing from each other, in graduated form and position, present themselves successively to the eye at very short intervals of time and close to each other, the successive impressions which they produce on the retina, will unite without confusion and we think that we see one object only which gradually changes both form and position."*

All the essential requirements for the cinematograph are seen here. The necessity of arresting the image before the eye during a véry short time is solved by the optical illusion which furnished a stationary image by the aid of a turning disc and a mirror (in fact: viewing each image through an opening in the same disc). I have copied these long passages showing how Plateau's ideas were followed in the evolution tending to this prodigious result, which to us seems so simple. Plateau, in addition, not only investigated the problem of vision but he is justly named first, having preceded all others.

Although he wrote: "I am entirely unfamiliar with the execution of this instrument which leaves much to be desired in many ways" (9), it has repeatedly been stated that Plateau constructed the phenakisticope — also called phenakistiscope — and he sent it to Faraday through Quetelet in November 1832. He had at this time "executed with great care" designs which were adopted in an apparatus constructed in London under the name of *fantascope*. This latter name does not deserve to be preserved because it was known only as phenakisticope. At the same time as Plateau, Stampfer, a Viennese, constructed an apparatus which he named "Stroboscope".

While constructing the fantascope and the stroboscope, their inventors devoted themselves to the study of optics and the laws of vision. They intended only, and so did those who followed them, to have their apparatus serve to determine the phases of a movement which might be printed and reproduced on the phenakisticope and still less to fix the image by some kind of an action because this was impossible by manual design. The examples which are quoted of the records of motion like, for instance, that of the clouds, of a pendulum, of gears, had no claim to scientific pretension because the exactness of the drawings was too conventional. When photography appeared in 1839, by the process furnishing an infallible copy, it changed these things.

PHOTOGRAPHIC MOTION PICTURES

The appearance of photography on the scene, Claudet says, enabled those who were familiar with the phenomenon produced by the phenakisticope to see the advantage offered in applying photographic images owing to the extraordinary degree of exactness which they possessed and which no manual process could possibly approach. As a matter of fact, it seems that the idea of applying photography to the phenakisticope had its birth at once and spontaneously. But one will search in vain to find where this idea was expressed for more than ten years. Plateau, it is said, considered in 1849 equipping his apparatus with photographs and stereoscopic designs. This was difficult; in 1849 there existed only one stereoscopic apparatus by Brewster constructed by London. Again it was the discovery of stereoscopy and not that of photography which opened the eyes of the investigators and showed what could be done by the photographic image. Contemplating objects motionless in relief, photographers suddenly realized that what they lacked in order to produce lifelike images and faithful copies of nature was movement.

The first who clearly observed these things or who at least transformed this desire into action was the optician Jules Duboscq. His little known attempts date from 1851, or later perhaps, from the beginning of 1852. Claudet is said to have begun the same researches sometime after Duboscq; his apparatus was constructed and in use in May 1852. (10) Duboscq, as we know, had constructed Brewster's stereoscope in 1850, later he devised new arrangements which he patented (February 16, 1852). Among the models of his invention is found an apparatus with revolving mirrors, where the two dissimilar figures — viewed by reflection — are no longer placed side by side, but one above the other. (11) The photographs are placed on the interior surface and are reflected in the mirrors; they turn with their backs to the spectator and shine horizontally on the screen which is held in the hand. The mirrors are movable on their axes, of the kind so that they may be adjusted and inclined at will, according to the reflection produced in the plane of the two eyes. The images are viewed through two lens tubes.

It was this apparatus which was used for the phenakisticope under the name of *Stereofantascope* or *Bioscope*. (12) The stereoscopic photographs were placed on the disc of the fantascope instead of sliding horizontally. "The two mirrors reflect the two image zones on to the same horizontal line, where the images can separately meet on the axis of each of the prismatic lenses of the stereoscope. In this manner, during the rotation of the disc, each eye perceived separately one of the

249

series of photographs and the coincidence of the images produced the sensation of moving figures in relief." "Duboscq (13) made another change in his instrument. In place of the vertical disc of Plateau, he used a cylinder which turned on its vertical axis and fastened the two series of photographs on two zones in the interior of the cylinder, one above the other, and below the zone apertures for the viewing of the figures. By the aid of two mirrors, as in the first apparatus, each series was reflected in one mirror and the effect of relief was produced at the same time as that of movement."

In order to complete the illusion and show the picture true to life, it was necessary to make, without interruption, a sufficient number of photographs, at very short intervals, during the action of the subject. At first, the technique had not sufficiently advanced to permit this, the gestures of the model had to be suspended, a negative had to be taken, the movement had to be advanced a little, another negative had to be taken, and so forth. The images became as faulty as if drawn by hand. Duboscq overcame this difficulty by reproducing machines in action. It is plain that in placing the machine in the successive position of its movements in order to take the pictures at certain intervals, all errors were avoided, each element of the machine necessarily following a predetermined and invariable course. Certain series were composed of thirty-two images representing one action. (14) Besides, Duboscq employed at first for commercial requirements rather than as an expression of truth, people dancing, fencing, etc. Wheatstone and Claudet, shortly after Duboscq, also endeavoured to give motion to stereoscopic pictures. Wheatstone seems to have abandoned it and Claudet obtained only "partial success". Many others followed them, whose work is forgotten, until the similar apparatuses of Marey, Edison and Demény attracted attention, and until Louis Lumière discovered the complete solution of the problem and thus achieved glory. But this exceeds my program.

It must be remembered that this long genesis of cinematography had three distinct periods. The first ending with 1851 includes the phenakisticope of Plateau and the earlier researches. This is the period of pure theory. The investigators moved in an unknown field of science and formulated the laws of phenomena unobserved until then. But their work met with only indifferent application and their effort led nowhere. The second period is the photographic phase, that of the bioscope of Duboscq to the kinetoscope of Edison (1851-1891). The third period runs from the cinematograph of Lumière (1895) to the present. The second period thus marks the beginning and culmination of this idea: photography could copy, preserve and reproduce an action regardless of the subject, to which it could give, by the aid of images, the illusion of life. This period was misunderstood in its beginning, because the inventors of primitive apparatus were misjudged under the pretext that they had only constructed playthings, and were ignorant of the future importance of their work. No viewpoint could be more erroneous.

Duboscq presented in the beginning of 1853 his theory of stereofantascope, with other instruments invented by him, to the Société d'Encouragement pour l'industrie nationale which appointed a committee to examine them. (15) Edmond Becquerel made the report on the electrical apparatus; Lissajoux (1822-1880) reported on the stereoscopes and the stereofantascope; both requested and obtained for Duboscq a platinum medal and a gold medal. This is hardly in keeping with the construction of a plaything, nor is it supported by the language of the reporter: "The panoramic stereoscope was combined by M. Duboscq with the phenakisticope, and he thus attained the double effect of relief and movement. This apparatus is, moreover, remarkable for the merit of having overcome the difficulty . . . . Your committee on economic arts requests that you express to M. Duboscq your full appreciation of his work, and that this report be printed in the Bulletin with the design and description of the apparatuses of which he is the inventor." Let us abandon, then, forever the ridiculous assertion that Duboscq, Claudet, and those who followed them, constructed toys.

Their aim was to supply to scientists, in the laboratory, an apparatus which would reproduce faithfully the phases of any action in order to study them more closely. And again, they desired to give to two or three observers the astonishing spectacle of moving figures in imitation of life. The resources which the photography of their time could put at their command were not sufficient for success, but they had a perfectly clear conception of the entire problem. The more recent inventors whose names are acclaimed, like Marey, Edison and Demény have added nothing to the ideas of Duboscq and Claudet; their success is wholly based on the efficient resources furnished them by the development and progress of photography. I have elsewhere (16) cited the names of some of these unknown forerunners, but this is not my subject today. It was necessary to show what they hoped to attain, with their apparatus in this period long past.

Claudet says (17) "Photography and stereoscopy in their marvelous and perfect ensemble have not been called on to complete the phenakisticope which, without their aid, would have remained a scientific toy, good enough for a single view . . . . In this manner, and nothing could be more curious in physics than a perfect combination of the stereoscope, the phenakisticope and photography, by which one could reproduce the extraordinary phenomenon of figures moving with all the illusion of natural relief. An art capable of making objects seem like *moving sculptures* would certainly be all that science could ever create, as most extraordinary and most marvelous." Dumont also exhibited (1862) his "stereoscopic and phenakisticopic apparatus". (18) "This apparatus permits me to pose before my lenses objects and persons in motion which are reproduced in all the successive phases of their movements, and with intervals of time which in reality separate these phases. These series of images may also be used, for instance the movements of a dancer, that of several soldiers, that of a machine, etc., either for the pleasure of the eyes or instruction."

Cook (1867), in describing his photobioscope (19), states: "If I am correct, and I have a perfect right to believe this, we are going to see another complete revolution in photographic art. Landscapes in which the trees sway in the wind, leaves trembling and scintillating in the sunshine, boats, birds gliding over the water agitated by waves, the manoeuvers of armies and navies and any other imaginable movements can be taken at will and serve for instruction." Will you say that he did not see the cinema function? It is interesting to recall these quotations. Demény, speaking in 1892 of his phonoscope, said: "I have joined stereoscopy with zootropy and have made toys which have remained museum pieces because they were too delicate." (20)

To the laboratory apparatus designed for a single spectator, to the idea of Duboscq, Louis Lumière, in 1895, added this other source of public spectacle. This was the supreme effort, the entire solution, and the final glory, but in the glamour of the triumph, we must not relegate to the sombre shadows those who started it on its way: the humble pioneers of the beginning. Above all we must remember Duboscq.

PHOTOGRAPHIC MOTION PICTURES
REFERENCES: CHAPTER XLV

1. *De Natura Rerum*, vol.IV, pp.770, 778.
2. M.Clerc writes: "It is generally recognized that persistence of vision has nothing to do with sensation of movement in cinematography; this was established by Flinke, and confirmed by Goldberg.
3. *Dictionnaire raisonné de Physique* (Analytical dictionary of physics) by Brisson, Paris 1781, 3 Vols. Under one of the plates in Vol.II, p.736 is the word "Visible".
4. *Leçons de Physique expérimentale* by Abbé Nollet, Paris 1765, Vol.V, p.493.
5. *Transactions philosophiques*, 1825, p.131.
6. Plateau: *Dissertation sur quelques Propriétés des Impressions produites par la Lumière sur l'Organe de la Vue* (Dissertation on some properties concerning the influence produced by light on the organ of vision) Liège 1829; *Correspondance mathématique et physique de M.Quetelet*, Brussels, vol.IV, 1828, p.393.
7. *Annales de Chimie et de Physique*, 1831, vol.48, p.281. Le François: *Dissertatio inauguralis de quibusdam Curvis geometricis*, etc. (Inaugural dissertation on certain geometrical curves) Ghent 1830.
8. *Des Illusions d'Optique sur lesquelles se fonde le petit Appareil appelé récemment Phénakisticope* (Optical illusions on which the small apparatus is based called recently Phenakisticope) by Plateau. *Annales de Chimie et de Physique*, 1833, vol.53, p.304.
9. *Correspondance mathématique et physique de l'Observatoire de Bruxelles*, 1833, vol.VII, p.365 — *Annales de Chimie et de Physique*, Paris 1833, vol.53, p.304.
10. *La Lumière*, May 22, 1852.
11. De La Blanchère, *Monographie du stéréoscope*, Paris 1860, p.49.
12. Moigno, *Cosmos*, November 14, 1852, vol.I, p.703.
13. *Bulletin de la Société Française de Photographie*, 1865, p.292.
14. *Bulletin de la Société d'Encouragement*, 1857, p.712; *Bulletin de la Société Française de Photographie*, 1857, p.75.
15. *Bulletin de la Société d'Encouragement*, 1856, pp.135, 183; 1857, pp.492, 707.
16. *Bulletin de la Société Française de Photographie*, 1920, p.171.
17. *Bulletin de la Société Française de Photographie*, 1865, p.287.
18. *Bulletin de la Société Française de Photographie*, 1862, p.34.
19. *Bulletin de la Société Française de Photographie*, 1867, p.201.
20. George Demény, *Les Origines du Cinématographe*, Paris, 1909, p.23.

CHAPTER XLVI

Daguerre from 1839 to 1851

DURING these changes, while improvements added one after the other made daguerreotypy almost a new thing, Daguerre, to whom I have not referred lately, did not remain impassive. His contract obliged him to deliver any improvements which he might make later, indicating that he intended to seek for such improvements. But he was soon overtaken by the innumerable investigators who, everywhere, experimented with his process. It was not without fear and irritation that the inventor saw his discovery tormented by so many men eager for changes. When Donné in September 1839 submitted to the Académie des Sciences daguerreotypes transformed into etched plates, Daguerre protested "against the modifications to which his process had been submitted", insisting that photographic images would not readily lend themselves to be etched or engraved. When giving his reasons, he recited his own attempts, he was led to speak exhaustively of his discovery. It is unfortunate that he is silent on the most important points; this is the only history of his work which we have from his own hands.

In October, in December and in the following January, Daguerre made some practical but unimportant contributions. In 1841 he found, or thought he had found, an entirely new process "truly inspired" according to the word of Arago. Daguerre electrified "the plate in the camera and obtained an image with such speed that he could photograph a marching crowd, the sea during a storm", in sum, record the most rapid movement. But the announcement of this success was premature. Arago had to correct it, deny it, and, in the muddled explications, blamed the mistake on a secretary. (1) No more was heard of it. In 1843, Daguerre having recommended a new method of polishing, Belfield and Léon Foucault did not share his opinion. The inventor emerged from his retirement and entered into a controversy with both of them. (2)

His most interesting and last communication dates from 1844 and deals with a change in the sensitized coating of the daguerrean plate.

FORMULA:

Polish the silvered plate with sublimate and rotten stone, then with iron oxide until it has a nice black colour; repeat the same operation again with cyanide of mercury and iron oxide; and a third time with a mixture of these two solutions:

254

1. $\begin{cases} \text{Gold chloride} & \text{1 gr.} \\ \text{Hyposulphite of soda} & \text{4 gr.} \\ \text{Distilled water} & \text{1 liter} \end{cases}$

2. $\begin{cases} \text{Platinum chloride} & \text{0.25 gr.} \\ \text{Distilled water} & \text{3 liters} \end{cases}$

The plate is then iodized in the usual manner, all other operations remain unchanged. (3)

It seems that the results were excellent; however I cannot find that this formula was ever employed by others. The only thing that has been retained from this formula is the use of platinum and it is probably the first time that it was used in photography. At the end of this year, Daguerre no longer took any part in the improvement of the daguerreotype, and retired to his house at Bry-sur-Marne, where, at that time, he resided.

Of the different homes which this famous man had occupied since his arrival at Paris in 1804, we know only that which he occupied about 1820 in the rue de Crussol. (4) During his early years in Paris he lived with his teacher Desgotti, at the Cinq Moulins, at the Barrière Poissonnière. The rue de Crussol, where long after we find him again, was near the Diorama where Daguerre moved after 1822. The Diorama was constructed on the site of the Hotel Sanson (5) and comprised two parallel buildings with a house for his own use on the rue Sanson. The building nearest to the boulevard served as the theatre. It was lighted by glass panels in the ceiling, and by five immense windows which looked out on the fountain of the Chateau d'eau. The other building was probably used as a studio and a storeroom for the properties necessary for the decoration. The garden and a pavillion, evidently remaining from the house of Sanson, formed the corner of the rue des Marais-du-Temple where it was No. 5, and where Daguerre lived. An illustration by Lancelot which appeared in the *Magasin pittoresque* of 1868 often reproduced shows the number as 15, an error which has deceived more than one historian.

The headings of letters (6) and the annuals of the time agree that the address of Daguerre was 5 rue des Marais-du-Temple. The survey records also describe the rue Sanson beginning between numbers 12 and 14 of the rue de Bondy and finishing at No. 5 rue des Marais.

We know that on March 3, 1839, owing to the clumsiness of a stagehand, a fire destroyed the Diorama. Daguerre was no business man; he had made a lot of money and saved very little. In addition, his income was used to repurchase the shares of the Société du Diorama, because he wanted to be the sole proprietor. Thus, almost his entire fortune was invested in this and the fire ruined him. Daguerre at this time was fifty-two years old.

After the catastrophe, Daguerre moved to No.17 Boulevard Saint-Martin opposite the theatre l'Ambigu-Comique. It was in this humble lodging, as described by Jules Janin (7), that he received the marks of esteem of the entire world when the daguerreotype was announced, as related above.

In 1840, he bought a property at Bry-sur-Marne, which was then a small village (8), and went there to live in January 1841. (9) The house, which dated from the seventeenth century, was very modest but was set in a spacious garden, and Daguerre made improvements on the property. Incapable of being idle and having an artistic taste, he was anxious to remodel the landscape. He employed workmen, re-designed the garden, moved rocks, changed the perspective, so that this gay Parisian landscape took on the aspect of a Swiss scene on a reduced scale. Of course he also had a studio for painting and a dark room for photography. A square tower twenty meters high dominated the valley and furnished him with an observatory.

Daguerre had one sister, but it seems that they were not very intimate. His close family seems to have been that of his wife, Louise-Georgine Arronsmith, whom he married in 1812. Mme. Daguerre, born in 1790, had two brothers and a sister. One of these brothers died in 1820 and left a daughter, Marguerite-Félicité, intimately called Félicie —a few months old, who lived sometimes at Mme. Daguerre's house and sometimes at that of her brother. After the death of this brother, Daguerre and his wife took this niece to live with them and, from this time on, considered her as their own daughter. This was the family circle in which Daguerre spent his last years.

His old friends Ysabey, the painter, J.-B. Dumas, the chemist, the sculptor Carpentier, Grevedon, Sibon, Jazet, Cayeux, Bouton, Chevalier, and others, visited him there: or sometimes he went to Paris and there discussed art with them, talking about form, colour, and above all, light, the passion of his life. It was during these visits that he regularly attended the meetings of the Société libre des Beaux-Arts of which he was a member. The inhabitants of Bry also showed their respect for him by electing him a municipal councillor. And in their often violent discussions, he lavished on his colleagues counsels of moderation and

wisdom, because age and probably success had softened the hot-tem-
pered artist and had made a sage of the adventurous young man of the
past. This unusual role enhanced Daguerre's reputation. One likes to
think of this famous inventor as the peaceful, small-town citizen, paying
a visit to the venerable chatelaine Mlle. de Rigny, or discussing quietly
with his neighbor and friend Mentienne, under the century-old elms,
which line the market-place of Bry.

And so the time passed in leisure but not in idleness; Daguerre
painted, he executed there at Bry the most original work of his career as
a painter. It is a painting in perspective of the church at Bry, placed in
the back of the choir behind the main altar, and represents a nave which
seems to extend the real nave of the church. It was necessary in order to
place this canvas, which was 6m. high and 4m. wide, to alter the apse
and interior of the church; the expenses were paid by Mlle. de Rigny.
This strange work, unique of its kind perhaps, was dedicated in June
1842; it is little known and seldom visited today. Notwithstanding the
loud admiration of his contemporaries, I must say that it did not give
me a complete illusion. Either time has deteriorated it or our eyes are
less obliging.

The inventor also searched for a means of fixing pastel drawings which
he made for his pleasure; and in addition he practiced almost all the
different methods of drawing, even lithography. What he liked best was
to draw on glass with some black, using his digit as a stomp. He backed
these with white paper in order to obtain the lights and his results show
great vigor. These drawings, sometimes called smoke drawings, were
rapidly spreading. (10)

Of course, Daguerre also made daguerreotypes. We have seen that he
made them in order to perfect the process and that after 1844 he ceased
his researches. It also seems that after this date he did not make many
photographs. Images by Daguerre made after 1845 are extremely rare.
He also had a great repugnance against having his own portrait made
by the numerous operators who requested it of him. Almost all met with
his refusal. Did he suppose that his process, altered by too many inventors, would become a stranger to him? Or again, did he foresee in so
much progress, in new applications and the coming of photography on
glass and paper the approaching end of daguerreotypy at its climax and
in all the radiance of its glory? Or did he simply desire rest?

The Revolution of 1848 disturbed the peace of the inhabitants of Bry
and turned Daguerre from his usual occupations. In order to reassure

the frightened lady of the manor who remembered 1793, he organized a kind of a national atelier on her grounds and made in her park an extended development of his ideas as a landscape painter. He scattered piles of rocks, lakes, grottoes, cascades and rustic bridges all over the prosaic park of the castle of Bry; he went so far as to put up buildings with classic perspectives in appropriate surroundings, and the passerby was astonished to find at the turn of the road the remains of a gothic chapel adjoining a ruined castle.

Such were the last occupations of his life. Age had shrunk him, but he was not ill. Nobody could foresee that his robust health was undergoing a change when, on July 10, 1851 about eleven o'clock, seating himself at the table, he was taken with a violent illness and rapidly lost consciousness. His wife and niece, unable to revive him and trembling with anxiety, sent for their neighbour Mentienne who quickly responded. But Daguerre expired in their arms within the hour. So came the end of this famous man; he was 63 years and 7 months old. The announcement of his death stirred photographers, artists and scientists, not only in our country but in the whole world. A great number of the public remained indifferent because crowds have short memories.

The Municipal Council at Bry offered the necessary ground for his interment and the Société libre des Beaux-Arts also opened a subscription for the erection of a monument. (11) This movement was supported by the journal *La Lumière*, which generously suggested that Niepce be united with Daguerre in this monument. The obsequies were held in the church and cemetery at Bry on July 12, 1851 in the presence of a great crowd; but the tomb was not dedicated until November 4th of the following year. (12) It is a simple monument, a medallion on a polished stone enclosed with an iron grille. Notwithstanding that, since 1893 (13), the Société Française de Photographie has been charged with its care, the stone has deteriorated and one can hardly trace the inscriptions engraved on it.

The great inventor at his death left to his widow nothing but penury. For some time previous nothing or very little had remained of the great sums of money which he had earned. Mme. Daguerre had nothing to support herself and her niece but half of her husband's pension, about three thousand francs, which reverted to her. In order to establish this niece, she was obliged, in 1853, to sell her property to the congregation of the Ladies of St. Clotilde, in the rue de Reuilly, at Paris, who there established a house of retreat. She reserved in perpetuity a residence in the studio, and there, six years after her husband, she died on March 24, 1857. She was buried by his side.

Daguerre's house with some of its furniture was sold. The nuns acting as trustees for the conservation of the past, took scrupulous care not to change anything; but during the siege of Paris, in 1870, furious attacks were made on the village of Bry (Nov. 30th and Dec. 1st and 2nd) and the house was destroyed. (14) Reconstructed after another plan, it was, after the expulsion of the religious orders, repurchased by Mentienne, who owns it today (1925). The garden remains largely as laid out by Daguerre, only the residence is changed.

Unfortunately it was not only the house which was destroyed in 1870. Mme. Daguerre, after the death of her husband, offered to the Minister of Fine Arts, the apparatus, prints, research material, even the manuscripts, everything that seemed to her the most interesting of the inventor's possessions. (15) This was a considerable offering, because it required two wagons for their removal. It is claimed that all this was presented by the Minister to the Conservatoire des Arts et Métiers. However, the relics of Daguerre at the Conservatoire are very few in number and cannot possibly represent more than a small part of Mme. Daguerre's legacy. (16)

Notwithstanding this gift, a great number of daguerreotypes enclosed in grooved wooden cases, the correspondence, memoires, and a number of other precious relics remained in the possession of Mme. Daguerre, and, after her death, passed into the hands of Félicie Arronsmith, who had become Mme. de Sainville. She lived with her husband at Noisy-le-Grand, a village near Bry, which was also occupied by the German army during the siege of Paris. The houses at Noisy and Bry were both pillaged, and all that remained of Daguerre was destroyed or stolen by the German soldiers. Mentienne suffered the same misfortune; he had in his possession at Bry the voluminous correspondence of the inventor, which would have enriched our information on Daguerre if we knew where the documents were, or where to search for them. (17)

The monument at the cemetery at Bry is not the only one erected to the glory of Daguerre. A bust was erected of him in 1883 in a public square at Cormeilles-en-Parisis through the efforts of the Société Française des Archives photographiques. (18) The Société Française de Photographie also erected, in 1897, a bust of Daguerre in the principal square at Bry-sur-Marne. (19)

American photographers, in recognition of his genius, also erected a monument to him at Washington in 1890. (20) Undoubtedly there are others elsewhere of which I am not cognizant.

To reproduce Daguerre's portrait in these different places was not difficult because many models existed; his authentic portraits are numerous. One of the earliest is a miniature painted in 1820 by Millet de Charlieu (1786-1859), which Mme. de Sainville donated to the Louvre Museum in 1896. (21) In the same museum can be found a large painting by Heim (1787-1865), representing "Charles X distributing the awards at the Salon of 1824". Daguerre, who received the cross, occupies there a place among the principal artists of the period. He may be seen there in full face near the lefthand side of the canvas touching the pedestal of a statue. Most of his portraits, and the lithograph which was drawn in 1837 by his friend Grevedon, show him at the height of his energy and success, his features are softened and perhaps more regular than natural, radiant with charm, bold and intelligent, if not what he was, at least what he should have been in reality.

Of course, the daguerreotype also reproduced the features of its inventor. Although Daguerre did not lend himself easily to posing, distrusting the qualifications of the operators and the cruel exactitude of his process. In 1848 (22), the brothers Meade, well known photographers of New York, came to France and, having been introduced to Daguerre, induced him to be photographed. They took five or six portraits on daguerrean plates; their Parisian colleague Vaillat, who accompanied them, also made some exposures. These are the last portraits taken of the inventor. One of these plates is still in the possession of the Meade family, another is preserved at the Museum at Washington, one is owned by Nadar who received it from Vaillat's daughter; a last one, discovered in England, was presented to the Société Française de Photographie, in 1905, by Gaumont.

All these images are easily recognized owing to the identical arrangement of the pose and its background; Daguerre is seated, his cheek supported on his hand, his elbow on the table on which was the photographic apparatus. These images were reproduced by lithography. Carpentier, two years after the death of his friend, painted a large portrait in black and white from these daguerrean plates, which is now hung in the salon d'honneur of the Société Française de Photographie. (23) The photographer Nadar owns a second portrait on silvered plate of Daguerre in the last days of his life. The beautiful curled hair of the inventor, still abundant, is grey. The tense features, the thin face, betray his age.

DAGUERRE FROM 1839 TO 1851

Daguerre made numerous photographs in 1839 and 1840; he made many of persons of note and even of the sovereigns and so Germany, Austria, Russia and America own daguerreotypes by the inventor. In the last years of his life, he does not seem to have made any; at least if they exist, these plates have disappeared and those which remain are very rare. Thus it is impossible to make an authentic list of photographs made by Daguerre, not only on account of the loss of his archives, but because his work has been dispersed all over the world. Besides, up to now, no value has attached to these relics, and although there are daguerreotypes, impossible of identification, one may find, obtainable for a song, pieces from his studio, small tableaux, sketches, reproductions, etc., by Daguerre. We can only search for them.

1. *Comptes rendus*, 1839, 2nd semester, pp.411, 423, 512, 824; 1840, 1st semester, p.116; 1841, 1st semester, pp.23, 1228; 2nd semester, p.26.
2. *Comptes rendus*, 1843, 1st semester, p.588; 2nd semester, pp.356, 480.
3. *Comptes rendus*, 1844, 1st semester, pp.152, 187, 756.
4. *Etude sur la Vie et les Travaux de Charles Chevalier* by Arthur Chevalier, his son, Paris 1862, p.140. *Notice sur Daguerre* by Carpentier, Paris 1855.
5. The rue Sanson, ordered by Royal letters patent of October 25, 1782, was opened in 1784, crossing the garden of Sieur Robert Sanson, Chancellor of the Exchequer. One Sanson de Sanval was still proprietor of some buildings in this street in 1863. The name rue Sanson was changed to rue de la Douane in 1851; it was widened from 9.50m to 14m in 1856. The odd numbers were preserved in their original rotation.
6. Documents belonging to the Société Française de Photographie.
7. *L'Artiste*, September 1, 1839.
8. Less than 400 inhabitants at that period.
9. *Comptes rendus*, 1841, 1st semester, p.23.
10. *Des Arts graphiques*, by Hammann, Geneva 1857, p.33 — *Comptes rendus*, 1839, 2nd semester, p.429 — *La Découverte de la Photographie* 1839 by Mentienne, Paris, 1892, p.111.
11. *La Lumière*, July 10, 1851.
12. Mentienne, work cited, pp.113 and ff. give details of the ceremonies.
13. *Bulletin de la Société Française de Photographie*, 1893, p.379.
14. *Bulletin de la Société Française de Photographie*, 1889, p.212.
15. Some of the unpublished details contained in this chapter were furnished by the family of Mme. Daguerre or are taken from the archives of the Société Française de Photographie.
16. The photographic collection of the Conservatoire des Arts et Métiers was begun in 1881. Thirty years elapsed between the gift of the widow and the installation at the museum. This time was more than sufficient to destroy the relics, even their memory. *Bulletin de la Société Française de Photographie*, 1881, p.207; 1882, p.86.
17. A letter from Mme. de Sainville (in the archives of the Société Française de Photographie) contains the following: "I have not a scrap of paper left concerning my uncle and my aunt." Mme. de Sainville died in 1900 and was buried in the Daguerre vault where a place was expressly reserved for her. Mentienne, who is quoted here, is the son of the Mentienne in whose arms Daguerre expired.
18. *Bulletin de la Société Française de Photographie*, 1883, p.310.
19. *Bulletin de la Société Française de Photographie*, 1893, p.379; 1894, pp.236, 332, 570, 594; 1897, pp.308, 320.
20. *Rapport sur l'Exposition internationale de Saint-Louis de 1904, group 16*, (Report on the International Exposition at St.Louis, 1904, group 16) by Jules Demaria, Paris, 1905, p.69 — *Bulletin de la Société Française de Photographie*, 1890, p.119.
21. *Documents historiques de la Société Française de Photographie*.
22. According to Carpentier this happened in 1851, according to Nadar in 1849. *Bulletin de la Société Française de Photographie*, 1864, p.97; 1892, pp.159, 213.
23. *Bulletin de la Société Française de Photographie*, 1892, p.213; 1864, p.97.

CHAPTER XLVII

1851

THE remarkable year 1851 in which Daguerre died marks also the end of the daguerreotype and terminates the primitive era. Modern photography, as we practice it, is composed of the following essential elements: negative images on glass, positives on paper. And the great improvements which in time have developed, creating a universal science, which is employed almost everywhere: permanent images, reproduced by printers ink, colour reproductions, luminous projections, stereoscopy and animated photographs.

Up to that time, photography was a limited art, of narrow application. Restricted little by little to portraiture, it became an appanage of specialists, jealous of their studio secrets which they regard as a capital investment. Metal plates were expensive and the design they carried differed greatly from the engravings which one was accustomed to see. The prints on paper eliminated these objections; they were easy to obtain at a reasonable price, more accurate than any other design, they became popular and expanded photography. From 1851, dates the first association of French photographers; they took the name of *Société héliographique* in memory of Niepce. We recall these founders for their fame: Eugène Delacroix, Benjamin Delessert, Victor Regnault, Edmond Becquerel, Bayard, Baron Gros, Aguado — who has such a sumptuous tomb at Père-Lachaise — Arnoux, Baldus, Champfleuri, Chevalier, the engraver Cousin, Durieux, Fortier, Legray, Lemaître, Lesecq, Lerebours, Mestral, Montesquieu, Prince de Montléard, Niepce de Saint-Victor, Renard — Bayard's photographic operator — Francis Wey and Ziegler. What a mixture of literary men, scientists and artists who, however, did not continue the society very long, and those who wanted to preserve it abandoned this moribund society in order to found, in December 1853, the *Société Française de Photographie*, which is still in existence and which constantly grows in importance.

As a matter of fact, in January 1848 (1), some London amateurs met for the particular purpose of practising and extending the use of Talbotype under the name of the *Calotype Society;* but their association did not last and since the *Royal Photographic Society* only dates from January 1853, the *Société héliographique* is perhaps the first of its kind formed in the world. The society required and thus had to create a bulletin or journal for its proceedings. This was *La Lumière*, which appeared for the first time on February 19, 1851. The society and the journal had the same author, M. de Montfort, but the journal survived the society and lasted with varying fortunes until 1866.

"The journal and the society" says Belloc, "gave photography a marvelous impetus" and Lacan adds: "It is from this moment only that amateur photography dates." Take notice that practical photography was learned from this all over the world. But Belloc and Lacan are mistaken. It was neither *La Lumière* nor the *Société héliographique* which created amateurs or popularized photography. On the contrary, because the new art was taken up everywhere, because everybody realized what immense possibilities it offered, and because of the ease with which it could be practiced, amateur photographers desired a society and a journal.

Henceforth nothing could arrest the growth of photography. As technique improved, its applications increased more and more. It has furnished a process for scientific observation which perceives more patiently and more penetratingly than the human eye, by its exact reproduction of reality and a new means for the expression of human thought; marvelous resources which were not dreamt of by preceding generations. The history of this development will be the object of the second part of this work.

REFERENCES: CHAPTER XLVII

1. Glanes photographiques (Photographic gleanings) by De Brébisson, Paris 1848.

INDEX

*The order in which the author deals with the divisions of his subject is indicated in the CONTENTS pages at the front of the book.

**Many valuable bibliographical notes concerning the works cited throughout this volume may be found in the REFERENCES given at the end of each chapter. T.N.

INDEX

INDEX

don), 233; (Veresz), 233; (Pons), 233; (Saint-Florent), 233.
Conduche, 54.
Conqueret, 40.
Conservatoire des Arts et Métiers, 54, 75, 140, 169, 259.
"Continuing rays" (Becquerel), 204, 231.
Conception of photography, First, 59-68.
Copper plates used by Niepce, 66.
Cormeilles-en-Parisis, 108, 259.
Cornelius, Robert, 202.
Cromer, M., 104, 113.
Crystal lens, 10.
Cussell, Sir, 143.

DAGUERRE, Birth, 108; youth—famous as scenic painter, 108; marriage, 109; association with Bouton leads to Diorama, 110-12; first idea of photography and experiments, 114, 148; addresses Niepce, 105; experiments with phosphorescent powders and coloured glasses, 118-20; negotiations with Niepce, 125; visits Niepce, signs agreement of partnership Niepce-Daguerre, receives Niepce's description and demonstration of Heliography, 126-132; suggests to Niepce the use of iodine, 132-133; association with Isidore Niepce, 146, 153; recognizes light-sensitivity of silver iodide and observes development of image with mercury, 150-151; perfects his process—named daguerreotype, 151; new contracts with Isidore Niepce, firm name Daguerre-Niepce, 153; makes daguerreotypes in streets of Paris and attempts commercial exploiting of process, 154; daguerreotype and diorama processes acquired by French government which awards pension to Daguerre and Niepce, 154-161; is acclaimed by the world, 168; demonstrates his process and writes the official manual, 169; protests modification of his process, 254; introduces new methods and formulas, 254-5; retires to Bry-sur-Marne, 255; his last years, 256-8; death, 258; relics, 259; portraits, 260.
Daguerre, Mme., 109, 113, 114, 168, 256, 258; death, 259.
Daguerre's niece, 109, 117, 256, 258, 259, 260.

Daguerrean studios, 203, 205.
Daguerreotype, Genesis of process, 150-1; perfected, 153; attempt to exploit commercially, 153; offers from foreign countries, 154, 171; early examples of the process by Daguerre, 139, 154; Arago interested, makes preliminary report to the Académie, 154; contention re. priority of invention, 156,175-177; French government acquires process, 159-161; officially published by Arago in report to the Académie, 163-166; world-wide excitement following publication of report, 169-171; honors awarded Daguerre, 170-173; introduction of daguerreotype in America, 170, 174; in Germany, 171; in Austria and England, 172; and in France, 173; some early daguerreotypes, 173; the first portraits, 170, 173, 201-204; demonstrations of the process by Daguerre, 169; early modifications, 191-3; improvements in cameras and lenses, 193-7; exposures shortened, 192, 197; application of daguerreotypy in portraiture, 201-205; instantaneous photography, 208; in scientific work, 209; in enlarging, 237; stereoscopy, 241; improved methods of daguerreotypy by Daguerre, 254-5; portraits of Daguerre by Meade Brothers and Vaillat, end of the daguerrean era, 222, 263; official manual, 169; daguerreotypes engraved, 224.
D'Alembert, J., 34.
Darwin, Erasmus, 59.
Davanne, L.A., 56.
Davy, Humphry, 47, 51, 54, 56, 59; Memoir of Wedgwood's experiments, 60-63, 68, 84, 237.
Dechales, M., 235.
Degotti, 108, 113.
Delannoy, 191.
Delécluze, 175.
Desbordes, 207.
Design, Early examples of manual, 3-4.
Desmarest, 175.
"Dessin fumée" Daguerre's, 117, 257.
Diaphragm invented by Niepce, Iris, 86.
Diorama, 66, 105, 110-12; seen by Niepce, 119; destroyed by fire, 159; process described, 159.
Dippel's (bone) oil, 95, 101.
Djafar (see Geber).

267

INDEX

Herschel, Sir John W., describes action of hyposulphite of soda on silver salts, 51, 169, 176, 180; experiments with spectrum, 165, 231; chrysotype, 213.
Herschel, Sir William, discovers infrared rays, 231.
Homberg, 147.
Honours awarded Daguerre, 170, 173.
Hooper, W., 49.
Hubert, 173, 187.
Humboldt, A., 154, 172.
Hunt, Robert, 176, 213, 231.

IBBETSON, 175, 228.
Illustration of books by photography, 228-229.
Image, Theories of daguerrean, 191.
Infra-red rays (W.Herschel), 231.
Instantaneous photography, 204-5, 208; with Talbot's negative paper, 220.
Institut de France, 12.
Introduction describing heliography, 64-66, 125.
Invention of Photography, Date of, 97.
Iodide of bromine accelerator, 192.
Iodine, Niepce's use of, 102, 103, 104, 129, 131, 132, 150.
Iodine, Chloride of, 192-3.
Iris diaphragm invented by Niepce, 86.
Iron salts investigated, 50, 87.
Isenring, 172.

JANIN, Jules, 169, 256.
Janse, Z., 30.
Jobard, J.B., 172, 175, 178.
Jouffroy, Marquis de, 75, 79.
Journals of the Royal Institution, 59, 68.

KASTELIN, 50.
Keir, James, 59.
Kepler, J., 9, 25.
Kew on Thames, 80, 122.
Kircher, A., 25, 32, 35, 235.
Klaproth, M.H., 50, 89.
Kratochwila, 192.
Kunkel, J., 91.

LACAN, E., 46, 100, 137.
Lalanne, L., 39.
Lamy, Fr., 39, 40.
Lassaigne, 175, 185.
Lasteyrie-Dusaillant, Count, 77.
Lebon, G., 5.

Leblond, J.C., 39.
Lechi's colouring process, 208.
Leclerc, Abbé, 7.
Lefèbre, F., 39, 237.
Legends re. Daguerre's discovery of the use of mercury, 151-2.
Legray's waxed paper process, 220.
Lemaître, 97, 99, 101, 102, 103, 105, 117, 118, 126, 133, 142, 173, 192, 226.
Lemoine, 39.
Le Moyne's amphitypes, 222.
Lenses of camera obscura, 34; used by Niepce, 86; in daguerreotypy, 195-7, 205.
Leonardo da Vinci, 11, 13, 17, 23, 241.
Lepine, Dr., 136.
Lerebours, 173, 192, 196, 204, 205, 226, 227.
Leroy, C.F., 39.
Leslie, John, 59.
Letters of Niepce, 64, 75, 82-107.
Lewis, W., 49.
Libri-Carrucci, 10, 13, 17, 175.
Lieberkuyn, J.N., 75, 236.
Light, Chemistry of, 47-51; studied by Niepce, 65-66.
Lincei Society, 6.
Lisle, Rouget de, 41
Lithography, 77, 81.
Littré, M.P., 21.
Louis XII, 11, 101; XVI, 53; XVIII, 78; Louis Philippe, 159, 173, 202.
Lucanus, Dr., 172.
Lucretius, 245.
Lunar Society, 39, 59.
Luynes Competition, Duc de, 226.

Magiae naturalis (Porta), 7, 10.
Malacarne, 237.
Mandelot, Count de, 105.
Manganese, Study of, 87, 91.
Marly's hydraulic engine, 73.
Marolais, S. de, 38.
Marsiglii, Count de, 147.
Martin, A., 172.
Maurolycus, F., 14.
Mayer and Pierson, 46.
Mechanical reproduction of designs, 38.
Megascope, 39, 237.
Melloni, M., 10, 17, 177.
Melzo, François, 11.
Memoir of Niepce for Royal Society, 97, 122-3.
Memoir of Wedgwood's experiments, 60-63.
"Meniscus prism", 35, 105.

269

271

INDEX

THE LITERATURE OF PHOTOGRAPHY
AN ARNO PRESS COLLECTION

Anderson, A. J. **The Artistic Side of Photography in Theory and Practice.** London, 1910

Anderson, Paul L. **The Fine Art of Photography.** Philadelphia and London, 1919

Beck, Otto Walter. **Art Principles in Portrait Photography.** New York, 1907

Bingham, Robert J. **Photogenic Manipulation.** Part I, 9th edition; Part II, 5th edition. London, 1852

Bisbee, A. **The History and Practice of Daguerreotype.** Dayton, Ohio, 1853

Boord, W. Arthur, editor. **Sun Artists** (Original Series). Nos. I-VIII. London, 1891

Burbank, W. H. **Photographic Printing Methods.** 3rd edition. New York, 1891

Burgess, N. G. **The Photograph Manual.** 8th edition. New York, 1863

Coates, James. **Photographing the Invisible.** Chicago and London, 1911

The Collodion Process and the Ferrotype: Three Accounts, 1854-1872. New York, 1973

Croucher, J. H. and Gustave Le Gray. **Plain Directions for Obtaining Photographic Pictures.** Parts I, II, & III. Philadelphia, 1853

The Daguerreotype Process: Three Treatises, 1840-1849. New York, 1973

Delamotte, Philip H. **The Practice of Photography.** 2nd edition. London, 1855

Draper, John William. **Scientific Memoirs.** London, 1878

Emerson, Peter Henry. **Naturalistic Photography for Students of the Art.** 1st edition. London, 1889

*Emerson, Peter Henry. **Naturalistic Photography for Students of the Art.** 3rd edition. *Including* The Death of Naturalistic Photography, London, 1891. New York, 1899

Fenton, Roger. **Roger Fenton, Photographer of the Crimean War.** With an Essay on his Life and Work by Helmut and Alison Gernsheim. London, 1954

Fouque, Victor. **The Truth Concerning the Invention of Photography:** Nicéphore Niépce—His Life, Letters and Works. Translated by Edward Epstean from the original French edition, Paris, 1867. New York, 1935

Fraprie, Frank R. and Walter E. Woodbury. **Photographic Amusements Including Tricks and Unusual or Novel Effects Obtainable with the Camera.** 10th edition. Boston, 1931

Gillies, John Wallace. **Principles of Pictorial Photography.** New York, 1923

Gower, H. D., L. Stanley Jast, & W. W. Topley. **The Camera As Historian.** London, 1916

Guest, Antony. **Art and the Camera.** London, 1907

Harrison, W. Jerome. **A History of Photography Written As a Practical Guide and an Introduction to Its Latest Developments.** New York, 1887

Hartmann, Sadakichi (Sidney Allan). **Composition in Portraiture.** New York, 1909

Hartmann, Sadakichi (Sidney Allan). **Landscape and Figure Composition.** New York, 1910

Hepworth, T. C. **Evening Work for Amateur Photographers.** London, 1890

*Hicks, Wilson. **Words and Pictures.** New York, 1952

Hill, Levi L. and W. McCartey, Jr. **A Treatise on Daguerreotype.** Parts I, II, III, & IV. Lexington, N.Y., 1850

Humphrey, S. D. **American Hand Book of the Daguerreotype.** 5th edition. New York, 1858

Hunt, Robert. **A Manual of Photography.** 3rd edition. London, 1853

Hunt, Robert. **Researches on Light.** London, 1844

Jones, Bernard E., editor. **Cassell's Cyclopaedia of Photography.** London, 1911

Lerebours, N. P. **A Treatise on Photography.** London, 1843

Litchfield, R. B. **Tom Wedgwood, The First Photographer.** London, 1903

Maclean, Hector. **Photography for Artists.** London, 1896

Martin, Paul. **Victorian Snapshots.** London, 1939

Mortensen, William. **Monsters and Madonnas.** San Francisco, 1936

*Nonsilver Printing Processes: Four Selections, 1886-1927.** New York, 1973

Ourdan, J. P. **The Art of Retouching by Burrows & Colton.** Revised by the author. 1st American edition. New York, 1880

Potonniée, Georges. **The History of the Discovery of Photography.** New York, 1936

Price, [William] Lake. **A Manual of Photographic Manipulation.** 2nd edition. London, 1868

Pritchard, H. Baden. **About Photography and Photographers.** New York, 1883

Pritchard, H. Baden. **The Photographic Studios of Europe.** London, 1882

Robinson, H[enry] P[each] and Capt. [W. de W.] Abney. **The Art and Practice of Silver Printing.** The American edition. New York, 1881

Robinson, H[enry] P[each]. **The Elements of a Pictorial Photograph.** Bradford, 1898

Robinson, H[enry] P[each]. **Letters on Landscape Photography.** New York, 1888

Robinson, H[enry] P[each]. **Picture-Making by Photography.** 5th edition. London, 1897

Robinson, H[enry] P[each]. **The Studio, and What to Do in It.** London, 1891

Rodgers, H. J. **Twenty-three Years under a Sky-light,** or Life and Experiences of a Photographer. Hartford, Conn., 1872

Roh, Franz and Jan Tschichold, editors. **Foto-auge, Oeil et Photo, Photo-eye.** 76 Photos of the Period. Stuttgart, Ger., 1929

Ryder, James F. **Voigtländer and I:** In Pursuit of Shadow Catching. Cleveland, 1902

Society for Promoting Christian Knowledge. **The Wonders of Light and Shadow.** London, 1851

Sparling, W. **Theory and Practice of the Photographic Art.** London, 1856

Tissandier, Gaston. **A History and Handbook of Photography.** Edited by J. Thomson. 2nd edition. London, 1878

University of Pennsylvania. **Animal Locomotion. The Muybridge Work at the University of Pennsylvania.** Philadelphia, 1888

Vitray, Laura, John Mills, Jr., and Roscoe Ellard. **Pictorial Journalism.** New York and London, 1939

Vogel, Hermann. **The Chemistry of Light and Photography.** New York, 1875

Wall, A. H. **Artistic Landscape Photography.** London, [1896]

Wall, Alfred H. **A Manual of Artistic Colouring, As Applied to Photographs.** London, 1861

Werge, John. **The Evolution of Photography.** London, 1890

Wilson, Edward L. **The American Carbon Manual.** New York, 1868

Wilson, Edward L. **Wilson's Photographics.** New York, 1881